D0575156
logolounge | MASTERlibrary
3000 INITIAL & CREST LOGOS
DO NOT REMOVE | PROPERTY OF:
DATE RECEIVED:
RECEIVED FROM:
CONTRIBUTOR'S NAME:
MICHAEL DORET
JOE DUFFY
BILL GARDNER
TOM GEISMAR

volume 1

logolounge MASTER library

3000 INITIAL & CREST LOGOS

BEVERLY MASSACHUSETTS

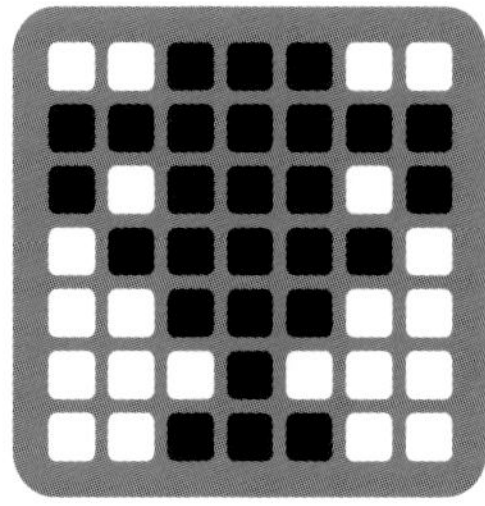

ROCKPORT PUBLISHERS

catharine fishel and bill gardner

First published in the United States of America by
Rockport Publishers, a member of
Quayside Publishing Group
100 Cummings Center
Suite 406-L
Beverly, Massachusetts 01915-6101
Telephone: (978) 282-9590
Fax: (978) 283-2742
www.rockpub.com

Library of Congress Cataloging-in-Publication Data
Fishel, Catharine M.
LogoLounge, master library. Volume 1 : 3,000 initial & crest logos / Catharine Fishel and Bill Gardner.
p. cm. — (LogoLounge, master library ; v. 1)
Includes index.
ISBN-13: 978-1-59253-567-5
ISBN-10: 1-59253-567-4
1. Logos (Symbols)—Catalogs. 2. Corporate image—Catalogs. I. Gardner, Bill. II. Title. III. Title: 3,000 initials & crests from LogoLounge.com. IV. Title: 3,000 initials and crests from LogoLounge.com. V. Title: Three thousand initials & crests from LogoLounge.com.
NC1002.L63F59 2010
741.6—dc22
2009027285

ISBN-13: 978-1-59253-567-5
ISBN-10: 1-59253-567-4

10 9 8 7 6 5 4 3 2 1

Design: Gardner Design
Layout & Production: *tabula rasa* graphic design
Production Coordinator: Lauren Kaiser / Gardner Design
Cover Image: Gardner Design

Printed in China

This new series is dedicated to the identity designer, able to charm a wealth of meaning from a handful of lines and savvy enough to know that the words, "There's nothing new. It's all been done before," is only an excuse for the lazy.

To Cathy, Troy, Brian, and Gail for starting the fire. To Lauren for stoking the fire. To Susan, Luke, Elisabeth, Ty, and Jami for enduring the fire. To Andrea and Molly for tending my flames.

—Bill Gardner

To Bill and the entire amazing LogoLounge team; to the fantastic Gardner Design team; to the ever-patient editors at Rockport; to all of the generous designers we work with; to my constant refuge, my sons and husband—thank you. You truly do make a positive difference in the lives of others.

—Catharine Fishel

LogoLounge.com is the world's largest searchable database of logo designs. The more than 110,000 logos are contributed by designers around the world. Members can post their logo design work; study the work of others; search the enormous database by keyword, designer's name, client, industry, and other attributes; learn from articles and news written expressly for and about logo designers; build lightboxes for inspiration; and much more.

For more details or to submit your own logos for consideration for a future book, please visit www.LogoLounge.com.

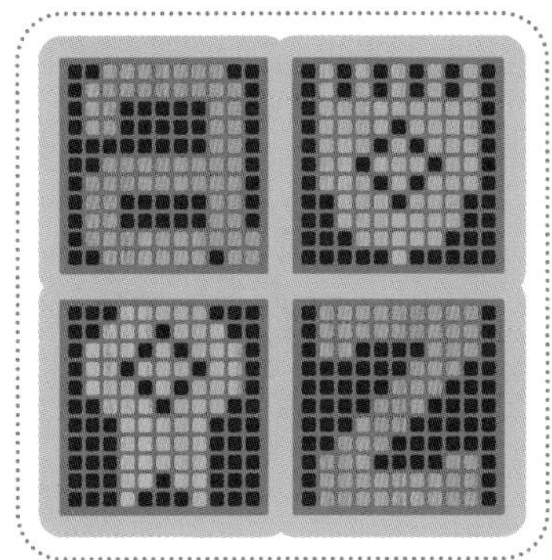

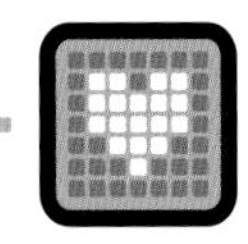

FROM THE
LOGOLOUNGE.COM
INTERNATIONAL
COLLECTION

introduction

LOGOLOUNGE
MASTER LIBRARY
INITIAL & CREST LOGOS

Some 4,000 years ago, craftsmen marked their wares with a simple glyph—an identifier that became a predecessor of initial logo designs today.

Imagine Demetri, *a fictitious Corinthian potter crafting large vessels for transporting olive oil some 4,000 years ago. If you could have asked this artisan about the meaning behind the small glyph he imprinted on the bottom of all of his wares, his answer would have been simple. The mark—three stacked, wavy lines—was meant to represent him and his small shop, which was located beside a wide stream—no more, no less. It was a mark that could be read by anyone, literate and illiterate alike (himself among the latter).*

That the weight of the lines or their color or the degree of their waviness could have additional meaning would have been superfluous information to young Demetri. In an age when people were defined by trade or location or ancestry, not by surname and certainly not by company name, Demetri was the potter who worked by the stream. That's all you needed to know.

The world's a much more complicated place today, and differentiation between potters and trades of all sorts is by necessity much more defined and refined. It's curious, though, that an identification system developed thousands of years ago for a largely illiterate society is enormously successful in today's much more literate world.

INITIALS

Literacy is a miracle of modern technology. Even five hundred years ago, the ability to read was still rare. Through the development of printing and now the electronic transmission of information, we have progressed from a society that recognizes glyphs as pictures that represent something to a people who can read and write letters. This is true in most societies except for those like China, where to read a newspaper or

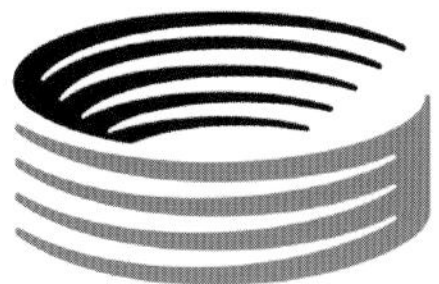

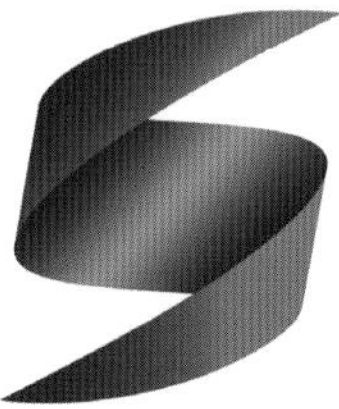

The use of an initial in a logo design provides a simple mneumonic device, but the simple character is rich with meaning. Each new initial design is completely different from all others, even though it uses as its base a very familiar alphabetic character. (All designs created by Gardner Design.)

TOP DOWN: Collins Bus Corporation, Conco Construction, Smart Tech, Surency Life and Health

write a letter, you must still be familiar with thousands of characters: Chinese, to name one example, is still a highly glyph-based language.

All modern Roman- and Latin-based letterforms represent at their core a pictogram from the past. But now they are used differently. They are components that can be used apart or in groupings to create a written language. It's a much broader and more expedient way to read and learn.

Curious, then, that with logo designs that use initial or single letters, we have come full circle: The single letter is turned back into a glyph.

Consider the Toyota logo. The *T* in its logo is a simple mnemonic that is easily read and remembered. But the letter is only the first level of mental association. The little ellipses that form the letter can suggest wheels or motion or speed or unity: Those are additional levels of meaning that transform the common letterform into a logo that is memorable, distinctive, and appropriate.

The letterform has been transformed back into a picture that we almost inherently understand represents Toyota. It lives in many levels in a more powerful way that the simple letter *T* cannot. It's like baking a cake: You can't just use flour. And the more ingredients you can add that blend harmonically and aren't unnecessary make for a better, richer experience.

A letter is one of the most basic elements toward which a designer can gravitate. If the conversation with the public can be started with this simple, familiar device, then the designer has achieved his first goal. If you see the letter *B,* you know immediately that it does not represent Nike, because that name starts with a different letter. The initial letter is the first hint that you can give a consumer.

The next step, though, is to transform it into a symbol that people don't have to "read." Think of the Volkswagen logo: You don't have to read *V* and *W* to understand the mark. The communication is much more visceral.

How is the transformation made? Think of it as a simple addition problem. If Morrison's Florist is the client, and the owner tells you that his company specializes in green plants and having the fastest delivery in town, the designer must take disparate factors—the client is a florist, but he also deals with green plants and he has speedy delivery—and add them together to form a complete sum.

So imagine that the designer comes up with a logo that is a letter *M* made entirely of twining vines, and the entire structure is canted ever-so-slightly forward. Adding all of the factors together allows all of the ideas to come together and mesh to form a simple, recognizable, yet entirely distinct initial design. Clearly, this new *M* is not for an iron foundry or a cleaning service. The viewer may not know or understand everything about the client just by looking at the logo, but he will be able to derive some information about that organization.

Using an initial letter as a logo solution is an option with endless possibilities. There are so many existing and possible varieties of *M*'s that even if it were the only letter in the alphabet, it would not be a confining factor for most designers. It's not even that important to be slavishly literal or true to the letter shape: An *M* could be wings or water or mountains and still be understandable as that letter. With just that single letter, you could say almost anything.

It's true that some letters are used more often than others in initial designs—*A*, *M*, *S*, and *E*, for instance—and not just because of the number of client names that start with those letters. An *M*, to name one example, has both symmetry and visual interest with its repetitive peaks and angles. The letters *A, E, H, I, N, O, S, T, U, V, W, X, Y,* and *Z* also have that same symmetry and rhythm.

An *R*, on the other hand, is a more difficult dance partner. When there's a leg sticking out or any other sort of asymmetry, the design is still possible, it's just trickier.

Ancient German boundary stones required no more than a coat of arms to identify property ownership.

CRESTS

We use the term *crests* in this book for lack of a better single-word descriptor. However, the use of the word is predicated on history that helps explain the origin of the category.

What can be referred to as a crest today is the result of a collision between two varieties of graphical information used in the twelfth century. First, in the days of heraldry, a lord, king, or other person of substance would send a person ahead to announce—or herald—his arrival. That person would wear livery in his liege's colors. Those same colors would also be displayed on the battlefield on a coat of arms that would appear on a combatant's shield: In that way, everyone knew who was on everyone else's team. Simple and effective identification.

The second variety of communication from that time was the family seal, such as might be used to stamp an important document. Like the coat of arms, a seal would only be possessed by noteworthy families or organizations.

So the stage is set in the minds of all peoples—literate or not—that persons or groups of note can be identified by a graphical element. Combine the information in the shield with the physical mark or stamp of the seal, and the result is what today is accepted as a variety of logo: a crest.

The crest is rich with information, and is also based in history. Break down a coat of arms, and you'll find eight basic elements in almost every one.

- **The design was based around a center shield, whose shape may vary.**
- **Atop the shield was the helmet. This could be an actual helmet or another component like an arm holding a sword or an animal.**

- **On top of the helmet was a crown or other "crowning" element that identified the rank of the family or person.**
- **At the very top was a banner or ribbon (often referred to as a crest) that carried written information, usually the name of the family or person.**
- **The mantling, sometimes formed from plant material or feathers, flowed down from the helmet on either side of the shield. It gathered the shield and tied it to the helmet.**
- **Around the base of the mantling were the supporters. This might be a pair of animals, for example, holding everything together.**
- **Underneath was a compartment, a base or foundation on which the supporters sat.**

Many individual heraldic elements come together to create a unique coat of arms.

- **At the very bottom was the motto, usually in the form of a ribbon.**

So much information! But how different is that from a modern-day logo that may contain one or more pieces of art, the name of a company, the name of its product or service, the company's establishment date, the company colors, a variety of graphical elements that refer symbolically to the company's philosophy (such as stars or plants), and maybe much more?

That task is the same today as it was then: Convey a plethora of information in a limited amount of space. Luckily for designers, the modern, consuming public accepts and understands a very refined graphical language that was established centuries ago. Perhaps the geographical location of each of the eight elements listed above isn't identical to that used in coats of arms, but the elements are largely the same. If designed well, there is a form and function to everything used in what we now call a crest.

There is also a visual hierarchy: The most visible element is usually the client's name. Next come elements that the client deems most important. There is usually some visual indicator of what the client does or provides. For a vineyard, for example, a bunch of grapes or wine glass might be included. The client might ask for an "established" date or some other indicator of quality or distinction. There might also be a logo or a tagline.

Because of their connection to history, crests today connect the psyche to a sense of nostalgia, quality, or heritage. Sometimes, especially for new companies or organizations, the crest can create an instant pseudohistory or heritage through the use of visual cues and bits of language. This is neither a good or bad thing:

The button is there to push, should the designer choose to use it.

There are certain applications that are better suited for crests than others. They are great for packaging and labels, providing a manageable lockup of a variety of text and visual information. When done well, each element isn't really "read" individually; instead, the lockup becomes recognized as a single element—think of the Anheuser-Busch logo.

The best crests have a distinct texture that is more important than any of their individual elements. They have an overall essence that stands out: The information is there, if anyone should choose to study it, but it's the global effect that people remember and recognize.

- Bill Gardner, founder of LogoLounge

Although each of these crest designs is very different, they all use design elements common to crests that evolved prior to and during the twelfth century. Each communicates a lot of information in a very limited amount of space. (All designs by Gardner Design.)

LOOKING FORWARD

Crests and initial logos are designs that are firmly rooted in history. But their relevance today remains strong. A well-rooted understanding of their history and development enables today's designer to not only use the tools more confidently, but more creatively as well.

That's the whole reasoning behind the Master Library series: to inform and inspire. Each book shares the origin of techniques; interviews with leading, contemporary logo designers; and a massive, highly focused, visual resource of 3,000 topic-specific logos. Everything was collected in one place in order to feed your work, and ultimately, improve value to the client.

For more information on the seven-volume Master Library series (future editions will also include Typography; People; Animals & Mythology; Shapes & Symbols; Nature & Food; and Arts & Culture) and other books created by LogoLounge, please visit: ***www.logolounge.com.***

Significant and PERSONAL

Joe Duffy, Duffy & Partners

Joe Duffy is principal and chairman of Duffy & Partners and is a leading creative director in the fields of branding and design. His firm's clients include market leaders such as Coca-Cola, Sony, Jack in the Box, and Wolfgang Puck, to name a few. His work is regularly featured in leading marketing and design publications and exhibited around the world.

Why have crests and initials remained so popular with designers and consumers over so many years?

It's primarily because they have meaning and because they are personal. They typically refer to a family or person or part of history. They can relate to the characteristics of a person or company and what makes them unique. Initials and crests represent people, primarily. I think that is why they are looked upon with some degree of meaningful nostalgia.

For example, I'm Irish. My family is from County Galway in Ireland. The "Duffy" name has a crest that goes back hundreds of years. I don't like the design of it, but I do like its significance. It represents the generations of Duffys who came before me.

Now, if it was also good design, you would then have both parts of the equation needed for real success: the meaningful part and the artistic part. Those crests or ligatures that are most successful achieve equity through both meaning and aesthetics.

A long time ago, someone unknowingly created the first crest or initial logo. When do you think it all started?

Interestingly in times like these—of economic and cultural uncertainty—crests and monograms deliver a sense of stability. They suggest that something has been around, or that it's legacy minded and built to thrive over time. Perhaps the first crest dates back to a time when people were looking for strength.

Commercially, it probably goes back to the first packages that were designed. That person had a desire to create iconography that was pleasing to the eye and that had some meaning that could be explained or expanded about a brand or company, something that would bring meaning to the company's audience. It probably goes back to the beginning of packaged goods.

Those that are most successful achieve equity through both meaning AND AESTHETICS.

What are the visual mechanics that make a crest work as a logo?

It helps the brain in terms of simple definition by creating a focal point. Having some framing device for the most meaningful parts of a brand language. That, plus placement on a package or a page, is what people will go to first when making a purchase decision.

Right now, I'm looking at a collage that one of our designers created during the research phase of a project. On the collage is an image of a Lucky Strike [cigarette] package—it's a design everyone knows. It's a crest of sorts with a very simple logotype. If you want to attract someone's eye to the center of a package in a crowded store—this is a good way to do it – create a "bull's-eye."

It's a carrier of a badge or an emblem—a simple red target. It's red and white, literally, a bull's-eye. If you build on that like the retail brand

1: International Truck logo

Target has done, and establish a way of speaking to the audience, using variations on the red and white target, then you've created messaging in a proprietary way—a brand language.

Crests are typically multilayered. On the International Truck logo we designed, it's simple. We took the old logo—the orange diamond road—and added other elements to it for added meaning. The black triangle in the middle of an orange triangle has meaning—it's a roadway—plus it has familiarity from the past—the old look of International Harvester.

Louise Fili on Sfoglia

As told by Louise Fili, Louise Fili Ltd., New York City

"Sfoglia (which is Italian for "sheets of uncut handmade pasta") originally started in Nantucket. When the owners decided to open another restaurant in Manhattan, they opted to rebrand. The original logo was neither good nor bad—just not up to par with the quality of Sfoglia, which is intimate and rustic, with exceptional pastas and extraordinary bread.

"The concept for the new identity came from the client's interest in heraldry, which led me to the notion of two islands represented by two mermaids. It was my original intention to label them Nantucket and Manhattan, but the client preferred to use the airport code for Nantucket, which the cognoscenti would recognize. (I, alas, did not.)

"I love the complexity and elegance of the logo, which perfectly represents Sfoglia's cuisine and aesthetic. It also looks quite striking in gold leaf on their front window."

It is a way of retaining brand equity, building on heritage. The dimensional, steel crest of the frame has to do with innovation, durability, and the history of their trucks.

I think the best logos that are done with a sense of nostalgia, such as crests, have meaning, and lead to more than just what is on the face of the design. There is more than just putting down flourishes and abstract bordering. All of a logo's parts are pieces to a puzzle that helps the viewer figure out what the company is all about—what they stand for, where they've been.

What's another crestlike logo that works in this way?

Fashion brand Ralph Lauren. I just saw their new banner outside their store on West Broadway in New York—it's a classic crest and it's all about nostalgia. It's an approach to fashion that's not just about clothing, but rather a lifestyle from another era that makes their audience feel better wearing those kinds of clothes. It's successful in that it puts people into a fantasy when life was more romantic or exotic. Look at all of the ligatures and crests and symbols used in that brand, and you see a wide range of icons that have to do with crests and icons from earlier times and various places. They complement the design aesthetic of the clothing, the marketing, and so on.

The Duffy & Partners logo is a new take on a monogram ligature as well. The *D* and the *P* connected in a fresh and simple positive/negative interchange—a suggestion of the dialogue central to creating fresh thinking and a key to our approach to design.

As a designer, I enjoy going through books like *LogoLounge* because I'm interested in the work from a design perspective—the simple logo on its own. But coats of arms, crests, initials, or whatever have to be attached to a broader brand language that establishes the brand meaning in a powerful way and sells product—at the end of the day, that's what it is all about.

It would be great if we could just look at it from an artistic point of view, but you have to realize that business side, too.

Exactly how do you think these designs imprint themselves on the brain? Why do they continue to work?

I believe they imprint on three different levels. First, they can work by blatant force—it is just in your face, for any reason. It can be loud or prominent. If I paint a big red devil on the side of a building, everyone will notice it. It can be somewhat outrageous—in itself or in its context. Billboards do that, book covers do that, packages can do that. So a logo can jump out at you because it is bold—not always a good thing. In fact, it can be obnoxious and irritating.

The next level of imprint is the artistic level. People are drawn to visuals that are pleasing to the eye. We like them because they remind us of other things, or because they're simply unique—maybe that color or that shape or the way those letters are rendered is new to us. They create an artistically pleasing presence in my mind.

Third is design that represents some other pertinent interest to the individual. Think of skateboarders—to attract their attention, I have

2 and 3: Basin White logo and identity

to know their visual language and the imagery that relates to their world. If I do that, the message will catch the eye and have meaning.

In designing an initial logo or crest, what are some factors of which designers should be aware?

Can you take a *G* or any other letter and turn it into something aesthetically pleasing? Sure. But you have to connect to the brand's essence and do so in a way that separates it from all of its competitors in a compelling way.

The logo is only one part of the brand language. An example is a ligature we did for Aveda Men—a simple *AM*. The client refers to it as their "dog." In a minimal way, it looks like a dog. I like the logo itself, but when you see it in the context of everything else—the photography, colors, and so on, that were used to launch the brand—you can see it is not just a simple ligature: It is part of a complete brand language that attracts the attention of the target audience.

Trevor Elliott on Zero G

As told by Trevor Elliott, Springboard, Los Angeles

"Zero G provides weightless flying experiences for consumers. It needed a new identity, but the client had no ideas or requests for this new mark. NASA and the military have planes outfitted to produce zero gravity, but this is for consumers, at $3,500 to $5,000 a ride—there is no competition.

"Our concepts went directly to weightlessness, not initials. Our brand board had feathers floating, apples floating, people floating. We also tried silhouettes of people floating, but that looked too much like iPod promo materials.

"Instead, I experimented with *sumi* ink on paper. The most 'off' experiments indicated flight—we needed weightlessness. But the organic energy was strong in these 'inkman' designs, so I made tons of scans and pieced them together.

"The client felt that inkman lacked accessibility: In fact, they told us to toss it out. Then I had a simple 'Aha' moment, reversing an arc over the top to form a *G*. They went from, 'Don't like it,' to 'Sold, done, it's over.'"

With crests, there is a tendency for designers to do too much. They fall prey to "how much can we cram into this" design, with colors and icons and borders and backdrops. You have to build a language that the viewer can understand and relate to.

Sometimes a designer may balk at considering an initial logo solution, believing that it's too simple a solution.

Keeping it simple can be the absolute right way to go forward. The logo in and of itself is not the end-all or be-all. I always go back to the Nike swoosh. It is one of the most recognized logos in the world. But if you were looking at it for the first time, it would have no meaning. It's the language that has built up around it through imagery and stories that makes it meaningful. It conjures up ideas of sports and great athletic performance, and the Olympics and all kinds of things. It has tremendous meaning. But on the face of it, there is very little there.

Another one from our office is Basin. It's a store that makes handmade soaps and lotions. They have now developed a higher-end version called

With crests, there is a tendency for designers TO DO TOO MUCH.

Basin White. The logo is a *B* that is half submerged—pretty simple. With the name "Basin" and knowing it is about soap, the simple crest helps a simple product line stand apart.

Fairly recently, we completed a new logo for Thymes. There is the company brand identity, and each of the product offerings has its own crest, or ligature. The Thymes *T* logo complements the individual product identities.

As the world shrinks, do you think that design solutions such as crests and initials will continue to be relevant? For example, would an initial design solution using a Roman letterform be effective in a country that does not use a Roman alphabet?

It all depends on the image a brand needs to project. Using a letterform that does not necessarily relate to me personally still can have meaning—or maybe it has even more meaning because it is from a different place with a different language. English letterforms presented to a Chinese audience that is interested in Western goods can be a powerful marketing message.

5

4: Thymes identity, **5:** Sulloc Cha logo

We recently did a crest for the large green tea brand there—Sulloc Cha. Its design has a South Korean look with English characters, all within a leaf motif. It relates more to what the product is than what the language says. One of their goals was to expand their audience outside of Asia. So they needed to have both an English and a South Korean look.

Schwartzrock Graphic Arts

As told by Sherwin Schwartzrock, Schwartzrock Graphic Design

"When I designed my own logo, I of course needed something that reflected my personality and what I do—illustrative logo design. The hardest part was working this awful name—Schwartzrock—into the design.

"The touch-words for my brand are 'quality' and 'professional.' I take my work very seriously—I even wear suits to the office—so I wanted a logo that would reflect that professionalism and yet also capture the whimsical aspect of my work.

"I chose a crest because it had a sense of civility and quality. I combined the stuffy border with cartoony type. So there's a dichotomy in the crest that reflects what makes me unique.

"All of the elements in a design like this are like putty. You have to work with them and squish them again and again until you come up with the right design."

Consistency and longevity

Tom Geismar, Chermayeff & Geismar

Tom Geismar is a pioneer in the field of logo and identity design, having created iconic marks for Chase bank, Xerox, PBS, Rockefeller Center, Mobil, and hundreds more. Founding partner of Chermayeff & Geismar, Geismar's elegantly lucid work has truly stood the test of time. He speaks here on how initial or ligature designs work and when and why their use is appropriate.

Why and how do people understand initials when they are used as identity elements?

If you step back from the situation a bit, initials are part of a category of logos that you could call "names." There are many types of names that are selected for a variety of reasons. There are proper names (often family names), like Armani or Braun. There are descriptive names, like the National Broadcasting Company or Best Buy. You have metaphors, like Jaguar for a car, or Giants or Eagles for football teams. You have found names which are arbitrarily applied, like Apple or Next. You have artificial or made-up names like Kodak, Xerox, and Exxon.

Then you have abbreviations, which include initials. If you go back to NBC, that's just shorthand for the actual company name. Think of BMW or IBM: They are just abbreviated names that we now accept as the replacement for the real name.

There are also acronyms like NASA or Esso, where the initials form a word that can be pronounced. They become words, but they are really initials, derived from National Aeronautic & Space Administration, and Standard Oil.

When a designer is trying to decide what to do when making a new mark, so much depends on the entity, and what you are saddled with in the first place. Maybe you have a long, complicated name like International Business Machines, or you need a design that is very evocative. An abbreviation may be a good direction.

It's hard for people to remember one set of initials from all of the OTHERS.

Those are all reasons why initials can work in identies. What causes them not to work?

Mainly, the problem is that there are already too many of them, especially in places like Washington, D.C., where everything has initials. Like crests, initials can tend to look official. But unless the entity has lots of exposure, and their initials have some unique attribute, it's hard for people to remember one set of initials from all of the others.

An abbreviation can also be confusing. We were talking with a very interesting group yesterday, and they referred to themselves as "CI."

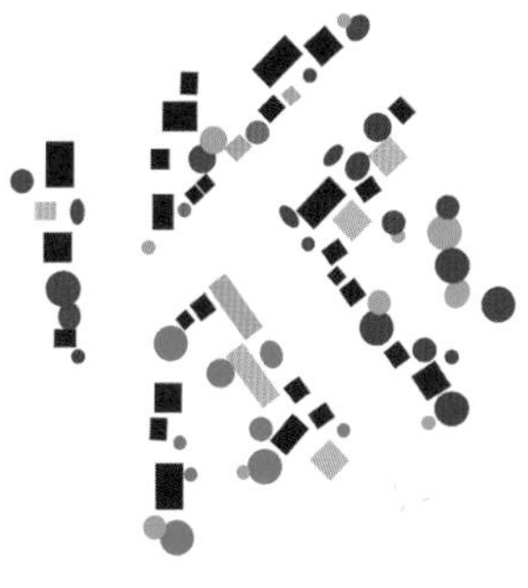

3

4

1: Armani Exchange logo, **2:** Owens-Illinois logo, **3:** Massachusetts Bay Transportation Authority logo, **4:** Robert F. Kennedy Foundation logo

Boris Ljubicic on Kutina City

As told by Boris Ljubicic, Studio International, Zagreb, Croatia

"Kutina, about 70 kms from Zagreb, Croatia, is referred to as a 'green town,' due to its many trees and parks. But it's also known for its petrochemical industry, which can be quite polluting. The mayor decided to change the visual image of Kutina into a green city of modern technologies.

"This logo is a representation of streets, trees, and houses, as a 2-D urban plan, whose shape is the letter *K*. The positive version perceives the logo in daylight, and there is a negative version as nighttime. The colors also represent the dynamics of development and the vivacity of children's play in the many parks. Also, the logo is like an electronic chip card, to show the development of a town of modern technologies. The slogan that Kutina will use with the logo is 'Kutina—The City of Technology.'

"Kutina is one of the first cities in Croatia that has had its visual identity laid out graphically. This solution is simple and complex—simple because it is only one letter and complex because it represents the city and the life in it. The mayor has decided to build a new part of the city based on this idea."

5

To me, that means "corporate identity," but their real name means something entirely different. Initials can be a real problem in that sense. They often can have unintended references for people outside your immediate community.

Initials can also be hard to remember. In Boston many years ago, the MBTA—Massachusetts Bay Transportation Authority—was changing everything around in its system. We asked, "Why not call the group *T*?" Everyone is familiar with relevant *T* words—trains, tracks, tubes, tunnels, trolleys, transportation, etc.—and no one can remember MBTA. *T* is still the logo today.

6

5: Massachusetts Bay Transportation Authority Identity
6: PBS logo

Can you describe initial design projects from your office that you feel are particularly successful?

PBS is a good example. Herb Lubalin created a logo for PBS that was based on the initials of the Public Broadcasting Service. It was a good logo, but it was causing problems. The individual public broadcasting stations, which did their own fundraising in their own communities, needed to have more of their own identities. The old logo made PBS look like one large network, when in fact it is a service for the whole group of independent local stations. We turned the *P* around and duplicated it to indicate the idea of the “public” in “public broadcasting.” This took the focus off of the initials.

The United Nations Development Programme is another interesting example. It’s a very long name, and all communications have to be in English, French, and Spanish. In English, its

You really can’t disassociate your view of the logo from your opinion OF THAT ENTITY.

initials are UNDP, but in French and Spanish, they are PNUD. We created a logo in which the visual look was the same even when the order of the letters had to switch.

What are examples from other offices that you admire?

The funny thing about logos is that if you ask people what they think are the best ones, invariably, they will name designs that are for very well-known entities, ones that they think of in a very positive way. This is because you really can’t disassociate your view of the logo from your opinion of that entity. For example, no one mentions the Enron logo as being outstanding. I think it is a very strong logo, but because of the company it represents, it is never mentioned.

I have always admired the IBM logo. It was a very tough design problem that Paul Rand solved quite neatly. Each letter gets wider and wider, but he found a way around that.

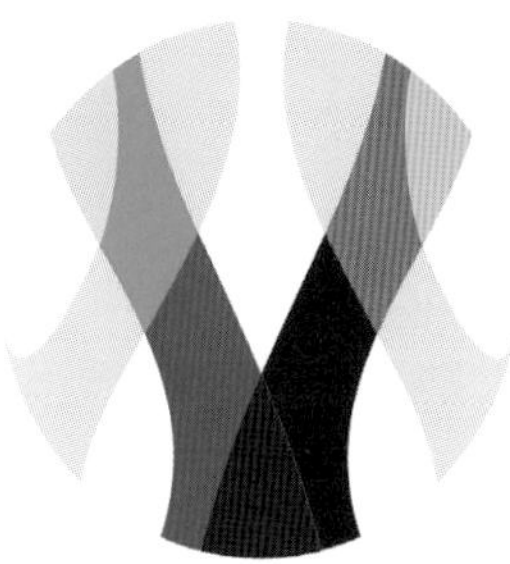

Denis Ulyanov on Mvlab

As told by Denis Ulyanov, Tula City, Russia

“Mvlab specializes in creating bioactive nutritional additives, curative cosmetics, nonalcoholic beverages, and other products for healthy diets using natural ingredients. The Russian company’s management decided to update its identity when it extended a product line.

“The key element in this design is the reflection of a shape. I wanted to reflect the multifacetedness and structure of the company, to show its mission. I wanted an emotional visual representation that indicated ‘global,’ ‘innovation,’ and ‘progress.’

“A ligature enclosed in a circle was the starting point for this solution. The idea was to represent a harmonious and inseparable union of science and nature, a main tenet of the company’s business. The reflection is of a shape based on attributes of labs, like a glass flask, or of a transformation and chemical reaction.

“The client eventually opted for a different logo that I proposed that may reproduce better and that is also a good match to the emotional ambience of the company. I support the client’s choice, but I consider this symbol to be a good solution to the task set, too: It is associational and it is genuine.”

I also think that 3M is an initial design that is very well done. It very clearly and boldly states what people have come to call the company, while the *MMM* logo it replaced displayed the name visually but not verbally.

Another example I have always liked is the *CN* that stands for the Canadian National Railway. Made of a single continuous stroke, the letter-forms suggest the idea of travel and movement, as well as reading very clearly and simply. The CNN mark, also made as a single stroke, uses bolder and more angular forms to suggest vitality and electronics, and as such is clearly different from CN, even though their initialized names are very similar.

The *ABC* mark for the American Broadcasting Company is another one that is based on a simple concept—recognizing that, in lowercase, the three initials can be essentially round, and by placing them within a larger circle, unites them into a bold, clear mark. In all these instances, the designer has found some element that makes the combination of initials distinctive and memorable.

If you change a design just for the times, you will be IN TROUBLE SOON.

Clearly, initial designs have been in use for many years, but would you consider them to be a more modern solution?

In the last half of the twentieth century, where things needed to be quicker because of the

development of TV and other media, initials gained a lot of favor. In the corporate world, there were many mergers and company transformations. This led to lots of odd names, and lots of initials.

Should such cultural or economic indicators steer a designer toward or away from design decisions? For instance, when the economy is poor, would a more austere initial design be a sensible direction?

We always take a long-term view. If you change a design just for the times, you will be in trouble soon. Logos only work when they have been around for a while and have been in people's minds for a while.

I think that when the economy is bad, there should be an even greater emphasis in getting your name out there and keeping it known. When you have to deal with reduced expenditures, you need to figure out ways to make the investment go farther.

Your work is well known for its longevity. What advice could you offer to others on creating logos and identities of any description that are not just of the moment?

As always, the particular circumstances determine what approach might work best. There are instances when a changing identity might be desirable. For example, many years ago we established the graphic identity for WGBH, the public television station in Boston, and especially its channel, number 2, as a three-dimensional number that could continually be reconfigured to reflect specific programming, holidays, or messages. MTV later adopted a similar attitude for their identity, using multiple depictions of the MTV initials. This kind of approach can work where there is a more or less captive audience, and variety and change are an important attribute of the entity.

Using a very current and fashionable graphic look might also be appropriate for some companies that want to be perceived as fashion leaders, and have a very distinctive name that is easily recognized, almost no matter how depicted. But we have found that, for most identities, it is best to use graphic techniques that will not quickly seem dated, because the reality is that it usually takes years for an identity to take hold in the public's imagination.

If the identity starts to look dated just when it's beginning to be recognized, that's a real problem. As someone once said, "Nothing dulls faster than the cutting edge." In this regard it is interesting to note that most of the leading-edge fashion brands have very classic graphic identities.

8

7: PBS identity materials, 8: WGBH logo

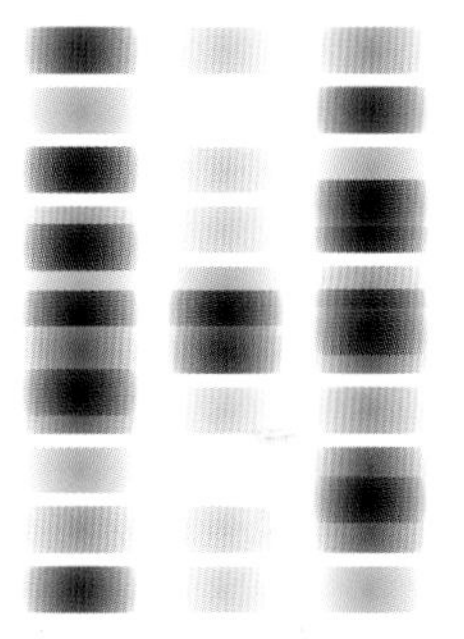

Roy Smith on Hooke Laboratories

As told by Roy Smith, Roy Smith Design, Norwich, England

"Hooke Laboratories is a bio-tech company that is searching for cures for human diseases. It offers contract research and products to the pharmaceutical and biotechnology industries.

"The founders were very open-minded when it came to their new identity. Their name was inspired by the seventeenth-century English scientist Robert Hooke, who was a less famous rival of Isaac Newton. He made significant contributions in the fields of physics, astronomy, biology, and medicine, and he coined the word *cell* to describe the smallest fragment of a human being.

"I produced quite a few concepts for the client, including designs with molecules, DNA spirals, test tubes, and the like. But this design was inspired by electrophoresis, a process that separates DNA into banding, which is visible with ultraviolet light.

"The solution really breaks a lot of rules of logo design—it's out of focus, there is not a line version of it, and it's somewhat monotone in color. When the client saw it, though, they knew this was the one."

Constellations for the Brain

Michael Doret,
Michael Doret Graphic Design

Michael Doret has long been respected and admired for his ability to combine design and illustration in identity designs that hearken from the past, yet feel completely contemporary. His clients have included such admirable names as Time *magazine, the NBA, the Graphic Artists Guild, Taschen Publishing, and Disney Imagineering. In this article, Doret shares how inspirations from the past inform his work today.*

What I like to do with my work is create what I call "constellations" of letters AND IMAGES

Your identity and logo design work is so distinctive. Where does your inspiration come from?

How I approach my work has a lot to do with my growing up in the 1950s in Brooklyn, near Coney Island. I was not really aware of how this environment had influenced me until a few years ago when I came across an old photo my dad had taken of my brother and me in front of the Tilt-A-Whirl in Coney Island. Looking at that photo, I realized that it contained many of the visual cues and elements that would later become very important in my work: bright colors, emblematic shapes, and wonderful, shaded, outlined, and dimensional letterforms.

So I had this epiphany: This was where and when my visual aesthetics were shaped! I remembered that I had been fascinated with lettered and hand-painted signs—from the enameled sides of Good Humor trucks, which roamed my Brooklyn neighborhood in summertime, to the huge billboards in Times Square I'd see when I visited my dad at work.

Nobody ever said my work was subtle—and now I understand why: Who I am and what I do was inspired and influenced by what we would now call the "Pop Culture" that surrounded me as I was growing up.

Much of your work is also very complex. How does the human brain process and recall a complex design like one of your crest logos?

I think one tends to see and remember patterns in images. What I like to do with my work is create what I call "constellations" of letters and images that somehow are tied together by the use of pattern, repetition, form, and color, and a very basic geometry. Any really good art should do that.

I think the origins of contemporary logos go back to ancient symbols, like the cross and the star, the circle and the triangle—geometric symbols that were imbued with magical properties by their creators. Think of medieval heraldry and of ancient vestments: We may not be conscious of it, but these forms are at the root of what we now call logos and corporate identity. These icons, shapes, and symbols are an important part of our past. Who knows whether or not our responsiveness to them might even go all the way back to the genetic level?

2

3

1: Cliff's Amusement Park logo, 2: Disney's River Country Water Park logo, 3: New York Knicks logo

Mirna Saletovic on Promel Projekt

As told by Mirna Saletovic, Hand Design Studio, Zagreb, Croatia

"Promel Projekt is a systems engineering company that specializes in traffic control through video and information systems, located in Zagreb, Croatia. It had an existing logo that was a bit outdated and too simple to effectively represent the full story of the company.

"There was no doubt that the concept for the new logo should visually follow shapes, colors, and symbols used in traffic. One idea came from traffic signals: The double letter *P* in the company name indicated the central symbol, and we could represent it as a light. The background uses a dark black for the color of asphalt. Yellow is used to represent the color of stenciled road symbols and traffic symbols.

"The client eventually selected another concept that we also presented: a *P* that was formed from the rounded shapes of highway interchange roads. We think both solutions sum up just about all of the company's activities. Client feedback has been very positive, and we are delighted with it."

Take a look at a couple of what I consider to be classic midcentury logos: the Sunoco Oil diamond, the Chevrolet chevron, or the Pennsylvania Railroad keystone. Why do we remember them so clearly, what makes these identities endure, and why have they become such beloved icons of our culture?

So you feel that the basic shape of a crest is part of the key to the enduring popularity of these designs?

There is balance and symmetry to these shapes. They are forms that for some reason appeal to us on a very basic level. A psychologist might better be able to tell us why these shapes have been so appealing over time. To me it's the inherent geometry that I find so attractive.

When I was growing up, I knew I would become either an artist or an astronomer, and I now realize there's a direct connection between the two. There is a grand geometry to the stars and the heavens; there's a great pattern that ties all things together. Perhaps my love for astronomy helps me see the patterns in all things—and informs my design work.

One design that covers both initials and crests is my logo for the Graphic Artists Guild. It embodies many of the things I've spoken about. It harkens back to ancient pictograms with its star shape, which has long been considered magical, and as in most classic monograms, all of the letters are intertwined. I chose this form so that the letters *G*, *A*, *G* would not appear sequentially as a word. All these elements are enclosed and tied together within a ring of text. The design has many disparate elements, but because of the math and geometry underlying the design, it ends up completely in balance.

This logo is a good example of pushing things to the limit. I do like to push things, but one has to be aware that there is a point beyond which a design becomes illegible or awkward. You have to be able to sense how far to push. You have to understand what the inherent possibilities of the letterforms in the design are, and you can't force letters into a design that won't accommodate them. If the guild's name had had different initials, such as *GDG*, this logo would have taken a very different form.

They are forms that for some reason appeal to us on a VERY BASIC LEVEL.

By using such familiar shapes, does the designer risk creating something unintriguing to the eye?

I believe successful design has to do with the departures and liberties you take. One thing I like to do is to look at a lot of old graphics, done by people who did not have formal design training. They made mistakes, but many were charming and interesting mistakes. Many of them did not know the rules, so they did not know they were breaking them. So there are times when I deliberately try to do it wrong—to learn from others' mistakes, and repeat them!

Sometimes in balancing all this geometry and symmetry, you have to throw a monkey wrench into the works and break some rules in order to keep things lively.

4

5

6

4: Graphic Artists Guild logo, **5:** Event Media logo, **6:** Chic-A-Boom logo

David Pache on WebMynd

As told by David Pache of dache, St-Cergue, Vaud, Switzerland

"WebMynd produces a computer plug-in that is meant to streamline the cumbersome process of bookmarking Web pages. It logs accessed data for word or character searches later.

"The client—a start-up—wanted bold coloring and a noticeable brand. They also wanted the logo or an element of it to be the link button the customer would click to download the product. So it had to be eye catching.

"As the project developed, I selected a multicolored *M* and *W*. The multiple shapes within the letterforms was meant to give the impression that it was a plug-in element consisting of many functions that could hold and store data from many sources. The colors are bold, but easy on the eye.

"The client actually only used the design for a limited time before changing the logo. But the comments I receive on it in my portfolio are very positive. It seems that multicolored solutions are very popular in an industry saturated with so many providers."

7

What are some examples of crests that you admire?

I always go back to the older stuff like those I mentioned earlier. There are many, many others including the Heinz logo, arching inside a pickle inside a keystone, or the Texaco logo within a star, or MGM with its lion surrounded by a crest made of unspooled, looping film. The Shell Gas logo is a shell, but it is also a crest. Over the years many of these have been updated, but they have all kept their essence. Think of the American Automobile Association "AAA" mark—three *A*s in an oval—you can't get more simple or memorable than that. Old car badges and logos have also been very influential to me. Ford, Buick, Chevrolet, and Oldsmobile—they are all so beautiful. I could go on and on.

What in your opinion causes a crest design to not work properly?

There can be a lot of elements to coordinate in these designs. One of the most important elements is color. Some designers don't understand how to use color, or at least don't use it in a way that I can relate to. Another problem can be too much information. When in doubt one should always err on the side of simplicity—eliminating elements that aren't 100 percent necessary for successful communication.

Another contributing problem is imitating without understanding—or blind imitation. There have been those who have chosen to ape the look of what I do. The problem with this is that instead of looking at my work, they should be looking at what *inspired* me. My work pays homage to certain historical precedents—but with a spin. Any designer interested in a specific sort of design should look to the original source of inspiration, not to any of their contemporaries.

I also advise young designers to forget about asking what program I work in. It's not important. A computer program can help with the process, but it is not an end in itself. Be aware of the history of design. You don't need to be able to cite dates or names, but if you are aware of historical trends, and study the work you love, you will be better equipped to pursue your goals. When you are overly concerned with the computer and what it can do, you will end up with something that is clean and slick, but that has no content and no soul. What makes any design successful is the *thinking* behind it, not how slickly it's done.

Does creating logos ever become any easier for you?

Before computers, I did very detailed pencil drawings to map out every angle. Everything was very carefully planned, elements aligned very carefully. I used drafting instruments as an architect would. A lot of that drudgery was eliminated when I started working on a Mac in

8

9

7: The Hollywood Dell signage, **8:** Tribeca Film Festival logo, **9:** Local Flavors logo

1995. The mathematics was inherent in the applications and made the drawing part a lot easier. But as I just said, it didn't eliminate the thinking part.

Coming up with good ideas is just as hard as it ever was. When I get a good idea, I can implement it faster and easier than before, but giving birth to good ideas is always a difficult process that never seems to get any easier. Seeing a successful design materialize before your eyes—and knowing it's your own creation—now that's a thrill that never gets old.

David Kampa on Costa Del Mar

As told by David Kampa, McGarrah Jessee, Austin, Texas

"Costa Del Mar makes high-end sunglasses for fishing that allow you to see below the surface of the water. They have a strong following among fishermen of all kinds and are mandatory equipment for many pros, guides, and the Coast Guard.

"Even though the sunglasses have a contemporary look, the brand is more adventure ready—rugged, sun bleached, windblown, and weathered. Inspiration comes from what you might find in a remote fishing destination, like fish taco shacks, surf shops, outfitters, and fishing guides.

"This design was the very last execution that I did for this project, the night before the presentation. The idea was to create a little 'instant history' for the brand by creating a design that felt old, as if it was a vintage Costa logo done years ago. The final logo felt authentic to our source of inspiration and classic to the Costa brand."

initials

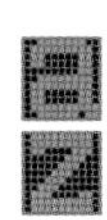

1

D = Design Firm C = Client

1A D Studio International C a Bank 1B D Straka-Design C T-Com 1C D Kinesis, Inc. C Amfit
2A D August Design Studio C August Design Studio 2B D August Design Studio C August Design Studio 2C D Giles Design Inc. C Alphabet Soup
3A D SmartArt Design Inc. C Artists for Creative Theater Inc. 3B D Mazemedia 3C D D&i (Design and Image) C A-Line
4A D Haute Haus Creative C Waterstone Development 4B D 13thirtyone Design C Ambiance 4C D FutureBrand BC&H

A B C

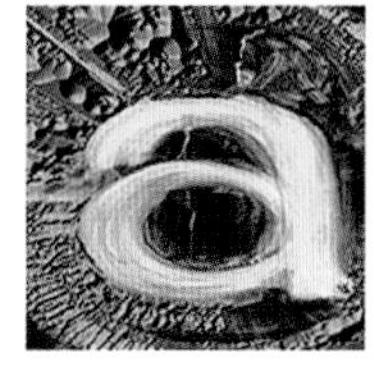

2

3

4

Ⓓ = Design Firm Ⓒ = Client

1A Ⓓ JoshuaCreative Ⓒ Hume Lake Christian Camps 1B Ⓓ Mosmondesign Ⓒ Education Board 1C Ⓓ LEKKERWERKEN Ⓒ Lekkerwerken 2A Ⓓ Impressions Design and Print Ltd Ⓒ Amlyn Group Ltd 2B Ⓓ McConnell Creative Ⓒ Automation Alley / Oakland County 2C Ⓓ Nastasha Beatty Designs Ⓒ Debbi Tisdale 3A Ⓓ chirag ahir design Ⓒ aakar 3B Ⓓ Biamerikan Inc. Ⓒ Al's board shop 3C Ⓓ Marlin Ⓒ Avalanche Snowboards 4A Ⓓ Valhalla | Design & Conquer Ⓒ Ascape Designs 4B Ⓓ Draplin Design Co. Ⓒ Ambission Clothing 4C Ⓓ Totem Ⓒ Alan Dalton

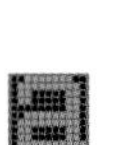

A B C

1

D = Design Firm C = Client

1A D Billingsley Concepts, Inc C Addison Title Co. 1B D Looney Ricks Kiss Architects, Inc. C Kite Realty 1C D Corder Philips C Crescent Communities
2A D Double A Creative C Double A Creative 2B D jeda creative C Allison Reisz 2C D Kessler Digital Design C Aslan Lamont Painting & Wallcoverings
3A D Sibley Peteet C Avenue One 3B D Sire Advertising C Apps Limited Partnership 3C D LSD C music of chamber spanish asociation
4A D grow C Aisha Hussain Al Fardan 4B D Haute Haus Creative C warterstone 4C D CONCEPTO WORLDWIDE C Alebrands

A B C

1

2

3

4

D = Design Firm C = Client

1A D Ambassadors C Ambassadors 1B D cypher13 C Alex Henry 1C D Pale Horse Design C Adixion Clothing
2A D Roman Design C Annette's Drapery Design 2B D Todd M. LeMieux Design C Austin Hill Inn 2C D MSI C 3Vodka
3A D Bean Graphics C St. Paul UMC Youth Group 3B D DUEL Purpose C Alexander's Flooring 3C D huber+co. C Arena District Athletic Club
4A D PETTUS CREATIVE C A'ccents Home & Garden 4B D CAPSULE C America's Team 4C D Letter 7 C AZ Adventures

A B C

1

2

3

4

D = Design Firm C = Client

1A D Dennard, Lacey & Associates C Antillia Capital 1B D LSD C Al Aire Books Editor 1C D bob neace graphic design, inc C Ayesh Lawyers
2A D Corporate Image Consultants, Inc. C Craft Services, Inc. 2B D G&G Advertising C Alexandar Outfitters 2C D Hand dizajn studio C Amteh
3A D Strange Ideas 3B D Sandstorm Design C Alliance 3C D Gardner Design C Action Scouts
4A D Haute Haus Creative C Alpine Paving 4B D Spangler Design Team C Advantage Rent A Car 4C D Tower of Babel C Ashbrook High School

A B C

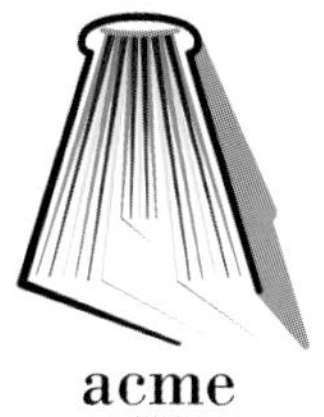

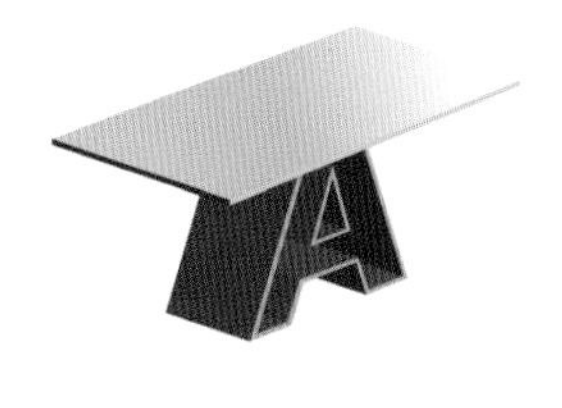

1

2

3

4

D = Design Firm C = Client

1A D Interrobang Design Collaborative, Inc. C White Packert Photography 1B D Fumiko Noon C Assemble
1C D Rick Carlson Design & Illustration C Atlantic Countertops 2A D Scientific Arts C Advantec 2B D Red Clover Studio C Alliance Homes
2C D Viziom C Almaga 3A D PixelGood. C Firefighter Achievers Association 3B D Shawn Huff C Austin 3C D Glitschka Studios C Campbell-Ewald
4A D Bridge Creative C All-In Chips 4B D Image Communications, Inc. C Aberdeen Switchplates 4C D ArtGraphics.ru C Akku-Vertrieb

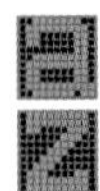

A B C

1

2

3

4

D = Design Firm   C = Client

1A D UNIT-Y C Sailings Inc 1B D Heisel Design C All Phase Construction 1C D Tran Creative C Abbotswood Design Group
2A D Swanson Russell C MinnKota 2B D Struck C Alchemy 2C D The Caliber Group C The Alliance Group
3A D Ad Impact Advertising C Avenger Yachts 3B D UNIT-Y C Aware 3C D Factory Creative C Axis Realty Group
4A D Diagram C Autostrada Wielkopolska 4B D Judson Design 4C D 01d C Aluplast

A B C

1

2

3

4

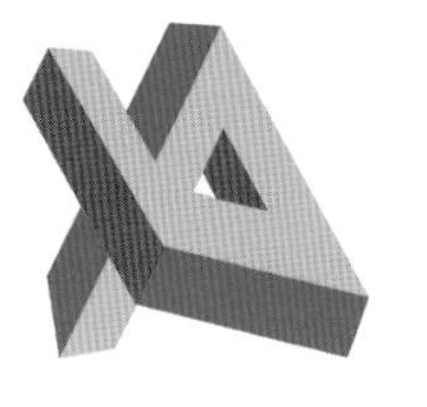

D = Design Firm C = Client

1A D Studio International C Arheology Museum 1B D M3 Advertising Design C Katrina Ferry 1C D Cfx C Altus Properties
2A D Mattson Creative C Lennar Homes 2B D The Flores Shop C TouchPoints Public Relations 2C D Tactical Magic C Alliance Africa
3A D Landor Associates C Ackermans 3B D Pixelube C RealNetworks 3C D Kern Design Group C Anderson Analytics
4A D Carmi e Ubertis Milano Srl C Ascherio 4B D Diana Graham C Argent Corporation 4C D Shelley Design+Marketing C Lee Ashmore P.A.

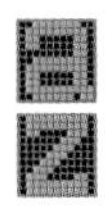

A B C

1

2

3

4

D = Design Firm C = Client

1A D Lienhart Design C American Midwest Financial 1B D Jeff Kern Design C iMarlin, The Marlin Network 1C D SoupGraphix Inc. C Active Motorsports
2A D Pure Fusion Media C Ameritrans 2B D Ikola Designs C Airtronic 2C D Landkamer Partners, Inc. C Applicast
3A D switchfoot creative C Aggregate Media 3B D Adstract Art C Rann Property Adval 3C D Canvas Astronauts & Agriculture C BrigadeQM
4A D Marlin C Advanced Industries 4B D Romulo Moya / Trama C Artec Buenos Aires 4C D Jonathan Rice & Company C Accent Capital

A B C

1

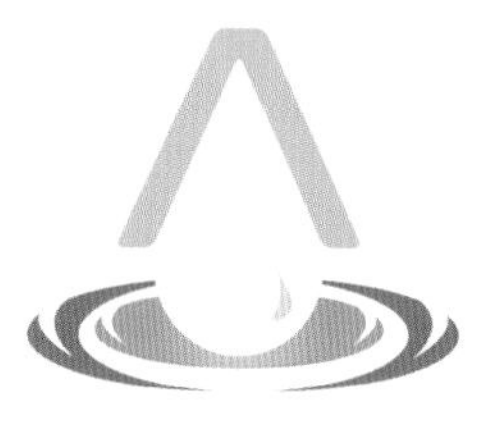

2

3

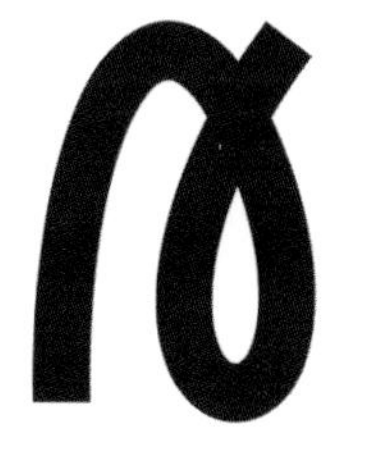

4

D = Design Firm C = Client

1A D Steven O'Connor C Allscripts 1B D Westwerk DSGN C AuraSoothe 1C D Scott Oeschger Design C Alstin Advertising, Inc.
2A D Jeremy Stott C Arteis 2B D MANMADE C NASA 2C D Abiah C American Abstract Agency
3A D Hazen Creative, Inc. C Apogee Lifestyle 3B D Ulyanov Denis C Altromine 3C D Sebastiany Branding & Design C Arte na Rua
4A D cincodemayo C Auvit de Mexico 4B D Jeffhalmos C Association of Condominium Managers of Ontario 4C D Brainding

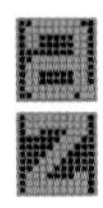

A B C

1

2

3

4

D = Design Firm C = Client

1A D Entropy Brands C Allaglo 1B D IE Design + Communications C Altus Positioning Systems 1C D ballard::creative C Autolease
2A D Bernas Design C Qualcomm Inc. 2B D KOESTER design C Mobil Land Development 2C D 28 LIMITED BRAND C Fokus
3A D David Gramblin C Allen Athletic Consulting 3B D Haven Productions C Asterion on the River 3C D The Martin Group C Account One
4A D Gardner Design C authentus 4B D Sonia Jones Design C Doug Schaub 4C D Range C The Avalon Group

A B C

1

FINANCIAL ARCHITECT

2

3

4

D = Design Firm C = Client

1A D ErikArt Design C Avatar Cottonwear 1B D Laura Manthey Design C Financial Architects 1C D Koetter Design C Apex Physical Therapy
2A D Hinge C Arlington Symphony 2B D joe miller's company C Arts Council Silicon Valley 2C D Dara Creative C Amethyst Irish Jewellery
3A D Luke Despatie & The Design Firm C Amuse 3B D Ezzo Design C Aromas Italianos 3C D DUEL Purpose C UrbanSpace Realtors
4A D Gardner Design C authentus 4B D Michael O'Connell C Museum of Contemporary Art Jacksonville 4C D fallindesign studio C AEROSCAN

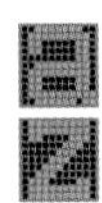

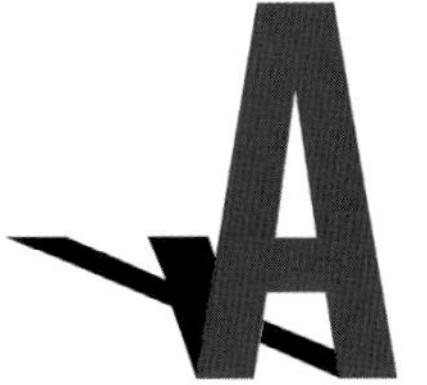

D = Design Firm C = Client

1A D Sudduth Design Co. C Crome Architecture 1B D Insight Design C Advanced Aviation Inc. 1C D Mungioli Design C Anthony Mungioli Design
2A D Flipcide C Abyss 2B D Josh Higgins Design C Apostrophe Films 2C D Home Grown Logos C Axiom Media Corp.
3A D yarimizoshintaro 3B D Turnstyle C Averetek 3C D ParkerWhite C Apptek Industries
4A D Octane 4B D Extrabrand C Alex Consulting 4C D Letter 7 C Abel Business Institute

A | B | C

1

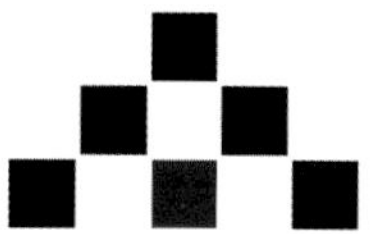

2

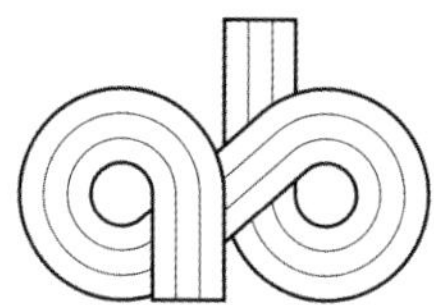

3

4

D = Design Firm C = Client

1A D Logoboom C Art Logic Studio 1B D PositiveZero Ltd. C Aest 1C D Pat Taylor Inc. C Adams Clay Tile
2A D Alan Barnett, Inc. C Alan Barnett 2B D Jenn David Design C Andreas Branch Photography 2C D Karl Design Vienna C Burmahilfe Austria
3A D Allen Creative C Allen Creative 3B D Creative Soapbox C Tracy Andrus Consulting 3C D Sebastiany Branding & Design C CA—Camara de Arquitetos
4A D Anoroc C Clay Aiken 4B D Hazen Creative, Inc. C Angela Gengler and Carlos Dobkin 4C D Werner Design Werks C College of Visual Arts

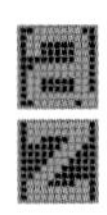

A B C

1

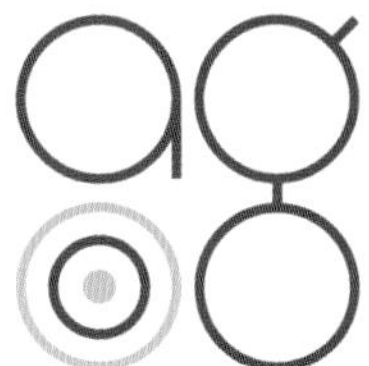

2

3

4

D = Design Firm C = Client

1A D Charles Henry Graphic Arts C Accel-Energy Services 1B D Axiom Design Collaborative C Academic Gameplan 1C D Hazen Creative, Inc. C William Galligan
2A D Advertising Intelligence C ai 2B D Denis Olenik Design Studio C AL Technologies 2C D Glitschka Studios C MacAgent.com
3A D KROG, d.o.o. C Andrej Mlakar, Ljubljana 3B D Selikoff+Co C Alan Metrick Communications 3C D Ulyanov Denis C Amedia group
4A D Oscar Morris C Oscar Morris 4B D maximo, inc. C AVID 4C D Advertising Intelligence

A B C

1

2

3

4

D = Design Firm C = Client

1A D GOTCHA DESIGN 1B D Steven O'Connor C Allscripts 1C D Form C London Records
2A D Dotzero Design C Alternate Universe Events 2B D Dotzero Design C Alternate Universe Events 2C D Joel Krieger C Allen Michaels
3A D DDB SF C Altavie 3B D Kahn Design C MCIK Advertising 3C D DikranianDesign C Adrienne Vartanian
4A D lunabrand design group C Arizona Village Communities 4B D Roskelly Inc. C Vista Auto works 4C D Brainding

A B C

1

2

3

4

D = Design Firm C = Client

1A D Louise Fili C Blount Park 1B D Tandemodus C Belle Voche 1C D A3 Design C DR Horton
2A D Judson Design 2B D Karl Design Vienna C Burmahilfe Austria 2C D ShenZhen Tusk Advertising &Brand design Co.,Ltd C BaiMeiSi
3A D Giles Design Inc. C Boudros 3B D Steven O'Connor 3C D M3 Advertising Design C Brace Yourself
4A D markatos I moore C B—San Francisco 4B D MSI C Tractor Supply 4C D Double Brand C Bazar Poznanski SA

A B C

1

2

3

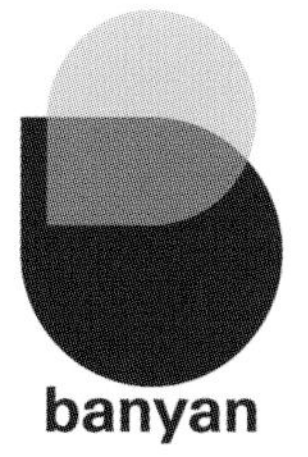

4

D = Design Firm C = Client

1A D Canvas Astronauts & Agriculture C BrigadeQM 1B D Z Factory C Out of the Ballpark 1C D The Joe Bosack Graphic Design Co. C Keystone Baseball
2A D Coolstone Design Works C Barrientos, LLC 2B D Steve's Portfolio C Point B 2C D CrossGrain Creative Studios C blabble.com
3A D Y&R Dubai C Bubbles Event Management 3B D 7th Street Design C Boshang Shopping Mall 3C D McConnell Creative C Ouimette / Brandscapers
4A D Laura Coe Design Associates C Blueshift Biotechnology 4B D Jawa and Midwich C Banyan 4C D King Design Office C Bridge Imaging USA

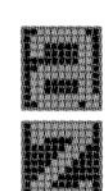

A B C

1

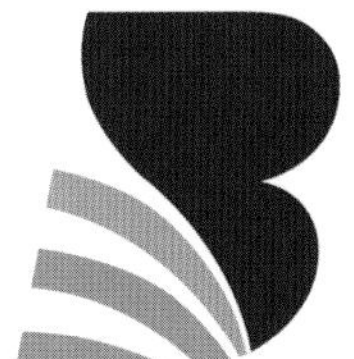

2

3

4

D = Design Firm C = Client

1A D Kiku Obata & Company C Brown Shoe 1B D Steven O'Connor C Terry G. Blackwell 1C D Gee + Chung Design C Broadband Sports
2A D Grey Matter Group C Parkland Properties 2B D Ulyanov Denis C Book Earl 2C D Alterpop C Barstow Industrial Park
3A D Gardner Design C Backroads Traveler 3B D Moker Ontwerp C Business Unusual 3C D Ikola designs... C Beulow Architects
4A D Parallele gestion de marques C Balios technologies 4B D Tunglid Advertising Agency ehf. C Kaupthing Bank 4C D 28 LIMITED BRAND C Balter Logistik

A B C

1

2

3

BLUEBERRY MEADOWS
PUBLISHERS

4

D = Design Firm C = Client

1A D David Kampa C Paul Bardagjy Photography 1B D Hornall Anderson C Best Collars 1C D MGPdesign C XS Energy Drink
2A D Collaboration Reverberation C Ocean Breakers 2B D Lichtsignale C Bluesmuse 2C D Sockeye Creative C Breault Industrial
3A D Blink Media Group 3B D 7th Street Design C Best Consulting Service 3C D Lesniewicz Associates C Bostleman Corp.
4A D Fiton C Birkifell 4B D Travers Collins & Company C Advertising Club of Buffalo 4C D Chris Rooney Illustration/Design C Blueberry Meadows

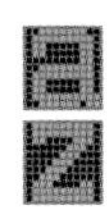

A B C

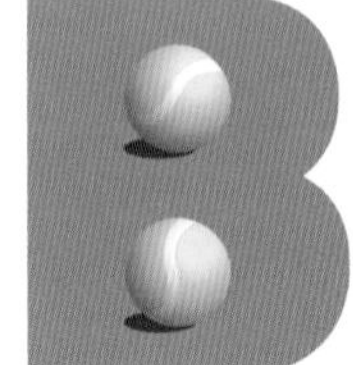

D = Design Firm C = Client

1A D Simon & Goetz Design C ballgreen gmbh & co. kg 1B D Deep Design C Bagnati Tennis Academy 1C D STUBBORN SIDEBURN C Magnet Eyes
2A D Entermotion Design Studio C Butler County 2B D Prejean Creative C Bordelon Law Firm 2C D Ventress Design Group, Inc C Bennett Communications
3A D Church Logo Gallery C Bethel Assembly of God 3B D Banowetz + Company, Inc. C Dr. Chuck Kobdish 3C D Tactix Creative C Benedictine H.S.
4A D Karl Design Vienna C Yacht Destination AG 4B D The Joe Bosack Graphic Design Co. C Boathouse Sports 4C D 28 LIMITED BRAND C Beneke

A B C

1

2

3

4

D = Design Firm C = Client

1A D Brandient C Brandient 1B D Invisible Associates C Blue Oak Projects 1C D Karl Design Vienna C Wilfling & Koertvelyessy
2A D Pivot Lab C Barkley Corporation 2B D Entermotion Design Studio C Brentwood 2C D The Laing Group C Broadspire Services
3A D Iperdesign, Inc. C Brusilow 3B D LSD C b_brator company 3C D Miller Meiers Design for Communication C Athenix Solutions
4A D RedSpark Creative C Belgrave Securities Limited 4B D Ikola designs... C Buffalo United Methodist Church 4C D Wox C Joao Fedor

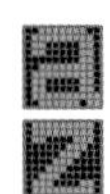

A B C

1

2

3

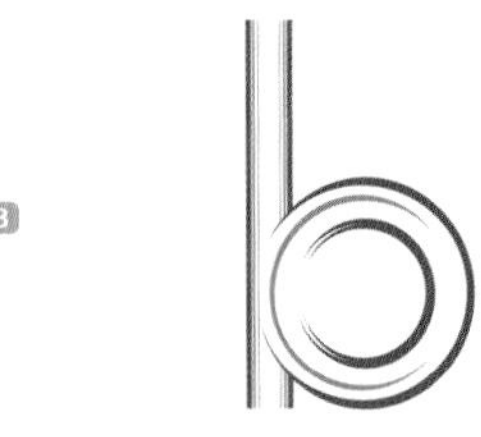

4

D = Design Firm C = Client

1A D RDQLUS Creative C Lorain Co. Visitors Bureau, Ohio 1B D Jerron Ames C Arteis 1C D 3 Advertising LLC C Brycon Construction
2A D Steven O'Connor 2B D Steven O'Connor 2C D Tran Creative C Bagmasters
3A D 1310 Studios C Bolection Door 3B D bryon hutchens | graphic design C Bryon Hutchens 3C D Angie Dudley C Angie Dudley
4A D I-MANIFEST 4B D MSI C Bed Bath & Beyond 4C D Vestigio—Consultores de Design, Lda. C Belfama

A B C

3

4

D = Design Firm C = Client

1A D Steven O'Connor C Amy Butler 1B D Carrie Dennis Design C Broadband Associates 1C D baCreative C Bill Aitchison Creative
2A D Vivid Envisions C Captain Promotions 2B D b5 Marketing & Kommunikation GmbH C bbcon 2C D UNO C Rancho Banchetti
3A D Blue Clover C Briones Engineering 3B D Pappas Group C Blackboard, Inc. 3C D BrandBerry C brandberry
4A D Braue: Brand Design Experts C Brandcode 4B D Boom Creative C Boom Creative 4C D Ross Hogin Design C Cutter & Buck

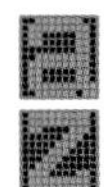

A B C

1

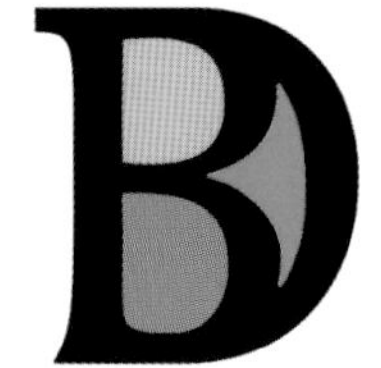

2

B.E.

3

4

D = Design Firm C = Client

1A D Gardner Design C BigDog Motorcylces 1B D Valladares, diseño y comunicacion C Bajo Deva 1C D Steven O'Connor C Dale Buelow
2A D ars graphica C herecomebetterdays.org 2B D reaves design C beth bannor designs 2C D B.L.A. Design Company C Scott Burgess, Burgess Editorial
3A D Steve Smith C Bliss Electrics 3B D Ulyanov Denis C Bankhouse Erbe 3C D Ulyanov Denis C Bankhouse Erbe
4A D Ulyanov Denis C Book Earl 4B D Dotzero Design C Brandywine Graphics 4C D Dotzero Design C Brandywine Graphics

A B C

1

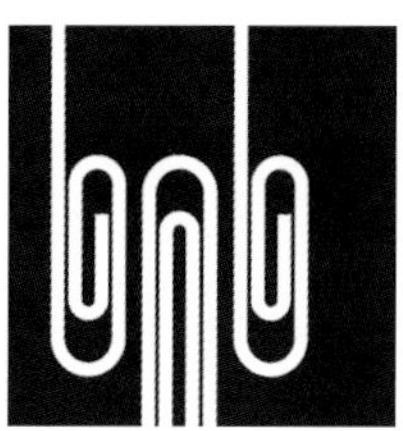

2

3

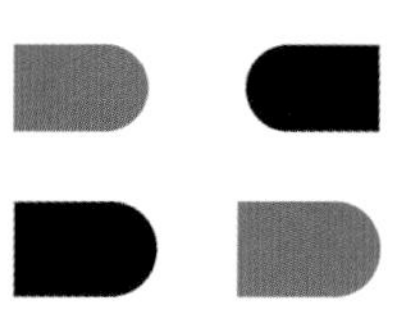

4

D = Design Firm C = Client

1A D Stefan Romanu C BN Business 1B D Murillo Design, Inc. C Kich & Co. 1C D rajasandhu.com C BuyPaper.com
2A D Jerron Ames C Arteis 2B D Gardner Design C Bradley Paper 2C D Karl Design Vienna C Braue / Q-Bioanalytic
3A D LeBoYe C Bungarampai Restaurant 3B D Offbeat Design C Blake Slade Photographers 3C D Rocket Science C Lion Brewery
4A D 3 Advertising LLC C Butt Thornton & Baehr PC 4B D Chase Design Group C The WB 4C D Freakstyle Media Group C Auto Assets

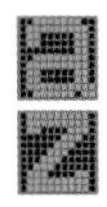

A B C

1

2

3

4

D = Design Firm C = Client

1A D Prejean Creative C City of Carencro, LA 1B D Dessein C Brian Coulson Construction 1C D Tandem Design Agency C Circa Estate Winery
2A D Haute Haus Creative C JPI 2B D Mauck Groves Branding & Design C Color FX 2C D Fitting Group C Conditionomics, LLC
3A D MSI C The Home Depot 3B D Gardner Design C Coleman 3C D Flow Creative C Streeter Place
4A D ADDWATER2 C Collabrus Inc. 4B D Effusion Creative Solutions C Cole & Cober 4C D Turnstyle C Centeris

A B C

1

2

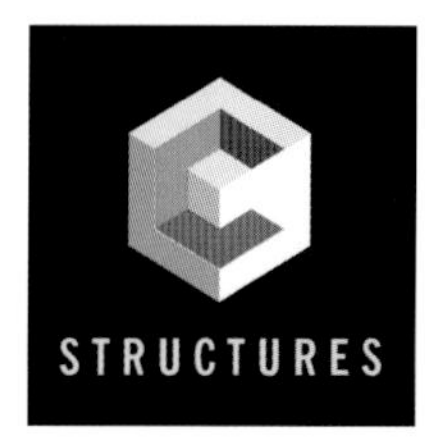

3

4

D = Design Firm C = Client

1A D Victor Goloubinov C Enviromental Centre 1B D Glitschka Studios C Glitschka Studios 1C D Bertz Design Group C Connecticut Career Choices
2A D Design Army C Capitol Communicator 2B D 5Seven C Capital One Financial 2C D brossman design C Glaxo Smith Kline
3A D Haute Haus Creative C Colorado Crossing 3B D Skybend C C Structures 3C D Lienhart Design C Garnet Community Bank
4A D Jenny Ng C crimson hexagon 4B D DAS Creative C Chance Business School 4C D Remo Strada Design C Cliffwood Partners

A B C

1

2

3

4

Ⓓ = Design Firm Ⓒ = Client

1A Ⓓ Galperin Design, Inc. Ⓒ Concept Construction Services, Inc. 1B Ⓓ Visualliance Ⓒ Cornoyer-Hedrick, Inc. 1C Ⓓ Mattson Creative
2A Ⓓ Incitrio Ⓒ SOS Printing 2B Ⓓ Tactical Magic Ⓒ Trey Clark Photography 2C Ⓓ Schwartzrock Graphic Arts Ⓒ Community Comics
3A Ⓓ ANS Ⓒ Cross Current 3B Ⓓ Keyword Design Ⓒ Marcia Carle Public Relations + Project Management 3C Ⓓ Tandemodus Ⓒ Chicago Jobs Council
4A Ⓓ Zaman Ⓒ The C Collection 4B Ⓓ Cfx Ⓒ Cfx, Inc. 4C Ⓓ Mirko Ilic Corp Ⓒ Mirko Ilic Corp.

A B C

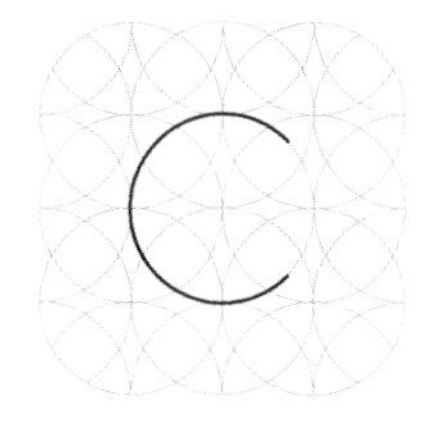

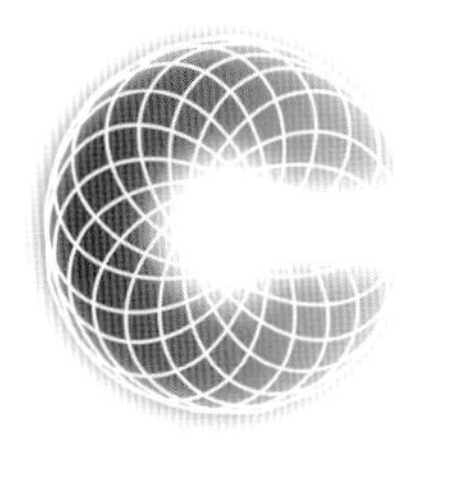

1

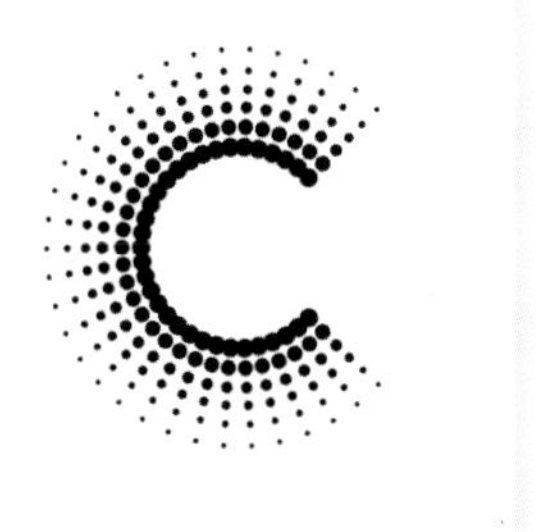

2

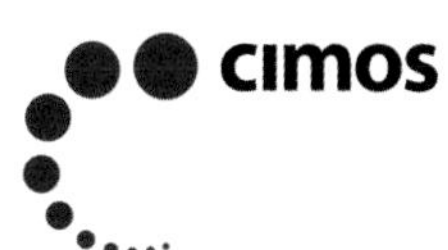

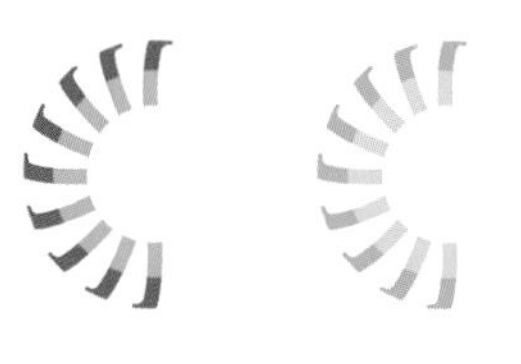

3

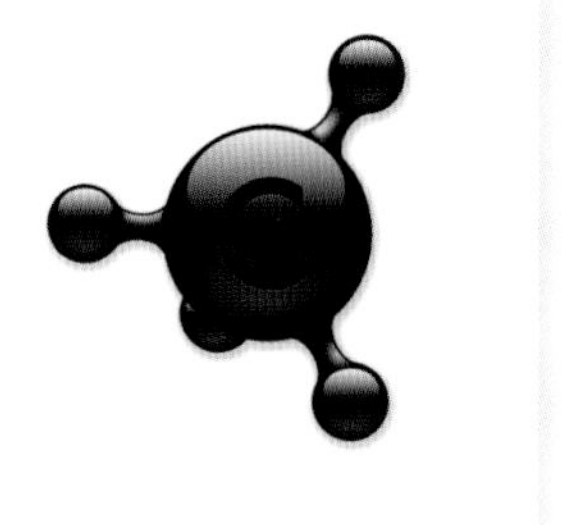

4

D = Design Firm C = Client

1A D FutureBrand BC&H 1B D Digital Flannel C Chad 1C D Gardner Design C Catalyst
2A D Haven Productions C Student Life 2B D this is nido C candeo 2C D Christian Palino Design C Cumberland Office of Children, Youth and Learning
3A D KROG, d.o.o. C Cimos, Koper 3B D twentystar C Copper Conferencing 3C D Nordyke Design C Connecticut College of Technology
4A D Little Jacket C Carol & John's Comic Book Shop 4B D 9MYLES, Inc. C Cryptek, Inc. 4C D Karmalaundry C Carbon

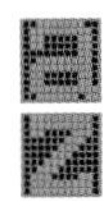

A B C

1

2

3

4

D = Design Firm   C = Client

1A D Catalyst Logo Design C Class VI 1B D Gardner Design C Community State Bank 1C D Richards Brock Miller Mitchell & Associates C Cypress Pediatrics
2A D Daniel Sim Design 2B D Westwerk DSGN C Chester's Kitchen & Bar 2C D Mortensen Design C Circle Bank
3A D The Image Group C The Collective 3B D Stephen Averitt C The Curve 3C D gsFITCH C Chapal World
4A D Octavo Design Pty Ltd C Construction Group 4B D 38one C Clever Creative 4C D Ardoise Design C Guy Connolly

A B C

1

2

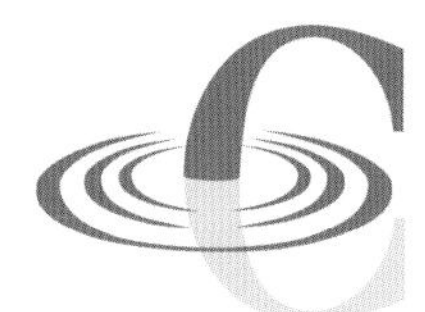

3

4

D = Design Firm C = Client

1A D Coastal Communities C The Coastal Companies 1B D DeFord Designs C MIC Systems & Software 1C D fuszion C Chanler Communications
2A D LSD C Castellón / Costa Azahar 2B D Rick Carlson Design & Illustration C Clean Water Scientific, Inc. 2C D America Online C AOL Web Properties
3A D AKOFA Creative C Cytexone 3B D Nicole Romer C Millbank 3C D Banowetz + Company, Inc. C Koll Development
4A D Eisenberg And Associates C Carbonet / Denbury Resources Inc 4B D Cinnamon Design C FDS Manufacturing, Inc.
4C D Gabriel Kalach • V I S U A L communication C Family Service League

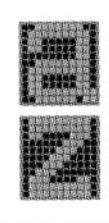

A B C

1

2

3

4

D = Design Firm C = Client

1A D RARE Design C Personal 1B D ER Marketing 1C D Maida Design C Jim Carpenter Construction
2A D True Perception C Chestnut Construction 2B D Strategy Studio C Camilli Economics 2C D Tactix Creative C Crum Bros.
3A D Gee + Chung Design C Castile Ventures 3B D fuszion C The Corcoran Group 3C D Harkey Design C Creek Ranch
4A D Jerron Ames C Arteis 4B D Mindgruve C Cresline Funding 4C D Tactix Creative C Meritage Corp.

A B C

1

2

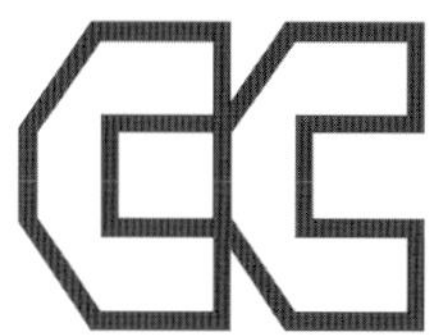

3

4

D = Design Firm C = Client

1A D Gardner Design C Corry Dance Academy 1B D EFL Design, LLC C cherokee casino 1C D R&R Partners C Clark County School District
2A D Vivid Envisions C Volleyball Team 2B D Ray Dugas Design C Corley Brothers Construction 2C D Scientific Arts C Cornell Concrete Constructions
3A D Stefan Romanu C Camera di Commercio Italiana per la Romania 3B D Hove Design Works C Carrie Davis Design 3C D Acute Cluster C TheCDStation
4A D Garza-Allen Designs C Deanna Cox Centurion and Carlos Centurion 4B D Digital Flannel C Chad Edward 4C D Jonathan Rice & Company C Champion Energy

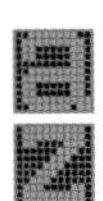

A B C

1

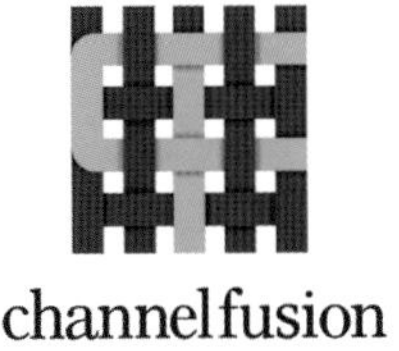

2

3

4

Ⓓ = Design Firm Ⓒ = Client

1A Ⓓ Integer Group—Midwest Ⓒ Channel Fusion 1B Ⓓ Taylor Martin Design Ⓒ Crystal Falls Golf Course 1C Ⓓ Brad Norr Design Ⓒ FastFunds
2A Ⓓ Mirko Ilic Corp Ⓒ Hampshire Hotels & Resorts, LLC 2B Ⓓ David Kampa Ⓒ Courney Mann Interiors 2C Ⓓ MultiAdaptor Ⓒ Catherine Owens
3A Ⓓ NOT A CANNED HAM Ⓒ Coredinates 3B Ⓓ bob neace graphic design, inc Ⓒ Power Chemicals 3C Ⓓ Tower of Babel Ⓒ Chris Pollock
4A Ⓓ MEGA Ⓒ Communique Interpreting 4B Ⓓ Tony Fletcher Design, LLC Ⓒ Captial Reach Webcasting 4C Ⓓ A3 Design Ⓒ DR Horton

B
C

1

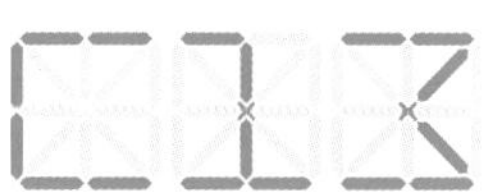

2

3

4

D = Design Firm   C = Client

1A D United States of the Art C Carsten Raffel 1B D David Clark Design C Four Winds Casino/Eslick Design 1C D Welcome Moxie C Clark's Register/Lucy Sisman
2A D Werner Design Werks C College of Visual Arts 2B D Mindgruve C Clear Water Outdoor 2C D cypher13 C cypher13
3A D Steve's Portfolio C JEG 3B D Steve's Portfolio C JEG 3C D Totem C GSK Dungarvan
4A D Blue Beetle Design C Details 4B D Diva Design C Diva Design 4C D Blink Media Group C Historic Delano District

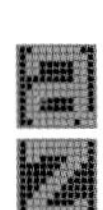

A B C

1

2

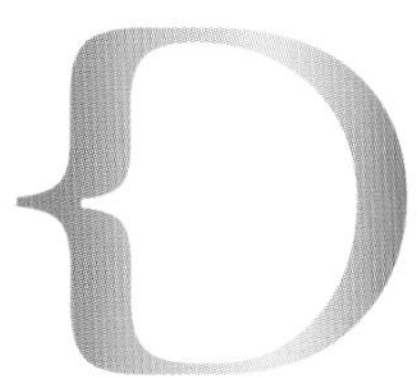

3

4

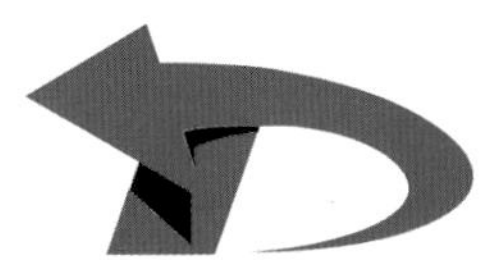

D = Design Firm C = Client

1A D Sanders Design C Dorchester Finance 1B D Judson Design C Dimensions 1C D Richards Brock Miller Mitchell & Associates C Dallas Legal Foundation
2A D Enlightened Design C The Insurance Design Center, LLC 2B D kickit communications 2C D RDY C DD
3A D Glitschka Studios C RTC Las Vegas 3B D LCD Incorporated C Dunlop Manufacturing 3C D reaves design C demand consulting
4A D Steven O'Connor C Mike Dunbar 4B D A. Shtramilo design studio C DataTransfer 4C D Steve Cantrell C DeWatering Industries

A B C

DOLE

1

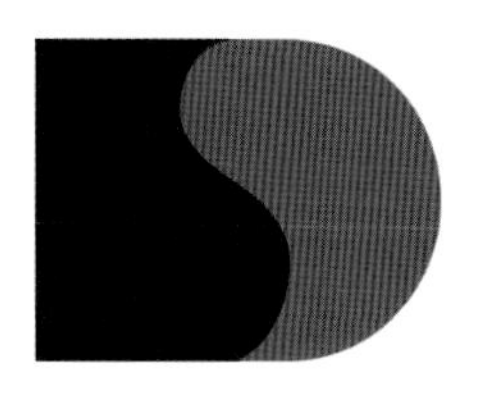

2

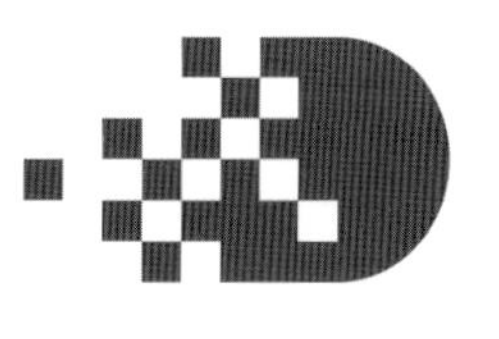

3

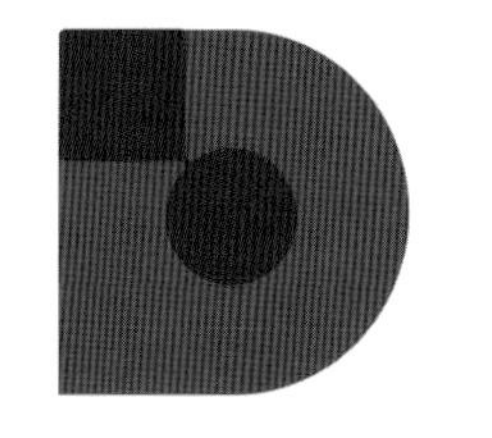

4

Ⓓ = Design Firm Ⓒ = Client

1A Ⓓ X RAY Ⓒ Dole 1B Ⓓ Hinge Ⓒ Dev Technology Group 1C Ⓓ Muamer Adilovic DESIGN Ⓒ SZR Dizajndzlluk
2A Ⓓ Gardner Design Ⓒ Devlin Trucking 2B Ⓓ Kendall Creative Shop, Inc. Ⓒ Scott Deakins Company 2C Ⓓ POLLARDdesign Ⓒ Digitech Solutions
3A Ⓓ Form Ⓒ Darling Department 3B Ⓓ Lesniewicz Associates Ⓒ Dunbar 3C Ⓓ Ikola designs... Ⓒ Digital Excellence
4A Ⓓ Sibley Peteet Ⓒ Dal Tile 4B Ⓓ GingerBee Creative Ⓒ Dundas Interiors 4C Ⓓ Lienhart Design Ⓒ Darby Graphics

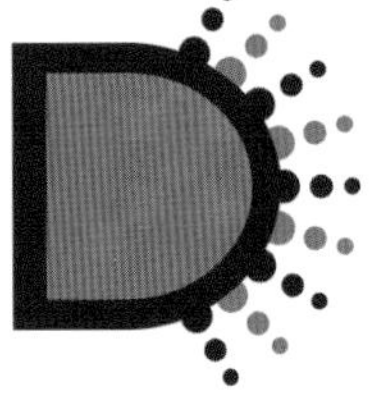
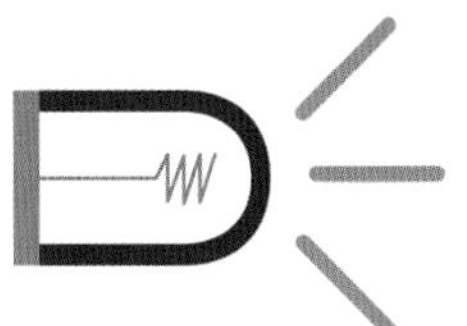

D = Design Firm C = Client

1A D Richards Brock Miller Mitchell & Associates C Dallas Chamber of Commerce 1B D Simon & Goetz Design C dinomoda / ekkehard dreyer gmbh & co. kg 1C D Selikoff+Co C Destia 2A D David Airey C David Airey 2B D Pat Taylor Inc. C Dana Research, Inc. 2C D Alin Golfitescu C the digimation archive 3A D Clive Jacobson Design C HariWorld 3B D Jacob Tyler Creative Group C Dalina Law Group 3C D Shelley Design+Marketing C Potomac Laser 4A D Michael O'Connell C Hercules Incorporated 4B D LOCHS 4C D Classic Lines Design C Dandelion

A B C

1

2

3

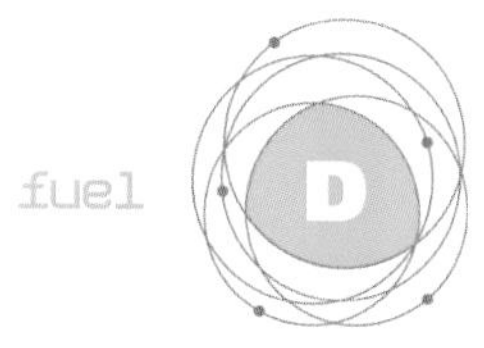

4

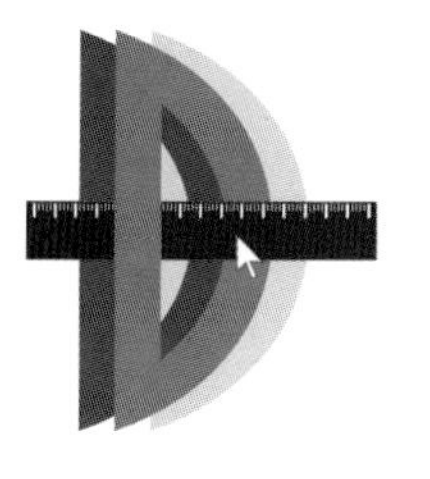

D = Design Firm C = Client

1A D Sheehan Design C Designcor 1B D LogoDesignGuru.com C Dynex Solution 1C D Cinq Partners C Delineate
2A D designlab,inc C designlab,inc 2B D design june C resonnances et cie 2C D Burd & Patterson C Drake University
3A D Flying Mouse Studio 3B D Miller Meiers Design for Communication C Darnell Inc of Kansas 3C D Rotor Design C Digital Clay Studios
4A D harlan creative C Datafied, Inc. 4B D Pennebaker C Dezyneco 4C D Stellar Debris, Inc. C Stellar Debris, Inc.

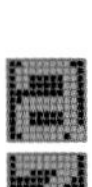

A B C

D = Design Firm C = Client

1A D MSI C Dalen 1B D Design Nut C Design Nut 1C D Born to Design C DayStar for: Fishhook
2A D Karl Design Vienna C FCB / Debitel AG 2B D D&i (Design and Image) C The City of Denver 2C D KENNETH DISENO C Delicat Fine Foods, Michoacan, Mexico
3A D Cinq Partners C Delineate 3B D skyymedia C Diamond Doctor 3C D Jelena Drobac C Jelena Drobac
4A D Habitat Design C The David Austin Group 4B D ballard::creative C DFW Painting 4C D Paragon Marketing Communications C Diet Care

A B C

1

2

3

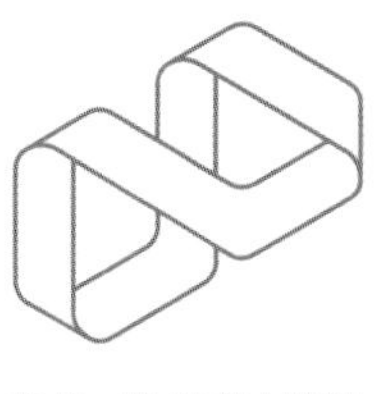

4

D = Design Firm C = Client

1A D Straka-Design C Diggin' Records 1B D 01d C Dykiro 1C D Spin Design C Dr. Deb, Inc.
2A D Carrihan Creative Group C Key Debt Services 2B D Carrihan Creative Group C Key Debt Solutions 2C D Dylan Menges C dzinejobs
3A D Chris Yin Design C Dun & Bradstreet 3B D Phony Lawn C Chandler Design 3C D Spork Design, Inc. C Dascenzo Creative
4A D Marlin C Derby Chamber of Commerce 4B D DTM_INC C DD Design 4C D DUEL Purpose C Digital Ensemble

A B C

1

2

3

4

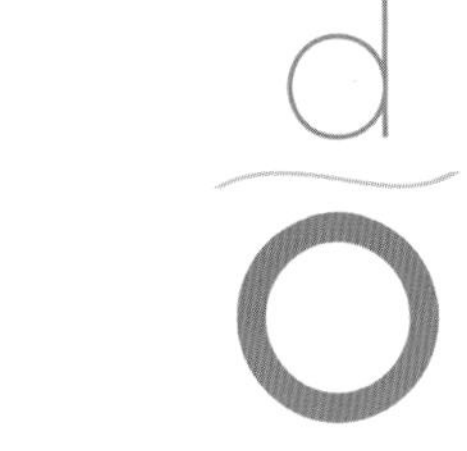

D = Design Firm C = Client

1A D Ulyanov Denis C Dating Free 1B D LogoMotto.com C DivergentGraphics.com 1C D Robot Creative C Denim Group
2A D Eric Baker Design Assoc. Inc 2B D Gabriel Kalach • V I S U A L communication C DDL 2C D PETTUS CREATIVE C LUX Designs LLC
3A D Integrated Media, Inc. C Design Massey, Inc. 3B D Philip J Smith C Design Now Concepts 3C D Kendall Creative Shop, Inc. C Dallas Nephrology Associates
4A D Organic Grid C Dennis O'Clair—Underwater Photography 4B D Hirschmann Design C Dorado Products 4C D stressdesign C SSK HR

A B C

1

2

ERASURE

EPIC EVENTS

event planning | marketing | pr

3

emerald

THE ELLIOTT

4

BLUE EQUITY

D = Design Firm C = Client

1A D Straka-Design C T-Com 1B D RARE Design C Deep South Incorporated 1C D Luke Baker C personal project
2A D Rhumb Designs, Inc. C Techway Services, Inc. 2B D Spec Creative C Epic Events 2C D Gardner Design C Elogen Skin Care
3A D UpShift Creative Group C Emerald 3B D Methodologie C RC Hedreen 3C D Mariqua Design C Elsewhere
4A D Peritus Public Relations C Blue Equity 4B D CF Napa Brand Design C Ehlers Estate 4C D Essex Two C Urban Growth Properties

A B C

1

2

3

4

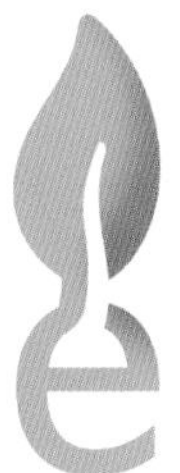

D = Design Firm C = Client

1A D Oscar Morris C Eastland Real Estate 1B D Flow Creative C Equinoxe 1C D Ross Hogin Design C Education First Consulting
2A D El Creative C Enchantment Cruise Line 2B D humanot C Endicott Gulls 2C D Steve Cantrell C Elite Getaways
3A D Haven Productions C Endurance Lawn Care 3B D Patterson Visual C Ernie Els LTD. 3C D HOOK C Ethanex Energy
4A D Gardner Design C Epic 4B D Fandam Studio C Evermed Clinic 4C D Strange Ideas

A B C

1

3

4

D = Design Firm C = Client

1A D e-alw.com C Euroinvestment, Poland 1B D Dessein C ecologia environment 1C D demasijones C EziPark Car Parks
2A D Ground Zero Communications C Executive Asset Management 2B D Mortensen Design C eShop, Inc. 2C D ENNEMM Ad Agency C Endurvinnslan
3A D Karl Design Vienna C Q / Stiftung Ettersburg 3B D Fossil C Fossil 3C D Campbell Fisher Design C E-Village
4A D Wrijfhout C Enter Electronics 4B D Alambre Estudio C Matz Erreka 4C D Dotzero Design C Ecos

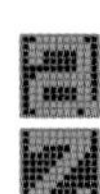

1

2

3

4

Delaware County eCenter

D = Design Firm C = Client

1A D Deere Design Group C Evolve Board Shop 1B D humanot C Entertainment Direct 1C D Brandstorm Creative Group C Emotion
2A D Denis Olenik Design Studio C Elara Systems 2B D Gizwiz Studio C Aritsara 2C D Kloom C Essociate
3A D The Flores Shop C eNIQUE 3B D Faith C Salon E 3C D Kahn Design C Envoy Systems
4A D bryon hutchens | graphic design C Effective Graphics 4B D GrafiQa Creative Services C Delaware County eCenter 4C D rajasandhu.com

A B C

1

2

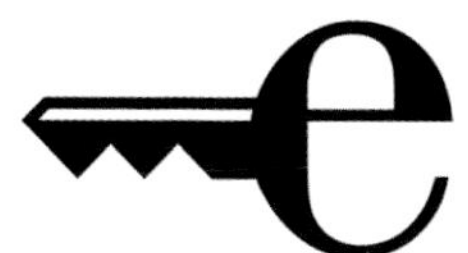

3

4

D = Design Firm C = Client

1A D Richards & Swensen C Evergreene Construction 1B D LogoMotto.com C Endorphin Sports Media, LLC
1C D Funk/Levis & Associates, Inc. C Eberhart Project Industries
2A D Shelley Design+Marketing C Code Angel 2B D Hirschmann Design C IBM 2C D Heck Yeah! C eLaunch Point
3A D Steele Design C Estamp 3B D EFL Design, LLC C Brunswick Bowling 3C D Karl Design Vienna C Preussen Elektra / Saatchi
4A D StudioNorth C Komatsu America 4B D Bridges Design Group C Enzo Investments 4C D Studio International C Electroproject

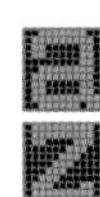

1

2

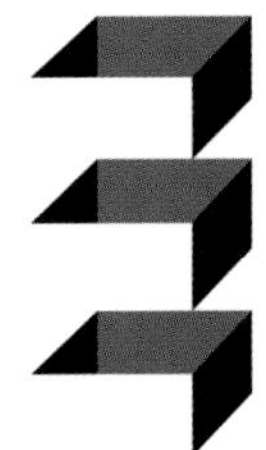

3

4

D = Design Firm C = Client

1A D Mikhail Gubergrits C ExpoFar 1B D Sibley Peteet Design—Dallas C Calise Sedai, MedcareXpress 1C D Tran Creative C Excel Entertainment
2A D CONCEPTO WORLDWIDE C Enter 2B D demasijones C Eword Development
2C D HERMANO S TALASTAS C Don Schaaf & Friends, Inc., for The EZRA Companies
3A D Rule29 C Entrenuity 3B D ZORRAQUINO C Epromotores 3C D Default C The Emperorhouse
4A D DBD+A Studio C Eggers + Associates 4B D Fangman Design C Texas EDGE 4C D James Clark Design C Elevations Credit Union

A B C

1

2

3

4

D = Design Firm C = Client

1A D Jeffhalmos C eVentures Financial 1B D Sebastiany Branding & Design C Monari Engineering 1C D Felixsockwell.com C felix
2A D 20FIRST C economy.one 2B D Chris Yin Design C Monster Cable 2C D Brandient C Domo
3A D Ken Dyment C Everwood Timberworks 3B D Hecht Design C Ellenzweig Inc. 3C D Whole Wheat Creative C Evans
4A D eight a.m. brand design (shanghai) Co., Ltd C e-cowell(china) co.,ltd 4B D Funnel Design Group C The Gooden Group 4C D Marlin C Eco-Works

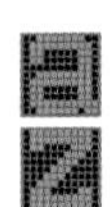

A B C

1

2

3

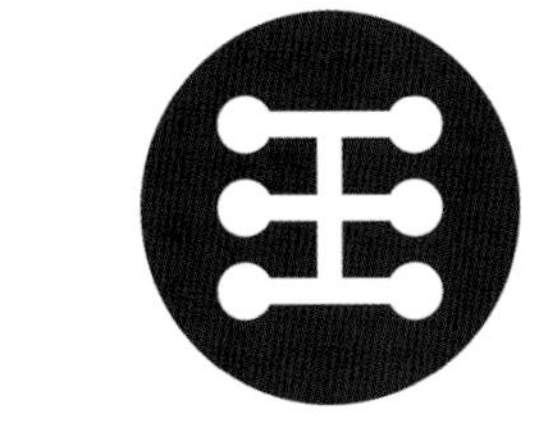

4

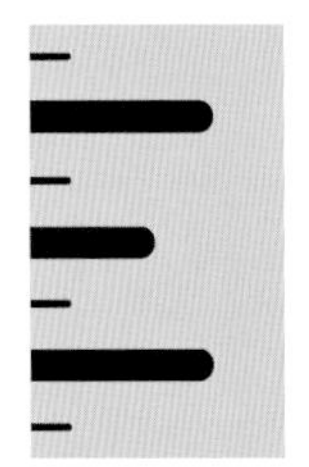

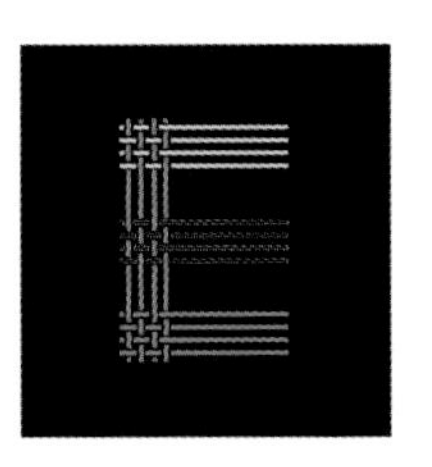

D = Design Firm C = Client

1A D Eyescape C Elite Vending 1B D 9MYLES, Inc. C erowe design 1C D Diagram C IGD Irlandzka Grupa Deweloperska
2A D Brady Design Ltd C Huntington Bank 2B D Dill and Company C Miss E 2C D Studio Limbus C Etre Jewelry
3A D Glitschka Studios C Expression Engine 3B D Cisneros Design C Energies Online 3C D Diagram C IGD Irlandzka Grupa Deweloperska
4A D Theory Associates C Elliott & Elliott Law Firm 4B D The Bradford Lawton Design Group C Easy Inch Weight Loss 4C D Paul Black Design C Poly Ellerman

A B C

1

ENDORTRAINING

2

3

4

D = Design Firm C = Client

1A D Factor Tres C Mauricio Diosdado 1B D Church Logo Gallery C Extreme 1C D Gardner Design C Epic
2A D MSI C The Home Depot 2B D Howling Good Designs C Linx Communications 2C D Minale Tattersfield and Partners Ltd C Express Dairies Plc
3A D Monigle Associates Inc. C Emprise Bank 3B D Essex Two C Equity Residentual Property 3C D Steven O'Connor C Ford + English Financial Group
4A D justpixels.com C big-e.com 4B D Latinbrand C Enigma 4C D ZupiDesign C EmpowerMed

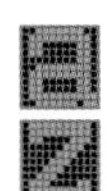

A B C

1

2

3

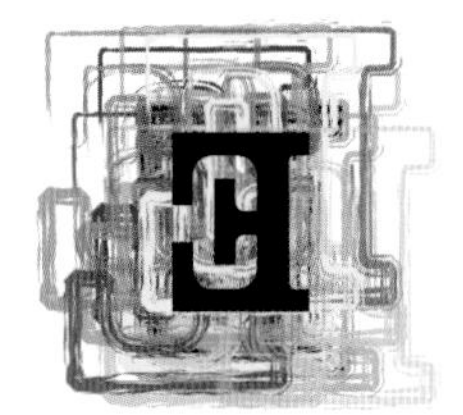

4

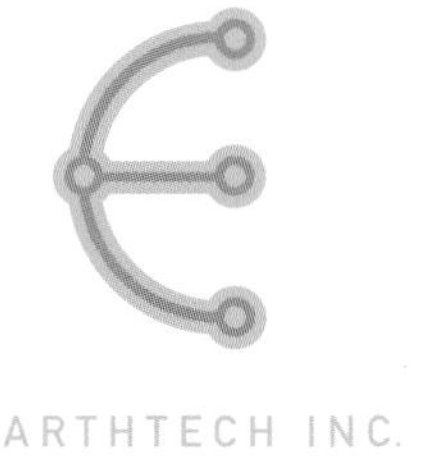

D = Design Firm C = Client

1A D Glitschka Studios C e environment inc. 1B D RADAR Agency C The Eppstein Group 1C D Double Brand C Epogeum Interacive Agency
2A D Whaley Design, Ltd C Erin Eithier, MN 2B D Studio18Group C Mark Edwards & Co 2C D Tran Creative C Excel Entertainment
3A D Tactix Creative 3B D Cappelli Communication Italy C Cappelli Communication 3C D Pinnacle Design Center C Enigma
4A D rylander design C EnTouch, Inc. 4B D Mosmondesign C Decoin Pty Ltd 4C D H2 Design of Texas

A B C

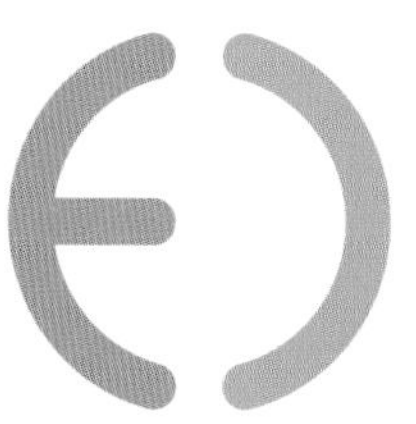

D = Design Firm C = Client

1A D Gardner Design C Epic 1B D Projoan Creative C Iberia Medical Center 1C D Karl Design Vienna C Outlaw GmbH
2A D Acme Graphic Design C Expresscopy.com 2B D Jonathan Rice & Company C Champion Energy 2C D EvenDesign C EvenDesign
3A D Karl Design Vienna C Saatchi / Preussen Elektra 3B D Ulyanov Denis C Book Earl 3C D Cause Design Co. C Ellipsis Enterprises
4A D Brand Bird C Emerald Graphics 4B D The Mixx C Knockout Management 4C D Nynas C East Shore

1

2

3

4

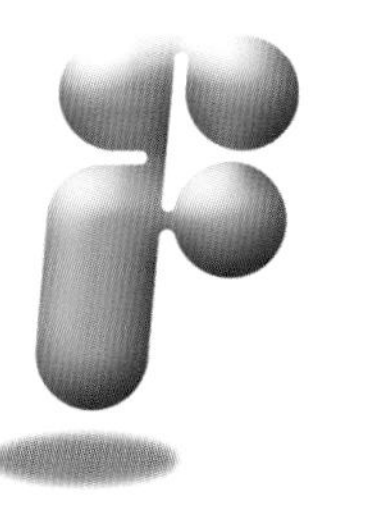

D = Design Firm C = Client

1A D The Robin Shepherd Group C Tech Ease 1B D DTM_INC C ETC 1C D Javen Design C Westend Equities
2A D Creative NRG C Drescher Holdings 2B D Leytonmedia C CLub EVE 2C D Diagram C E24 Internet Club
3A D Monster Design Company C Fleet Collision Services 3B D Tran Creative C Pharma Fusion 3C D Fusion Advertising C fusion advertising
4A D Stiles+co C FastCountry 4B D Grapefruit C The Cayenne Group 4C D o graphicstudio C fountainhead

A B C

1

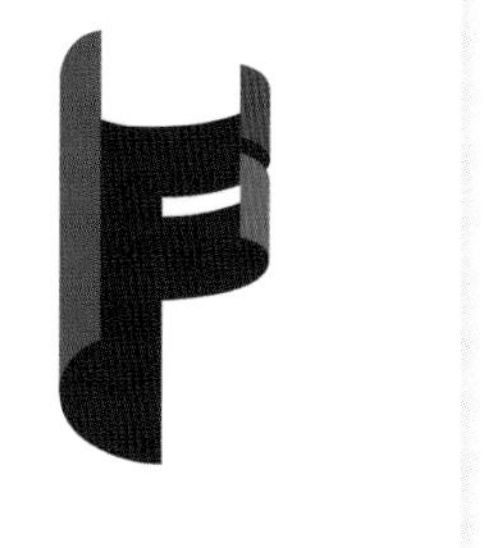

2

3

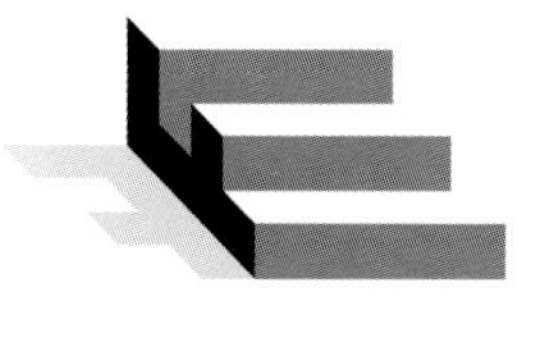

4

D = Design Firm C = Client

1A D Sage Corporation C Fundamentec 1B D Organic Grid C Freedom Film Festival 1C D The Bradford Lawton Design Group C Fleming
2A D Jeffhalmos C Real Facilities 2B D UTILITY C Fortis 2C D Think Tank Creative C Fife Oil Company
3A D Oscar Morris C Frost+Fuller Architects 3B D maynard kay C Fischer & Company 3C D Gardner Design C Flagstone Investments
4A D Gardner Design C Flagstone Investments 4B D 5Seven C service performance, inc 4C D Lienhart Design C First Financial Bank

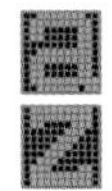

A B C

1

2

3

4

D = Design Firm C = Client

1A D Denis Olenik Design Studio C Fidelity 1B D Glitschka Studios C Fitness Experience 1C D Glitschka Studios C Upper Deck Company
2A D Advertising Intelligence C Fashion seasons 2005 2B D Tower of Babel C The Flower Company 2C D Back2Front C Kara Jeffers
3A D Rule29 C Furnace Films 3B D Jason Pillon C RightNow 3C D Wrijfhout C Flexcoat Industries
4A D Dotzero Design C Fortuna Group 4B D Rule29 C Furnace Films 4C D Stiles+co

A B C

1

2

3

4

D = Design Firm C = Client

1A D Spohn Design C Focus Performance Wear 1B D Fossil C Fossil 1C D Cacao Design C Fontegrafica
2A D Second Shift Design C Georgia Baptist Convention 2B D innfusion studios C FUSION Comics 2C D Velocity Design Group C Freedom Board Shop
3A D Methodologie C The Boeing Company 3B D Steve's Portfolio C JEG 3C D Dotzero Design C Fortuna Group
4A D Peel C Family Church Albuquerque 4B D Iron Creative Communication 4C D designlab,inc C Weissman's Dance

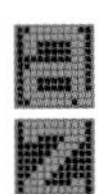

A B C

1

2

3

4

D = Design Firm C = Client

1A D Double A Creative C Frank Furness (Motivational Speaker) 1B D Felixsockwell.com C firefly 1C D Fleishman Hillard C The Joy Foundation
2A D STUBBORN SIDEBURN C magnet Eyes 2B D Tower of Babel C Tower of Babel 2C D Traction C Florence Freedom Baseball Team
3A D THINQ C Flack Construction 3B D UTILITY C Francis Carpentry 3C D McRae Creative Group, Inc. C Faison Capital LLC
4A D IGLOO57 Limited C Factory Clothing Company 4B D Hayes+Company C Don Fleming Developments Ltd. 4C D Gardner Design C Flagstone Investments

A B C

1

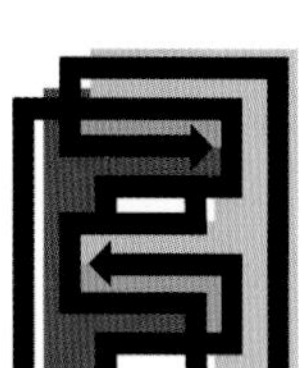

2

3

4

D = Design Firm C = Client

1A D Sandpaper Studio C The Floured Apron 1B D Think Tank Creative C First Aid Express 1C D Studio International C Tobacco factory Sarajevo
2A D Insight Design C Face-to-Face 2B D King Design Office C Wolfgang Puck Catering 2C D MSI C Tractor Supply
3A D Design Matters Inc! C Financial Graphic Service 3B D Emu Design Studio C francis james 3C D Ken Dyment C FreightLinks
4A D LogoMotto.com C Body Challenge Gym 4B D D&i (Design and Image) C Flipside Design 4C D United States of the Art C form-one.de

A B C

1

2

3

4

D = Design Firm C = Client

1A **D** Salty Design Foundry **C** Owen G. River 1B **D** paralleldesigned **C** ZEFER & Greenlight 1C **D** Burd & Patterson **C** Granger Community Church
2A **D** twentystar **C** Greenhaw Capital 2B **D** Les Kerr Creative **C** Ericsson 2C **D** Form **C** Perfecto / East West Records
3A **D** Landor Associates **C** Geo Cities 3B **D** Allen Creative **C** Missions of Grace (Grace Fellowship Church) 3C **D** Roskelly Inc. **C** St. Annes Hospital
4A **D** Banowetz + Company, Inc. **C** Randy Smoot 4B **D** LSD **C** yoblog 4C **D** A3 Design **C** Griffith Choppers, Inc.

A B C

1

2

3

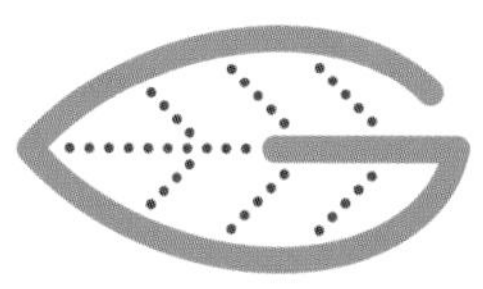

4

D = Design Firm C = Client

1A D Concussion, llc C Greenhill Air 1B D Campbell Fisher Design C Goodmans 1C D Ammunition C David Guest
2A D MSI C Golfsmith 2B D Logologik C Mazury Golf & Country Club 2C D LogoDesignGuru.com C Green Realty
3A D eggnerd C Greenhill Academy 3B D Liew Design, Inc. C Giving Global (now Universal Giving) 3C D Tandem Design Agency C Generations Management
4A D Elixir Design C Grandiflorum Perfumes 4B D two tribes gmbh C Galibier:Time 4C D Flaxenfield, Inc. C Groome Enterprises

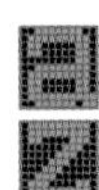

A B C

1

2

3

4

D = Design Firm C = Client

1A D zakidesign C Golden Wave Jewelry Design 1B D Kevin Creative C Pixellogo Custom 1C D Loop Design C Code Green
2A D Designer Case C G-Force Autoparts 2B D Squires and Company C Grants State Bank 2C D Paul Black Design C First Gibralter Savings
3A D BFive C John Green 3B D Atomic Wash Design Studio C GrayCell America 3C D Spectrum Brands / Schultz Creative C Omni Group
4A D Tomko Design C Good Impressions Printing 4B D Saltree Pty Ltd C Legacy Finance Group 4C D Ross Levine Design C Four J's

A B C

1

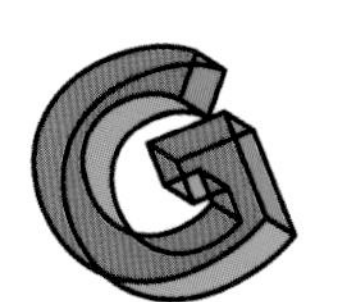

2

3

4

D = Design Firm   C = Client

1A D HOLAGRAPHIC 1B D Jackson Spalding Creative C Georgia Research Alliance 1C D Hubbell Design Works C Goodrich Theaters
2A D Ahab Nimry C Gilbert Industries 2B D Sabin Design C Greenberry Industrial 2C D Randy Mosher Design C John Gaynor Associates
3A D KITA International I Visual Playground C gene.sys biotechnology 3B D Liska + Associates Communication Design C Geldermann
3C D Squires and Company C Grants State Bank 4A D Karl Design Vienna C Doris Gassmann 4B D Karl Design Vienna C D. Gassmann Schmuckdesign
4C D Tunglid Advertising Agency ehf. C Center For Rheumatology Research

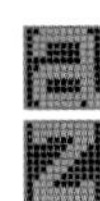

1

2

3

4

D = Design Firm C = Client

1A D R&R Partners C Gabe Gentile 1B D Gardner Design C Johnathan Goodwin 1C D Indicia Design Inc C Converged Communication Services
2A D Art Chantry C G Force 2B D Glitschka Studios C Geocaching.com 2C D Logologik C AIG/Lincoln Poland
3A D Mitre Agency C Goodrich Builders 3B D Kraftaverk—Design Studio C Gjaldheimtan 3C D Karl Design Vienna C D. Gassmann Schmuckdesign
4A D lunabrand design group C Gets It! Marketing 4B D Hayes+Company C GMerch 4C D Studio G C Studio G

A B C

1

2

3

4

D = Design Firm C = Client

1A D Dennard, Lacey & Associates C Grand Homes 1B D Banowetz + Company, Inc. C Randy Smoot 1C D Studio Tandem C Gaurded.Net
2A D Living Creative Design C GyoHwa International 2B D HuebnerPetersen C Travis Gray 2C D Greteman Group C Gregory Vinyl
3A D Creative Madhouse C God's Bible School & College 3B D Design Army C Goldman Law Group 3C D Strategy Studio C Jacobs Gardner Office Supply
4A D Roskelly Inc. C Guck Boats 4B D eye4 inc. C GeeSwell 4C D Hirschmann Design C Gart Properties

1

2

3

4

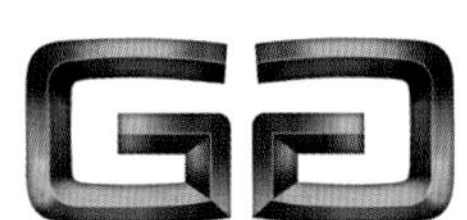

D = Design Firm C = Client

1A D Murillo Design, Inc. C Garza Architects 1B D BrandEquity C General Cinema Corporation 1C D Liska + Associates Communication Design C GCG Financial
2A D mugur mihai C Gold Coast Distribution 2B D Robot Creative C The Golf Club of Texas 2C D David Beck Design C Good Company Creative
3A D NeoGine Communication Design Ltd C Gillies Group 3B D Hutchinson Associates, Inc. C Godsey Design 3C D DTM_INC C DG
4A D j1s designs C Griffin Events 4B D Chermayeff & Geismar Inc. C GF Business Equipment 4C D BRUEDESIGN C Garage Gym

A B C

1

2

3

4

D = Design Firm C = Client

1A D Jerron Ames C Arteis 1B D Jan Vranovsky C Ales Zahradka 1C D Jerron Ames C Arteis
2A D Studio Simon C Corpus Christi Hooks 2B D A. Shtramilo design studio C Grand Gallery 2C D Tip Top Creative C Starwood Hotels & Resorts, Worldwide, Inc.
3A D Garfinkel Design C Garfinkel Design 3B D Eyebeam Creative LLC C H&G Contractors 3C D DAVID BARATH DESIGN C G13 Art Gallery
4A D A3 Design C Griffith Choppers, Inc. 4B D D&i (Design and Image) C Gorsuch Kirgis 4C D Maida Design C GK Designs

1

D = Design Firm C = Client

1A D Diagram C Kulczyk Foundation 1B D Church Logo Gallery C The LifeGate 1C D Hornall Anderson C GGLO
2A D 903 Creative, LLC C Gibson / Lewis Reunion 2B D Hornall Anderson C General Magic 2C D D&Dre Creative C GO Maintenance Services
3A D Deep Design C Sumitomo Rubber Co. 3B D Church Logo Gallery C GracePointe 3C D Jason Drumheller C Gerome Sapp
4A D 28 LIMITED BRAND C Schreiter 4B D Fine Dog Creative C Sharon Gutowski Photography 4C D T H Gilmore C T H Gilmore

B C

2

4

D = Design Firm C = Client

1A D Crackerbox C G.W.Engineering 1B D Gabriel Kalach • V I S U A L communication 1C D Oxide Design Co. C Generation 2
2A D MANMADE C Horizons 2B D Tactix Creative 2C D Bridges Design Group C Heirlooms Boutique
3A D Design One C Heritage Development Concepts 3B D Haller Design C Heritage Master Builders 3C D UlrichPinciotti Design Group C InvesTek
4A D juls design inc C Haven Homes 4B D Periscope C Hermantown Pilots 4C D MSI C Kmart

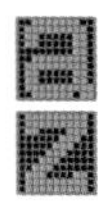

A B C

1

2

3

4

D = Design Firm C = Client

1A D ZONA Design, Inc C A&E Networks 1B D Walsh Branding C Holland Hall 1C D Range C Hexagraph
2A D Home Grown Logos C John Holden, Holden Physical Therapy 2B D Dennard, Lacey & Associates C Haggar Square
2C D CF Napa Brand Design C Hesperian Wines 3A D Riccardo Sabioni C Erick Harpole 3B D Richards Brock Miller Mitchell & Associates C Howard Homes
3C D design:tn C Hillview Financial 4A D Tactix Creative C Haven Homes 4B D Brandstorm Creative Group C Harbour One
4C D Bean Graphics C Heron High School

A B C

1

2

3

4

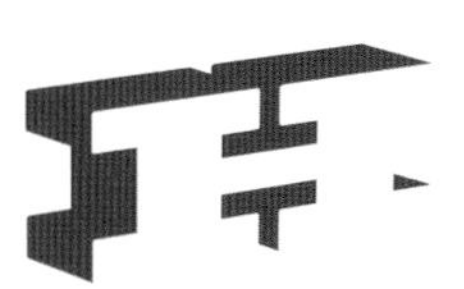

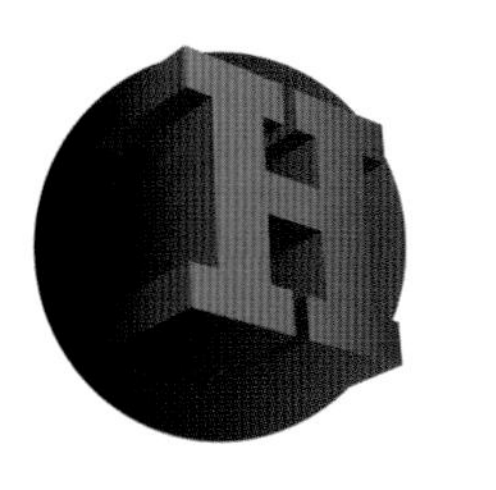

D = Design Firm C = Client

1A D Dotzero Design C House 1B D Greteman Group C Hearth and Home 1C D Richards Brock Miller Mitchell & Associates C Home Exteriors & Interiors
2A D Kahn Design C Steve Hansen 2B D Conduit Studios C Hawley & Hawley 2C D Dotzero Design C House
3A D DTM_INC C H+ 3B D Rufuturu C Hamand 3C D Stiles Design C HealthCare Facilities Development
4A D Stygar Group, Inc. C Hutton Construction 4B D Kahn Design C Hollywood.com 4C D Kahn Design C Hollywood.com

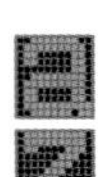

A B C

1

2

3

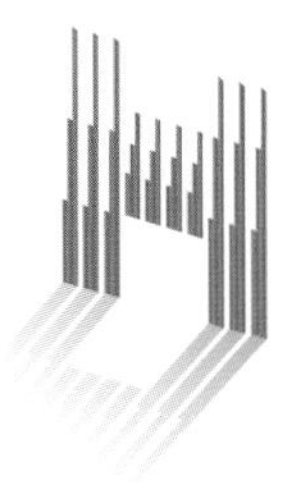

4

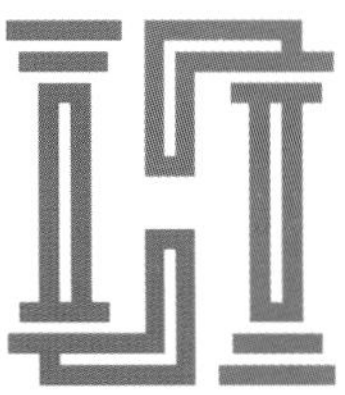

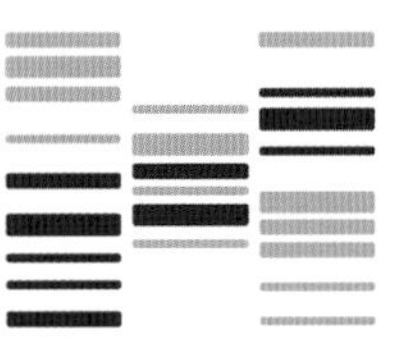

D = Design Firm C = Client

1A D DAGSVERK—Design and Advertising C Salus Ltd. 1B D Hazen Creative, Inc. C Hazen Creative, Inc. 1C D Hazen Creative, Inc. C Hazen Creative, Inc.
2A D Spinutech, Inc. C Michael Huff Construction 2B D neodesign C Han Lin Graphics Design Studio 2C D Strategy Studio C Consolidated Hydro
3A D Gardner Design C Hustler 3B D mccoycreative C Hansra IP LAW 3C D Sibley Peteet C Haggar Apparel
4A D Hazen Creative, Inc. C Hazen Creative, Inc. 4B D ceb design C Lavandale Home Inc. 4C D IF marketing & advertising C Helix Global Development

A B C

1

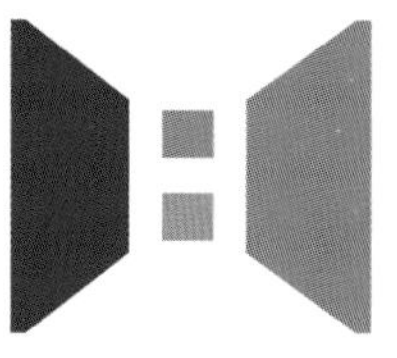

2

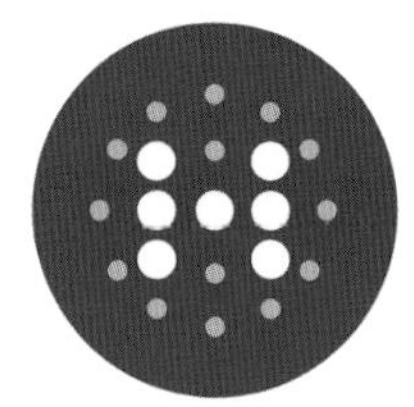

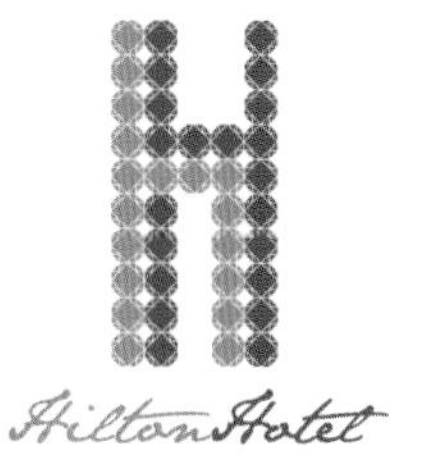

3

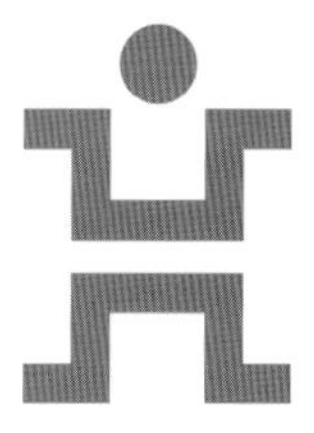

4

D = Design Firm C = Client

1A D Banowetz + Company, Inc. C Mercer Human Resources 1B D Element C Heritage Christian Church 1C D Rule29 C Hubbard Business Interiors
2A D Chris Yin Design C Helicomm 2B D juls design inc C Hyde Telecom 2C D Prana Design + Art Studios C Hiton Hotel
3A D 9MYLES, Inc. C Hansen Photo 3B D Gardner Design C Hustler 3C D Pure Identity Design C HITEK
4A D Shawn Huff C ShawnHuff.info 4B D Trilix Marketing Group C Iowa Hospital Association 4C D Steven O'Connor C David Holtz

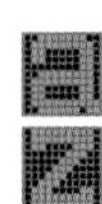

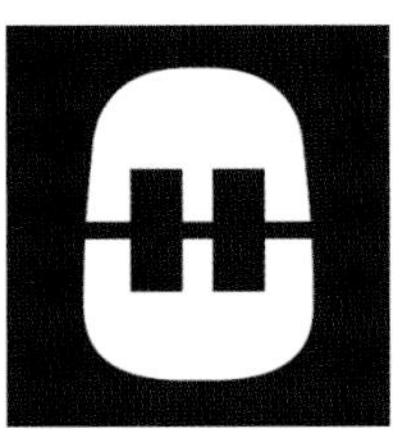

D = Design Firm C = Client

1A D Kahn Design C Hollywood.com 1B D Cassie Klingler Design C Hatch Landscape 1C D Ad Impact Advertising C QUBE Property
2A D Daniel Matthews C Horizon Finance 2B D Creative NRG C Hong's Black Belt Academy 2C D Pear Tree Design C Hendrickson Construction
3A D Gardner Design C Hullings Orthodontics 3B D ZupiDesign C House 3C D Tactix Creative C Homequest
4A D Church Logo Gallery C Hope Church 4B D studio-h 4C D Jeffhalmos C H.I.T

A B C

1

2

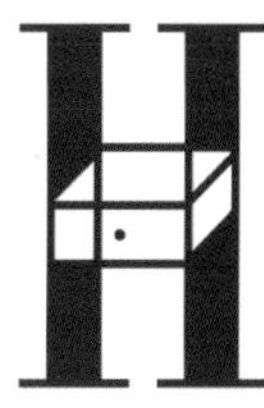

3

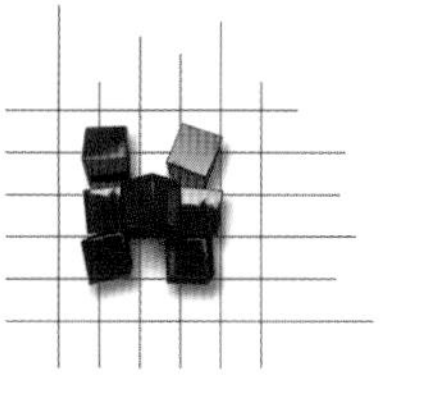

4

D = Design Firm C = Client

1A D Gardner Design C Hustler 1B D Karl Design Vienna C Landesbank Hessen-Thuehringen 1C D Gardner Design C Hustler
2A D Red Studio Inc C Holman Improvement 2B D Intrinsic Design C Handcrafted Constructed 2C D squiggle6 C Handsome Handyman
3A D Imaginaria C Univision Radio 3B D BLANK, Inc. C The Schusterman Hillel International Student Leaders Assembly 3C D KROG, d.o.o. C Hocevar
4A D The Joe Bosack Graphic Design Co. C MoneyBag Ent./ Interscope 4B D Paul Black Design C Hearthside Suites 4C D Studio International C HDD

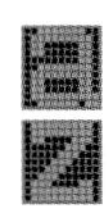

A B C

1

2

3

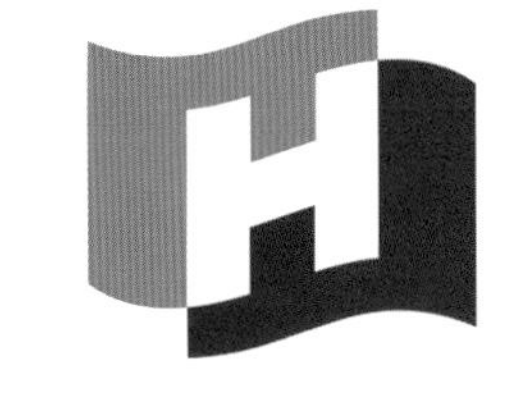

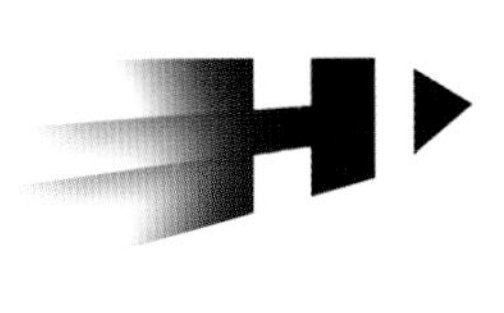

4

D = Design Firm C = Client

1A D Hand dizajn studio C Hand dizajn studio 1B D CF Napa Brand Design C Halter Ranch 1C D R&R Partners C Hampton Roads Transit
2A D Kraftaverk—Design Studio C HvassoSchool 2B D Schwartzrock Graphic Arts C Design Center 2C D lunabrand design group C ClubCorp
3A D Zed+Zed+Eye Creative Communications C Hilliards Insulation 3B D Element 3C D Strange Ideas
4A D Ulyanov Denis C First National Archive 4B D Dino Design C American Heart Association 4C D Alice Chae C Haley Builders, Inc.

A B C

1

2

3

4

D = Design Firm C = Client

1A D Dino Design C Bluefin Watersports 1B D Thread Design C Headcount 1C D Q C Hessen Chemie
2A D NeoGine Communication Design Ltd C Prime Property 2B D Howling Good Designs C Koulian Design 2C D ZORRAQUINO C Ercilla Hoteles
3A D Taylor Raber C Holy Fire Fellowship 3B D Richards Brock Miller Mitchell & Associates C The Hoglund Foundation
3C D Studio International C Croatian Documentation Center 4A D MINE(tm) C Hartman Griffin Associates 4B D dale harris C Hunter House
4C D Prejean Creative C The Richards Group / H-E-B Grocery Company

1

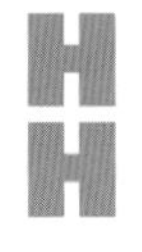
Homer+Helmcken
YALETOWN

2

3

HHK TRADING COMPANY, LTD.

4

D = Design Firm   C = Client

1A D Delikatessen C City of Hamburg Germany 1B D Letterbox Design C Chandlar 1C D Tomko Design C Health and Healing
2A D Valhalla | Design & Conquer C Helly Hansen 2B D Hirschmann Design C Marc Hirschmann 2C D Tielemans Design C Henness & Haight
3A D Draplin Design Co. C Hoss, Hoss & Hoss 3B D Hallmark Cards, Inc C Hallmark Cards, Inc 3C D face C Harrow College
4A D People Design C Herman Miller 4B D studio sudar d.o.o. C hercegovina produkt 4C D Looney Ricks Kiss Architects, Inc. C Poag & McEwen

A B C

1

2

3

4

D = Design Firm C = Client

1A D Kraftaverk—Design Studio C Hollrad (GoodAdvice) 1B D Steven O'Connor C Hilliard Rest 1C D Glitschka Studios C Salem Heights Church
2A D avenue:b C HSH Interiors 2B D Schwartzrock Graphic Arts C Design Center 2C D Studio Simon C Hudson Valley Renegades
3A D Blattner Brunner, Inc. C The Buncher Company 3B D Helius Creative Advertising C H2 Sports 3C D GingerBee Creative C Heller Homes
4A D Studio Simon C Kinston Indians 4B D Steiner&Co. C International Bank of Asia 4C D Ikola designs... C Ikola designs...

A B C

1

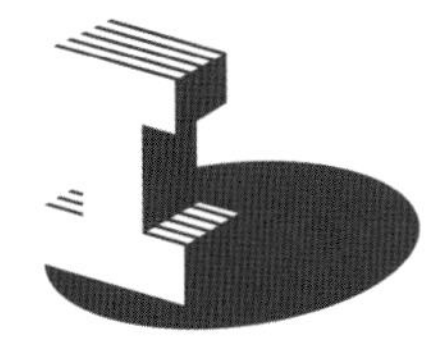

2

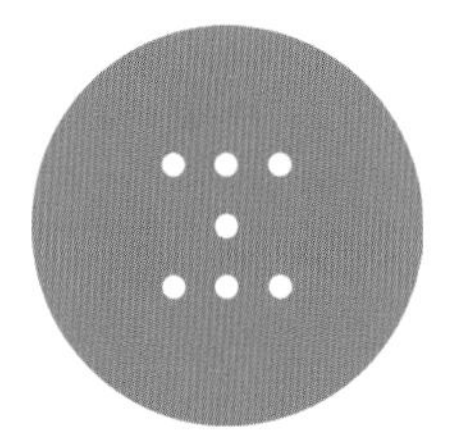

3

4

D = Design Firm C = Client

1A D Splinter Group C Imperial Construction Group 1B D Landkamer Partners, Inc. C Illustra 1C D Monigle Associates Inc. C Intust bank

2A D Saltree Pty Ltd 2B D Chimera Design C Digital Zoo 2C D Meir Billet Ltd. C Integrity Applications

3A D Carrie Dennis Design C Elk Grove Unified School District 3B D Ross Hogin Design C Internal Combustion 3C D Crave, Inc C Intellibrands

4A D The Martin Group C Integrity Office Solutions 4B D Kevin Creative C Insight Developments 4C D Miriello Grafico, Inc. C Iapyx Medical

A | B | C

1

2

3

4

D = Design Firm C = Client

1A D Chermayeff & Geismar Inc. C Irwin Financial Corporation 1B D Hexanine C Illini Life Christian Fellowship 1C D Business Identity Design C Ivery Investments
2A D MANMADE C Organised Noise 2B D FigDesign C InteliHome 2C D Kendall Creative Shop, Inc. C Inspire Properties
3A D MSI 3B D Bystrom Design C icom3 3C D Hornall Anderson C Intermation Corporation
4A D A3 Design C visit charlotte 4B D Ross Levine Design C Intervex Innovations 4C D Fitting Group C Capital Asset Management Group

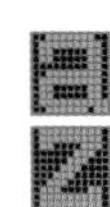

1

2

3

4

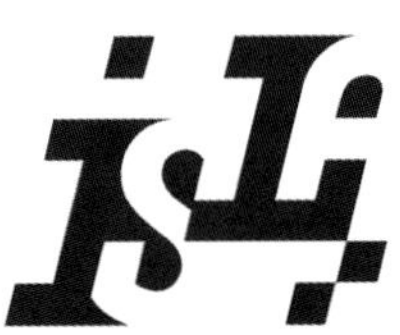

D = Design Firm C = Client

1A D Spire C ID Pro 1B D Effusion Creative Solutions 1C D Christian Palino Design C Interaction Design Association
2A D Ziga Aljaz C Interactive festival 2B D IMAGEHAUS C IMAGEHAUS 2C D Insight Design C NetWork Enterface
3A D Savage-Olsen Design Engineering Inc. C Imagin Office 3B D JK Design C Image Systems 3C D Schwartzrock Graphic Arts C Design Center
4A D Pepe Menendez C Latin American Chess Institute 4B D Identica Branding and Design C Harris and Company 4C D Landor Associates C ITT Industries

A B C

1

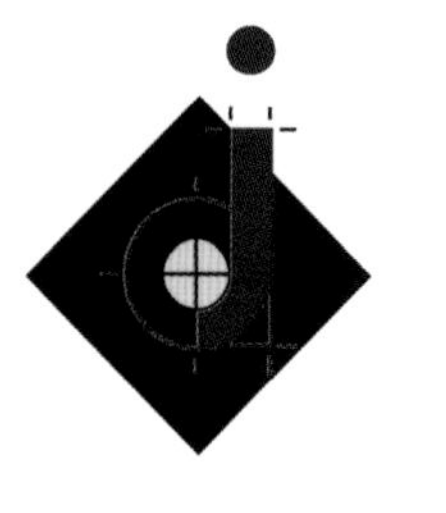

2

3

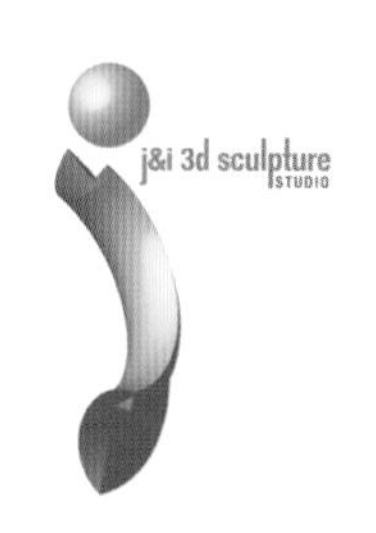

4

D = Design Firm C = Client

1A D Lienhart Design C Jean Grow 1B D James Clark Design C James Clark Design 1C D juls design inc C julsdesign
2A D Alice Chae C Jin Electric 2B D Clarke/Thompson Advertising C The Hudson Companies Incorporated 2C D Strategy Studio C Jamestown Packaging and Display
3A D pb&j creative C Jamie Dawson—webmaster 3B D Double A Creative C Jennifer Holz 3C D Living Creative Design C J & I 3D Sculpture Studio
4A D On Design, Inc. C John Apel Jewelry 4B D Lizette Gecel C The Sorrell Company 4C D dache C Jelena Blagojevic

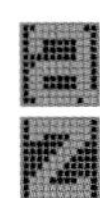

1

jay bird

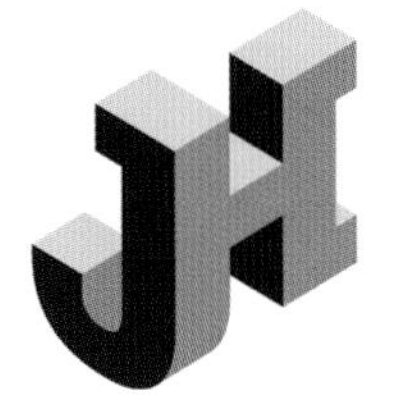

D = Design Firm C = Client

1A D BXC nicelogo.com C Jaybird Audio 1B D Gingerbread Lady C Jodie Chapman photography 1C D Iskender Asanaliev C Jinefem
2A D Splash:Design C Jazel Homes 2B D Chris Yin Design C James Jao Architects 2C D Gardner Design C Johnathan Goodwin
3A D 7th Street Design C JJY Shopping Mall 3B D Jarek Kowalczyk C Jarek Kowalczyk 3C D jKaczmarek C jKaczmarek
4A D Jarek Kowalczyk C Jarek Kowalczyk 4B D Rainy Day Designs C Johnson, Kunkel & Associates 4C D Brian Collins Design C Juristic Pilot

A B C

1

2

3

4

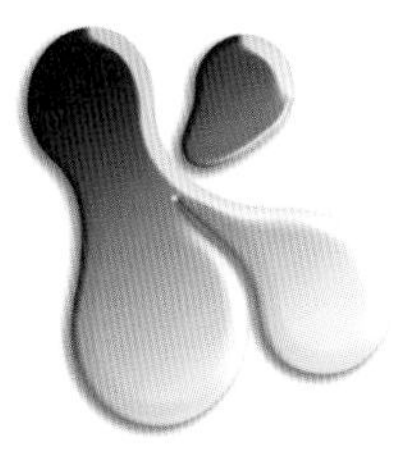

D = Design Firm C = Client

1A D Braínding C Julian Moyano 1B D Identity Kitchen C Kristen Parker 1C D Funk/Levis & Associates, Inc. C Jones & Roth
2A D Bridge Creative C SafetyWorks 2B D Gizwiz Studio C Kurt 2C D Tran Creative C Jane Scott Design
3A D Landkamer Partners, Inc. C Klaire Labs 3B D Lichtwitz—Buro fur Visual Kommunikation C Katovits Metal-Structure 3C D Gizwiz Studio C KISH BROWN
4A D Dragyn Studios C Karma Productions 4B D High Tide Creative C Kistler Fishing Rods Proposed 4C D KROG, d.o.o. C Biro za komunalo, Ljubljana

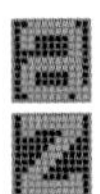

A B C

1

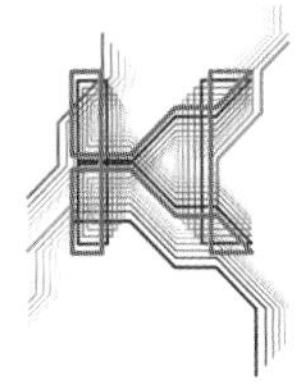

2

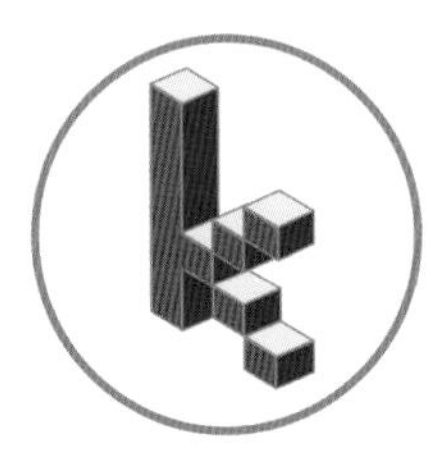

3

4

D = Design Firm C = Client

1A D Yoshi Tajima 1B D Studio International C Kutina city 1C D Interrobang Design Collaborative, Inc. C Kuppek Lanscaping Contractors, Inc.
2A D Judson Design C Kirby Construction 2B D Finch Creative C Kenalex Design 2C D Brook Group, LTD C Kroll Construction
3A D Gardner Design C Krehbil Architects 3B D UNIT-Y C Kapstone Paper and Packaging Corporation 3C D Lienhart Design C Kellogg School of Business
4A D Tran Creative C Kimmel Corporation 4B D Tran Creative C Kimmel Corporation 4C D Tran Creative C Kimmel Corporation

A B C

1

2

3

4

D = Design Firm C = Client

1A D Did Graphics C Kazheh Construction Company 1B D Tom Welch C Kevin Corn 1C D Dennard, Lacey & Associates C Crescent Capital
2A D Tran Creative C Kimmel Corporation 2B D Rhombus, Inc. C Kevin Kurbs Interior Design 2C D Diana Graham C Kaynee Shirt Corporation
3A D The Robin Shepherd Group C KALOS Engineering, LLC. 3B D The Robin Shepherd Group C KALOS Engineering, LLC.
3C D S Design, Inc. C A Karen Black Company 4A D Hiebing C Kinetico 4B D Pixellente C Kelvin Piñero 4C D KROG, d.o.o. C Presernova druzba

A B C

1

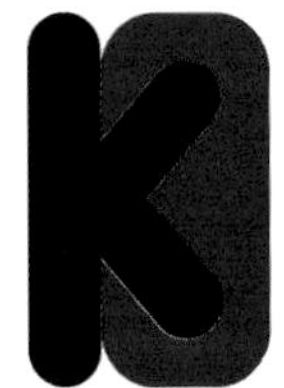

2

3

4

D = Design Firm C = Client

1A D Valmont Comunicación C Konnekt 1B D MacLaren McCann Calgary C K3 Design 1C D Beveridge Seay, Inc. C MarketResearch.com
2A D Judson Design C Unused 2B D tomvasquez.com C Kindred Kitchens 2C D Kessler Digital Design C Kessler Digital Design
3A D Planet Propaganda C Kaz Technologies 3B D Carrihan Creative Group C Key Debt Services 3C D paralleldesigned C Koret
4A D MINE(tm) C Cybernet Entertainment 4B D Diagram C Kulczyk Foundation 4C D Krghettojuice C Krghettojuice

A B C

1

2

3

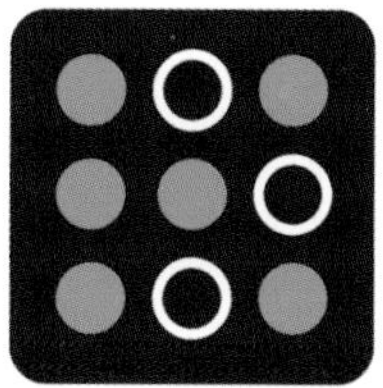

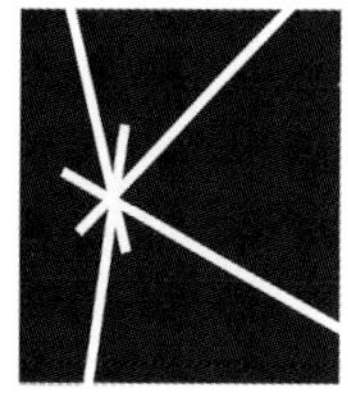

4

Ⓓ = Design Firm Ⓒ = Client

1A Ⓓ Tielemans Design Ⓒ Hot Rod Hill 1B Ⓓ Diagram Ⓒ Kulczyk Foundation 1C Ⓓ Bluespace Creative, Inc. Ⓒ Kahl Craft
2A Ⓓ Infiltrate Media Ⓒ Kustamyz 2B Ⓓ e-alw.com Ⓒ Key2Quality,Poland 2C Ⓓ Oluzen Ⓒ KotoHost
3A Ⓓ Studio GT&P Ⓒ GT&P 3B Ⓓ Kraftaverk—Design Studio Ⓒ Kerfi 3C Ⓓ richard zeid design Ⓒ The Keating Group
4A Ⓓ Tran Creative Ⓒ Kimmel Corporation 4B Ⓓ Tran Creative Ⓒ Kimmel Corporation 4C Ⓓ Thinking Caps Ⓒ Kendle Architects

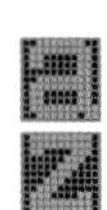

A B C

1

2

3

4

D = Design Firm C = Client

1A D Douglas Beatty C King West Fitness 1B D Ventress Design Group, Inc C John F. Kennedy Center for Research on Human Development 1C D Chris Rooney Illustration/Design C Cartridge King 2A D Sabet Branding C Kiai Sport 2B D Brains on Fire C Kaliburn 2C D D&Dre Creative C Karlson Construction 3A D KONG Design Group C Karcher Fire Stopping 3B D Gardner Design C Krehbil Architects 3C D Entermotion Design Studio 4A D Davina Chatkeon Design C Kasih Financial Advisors 4B D CONCEPTiCONS C CONCEPTiCONS 4C D IMAGEHAUS C Kuhlman Company

A | B | C

1

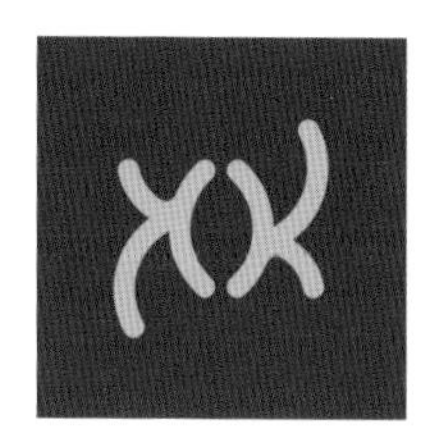

2

3

4

D = Design Firm C = Client

1A D Kevin France Design, Inc C Kevin France Design 1B D Newhouse Design C Kate Fisher 1C D Ross Hogin Design C Kevin Homes
2A D Living Creative Design C korean IT Network, San Jose, CA 2B D Mirko Ilic Corp C K Lounge 2C D Copia Creative, Inc. C Kristin Kobayashi Pilates
3A D Pink Tank Creative C Kafe Kulcha 3B D Funk/Levis & Associates, Inc. C Kelly King & Associates 3C D More Branding+Communication C Kitchen Design
4A D Steven O'Connor C Miller Design 4B D Archrival C Kopsa Otte 4C D Ellen Bruss Design C Continuum

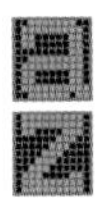

A B C

1

2

3

4

D = Design Firm C = Client

1A D Jennifer Braham Design C Kick Pleat 1B D Banowetz + Company, Inc. C Chef Kent Rathbun 1C D Modern Dog Design Co. C K2 Snowboards
2A D Cosmic Egg Studios C K3 Management Services 2B D Tower of Babel C Oregon Lottery 2C D Creative House C K12 Global Inc.
3A D PETTUS CREATIVE C LUX Designs LLC 3B D Richards Brock Miller Mitchell & Associates C Lincoln Hotels
3C D Funnel Design Group C Gardner Tanenbaum Group 4A D Brand Navigation C Leavitt's 4B D Dessein C Zen Resources
4C D Carmi e Ubertis Milano Srl C Linfleur

A B C

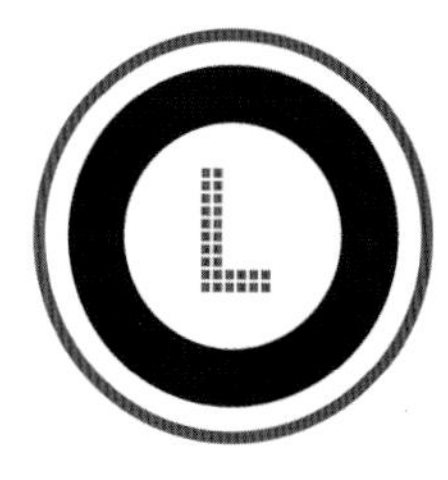

1

2

3

4

D = Design Firm C = Client

1A D Westwerk DSGN C Leighton Design Group 1B D Jovan Rocanov C Studio Linije 1C D mattisimo C Virgin Mobile
2A D Onoma, LLC C LeBoeuf, Lamb, Green & MacRae, LLP 2B D Z Factory C Linkergy, LLC 2C D Riccardo Sabioni C Craig Lerch
3A D Richards Brock Miller Mitchell & Associates C Landes Investments 3B D Simon & Goetz Design C lessings ag
3C D R&R Partners C Las Vegas Convention & Visitors Authority
4A D Dino Design C LeaderMark Homes 4B D Conover C The Lowry Company 4C D Tactix Creative

A B C

1

2

3

4

D = Design Firm C = Client

1A D Ramp C Local.com Corporation 1B D Oluzen C Constructora Langa 1C D Alterpop C Lafayette Library
2A D Carmi e Ubertis Milano Srl C Lupano 2B D maynard kay C Lazard Asset Management 2C D Diagram C Logzact Ltd.
3A D S Design, Inc. C Looper(r) Law Enforcement Supply 3B D The Joe Bosack Graphic Design Co. C Lagrange College
3C D Artrinsic Design C Lovinggood Middle School 4A D Felixsockwell.com 4B D David Kampa C Loophole Entertainment
4C D Hirshorn Zuckerman Design Group

A | B | C

1

2

3

4

D = Design Firm C = Client

1A D Cidma Group C Lagasse Group 1B D Eggra C UNMIK–EU Pillar 1C D Karl Design Vienna C Korbstadt Lichtenfels
2A D Fredrik Lewander C Maria Campos Björkquist 2B D Creative Madhouse C Liz Caan Designs 2C D WestmorelandFlint C Larson Electric
3A D Fekete + Company C The Leslie Group 3B D LIFT HERE, Inc. C LIFT HERE, Inc. 3C D Carmi e Ubertis Milano Srl C Uniweld
4A D christiansen : creative C Lifetime Learning 4B D Straka-Design C ProSieben 4C D Mazemedia

A B C

1

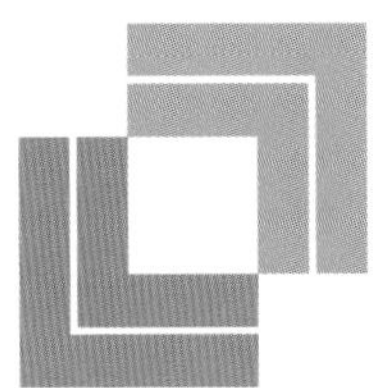

D = Design Firm C = Client

1A **D** Fixation Marketing **C** Lewis Limited 1B **D** Lukatarina **C** Luka Mancini 1C **D** DUEL Purpose **C** Launchpad Creative
2A **D** lunabrand design group **C** Legacy Ridge 2B **D** For the Love of Creating **C** Sam Hughes Photography 2C **D** Spoonbend **C** Lago Terra
3A **D** Insight Design **C** LaminateWorks 3B **D** David Clark Design **C** L2 Holdings 3C **D** Karl Design Vienna **C** Montscher Spedition
4A **D** noe design **C** Mercury Management Group 4B **D** Hula+Hula **C** Moderatto / BMG 4C **D** Mystic Design, Inc. **C** Matthews Mattress

A B C

1

2

3

4

Ⓓ = Design Firm Ⓒ = Client

1A Ⓓ Steven O'Connor Ⓒ Morehouse College / Spike Lee 1B Ⓓ Barnstorm Creative Group Inc Ⓒ Snomotion Whistler 1C Ⓓ Studio Simon Ⓒ Golden Baseball League
2A Ⓓ Corder Philips Ⓒ Mecca Investments 2B Ⓓ Niedermeier Design Ⓒ Queen Mary Tea 2C Ⓓ Giles Design Inc. Ⓒ Rancho San Miguel
3A Ⓓ MSI Ⓒ Monier Lifetile 3B Ⓓ Bystrom Design Ⓒ Martin/Maribeth 3C Ⓓ Primarily Rye LLC Ⓒ McLean & Co.
4A Ⓓ Sellier Design, Inc. Ⓒ Matt Yung 4B Ⓓ Extraverage Productions Ⓒ Mayo Chix 4C Ⓓ Banowetz + Company, Inc. Ⓒ Hotel ZaZa/Monarch

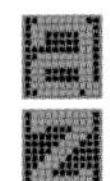

A B C

1

2

3

4

D = Design Firm C = Client

1A D Lysergid C Personal Brand 1B D mugur mihai C Gideon Cardozo Communications 1C D ivan2design C Madina Vadache couture
2A D Banowetz + Company, Inc. C The Mosaic Hotel 2B D Extraverage Productions C Medusa 2C D Clutch Design C Manitou, Inc.
3A D Intersection Creative C Mooney Design/Tom Mooney 3B D Bunch C Pero Mamic 3C D Studio International C City Museum Vukovar
4A D MacLaren McCann Calgary C Mike Meadus 4B D Haven Productions C Matjik Creative 4C D Liska + Associates Communication Design C Joan Maloney

A B C

1

2

3

4

D = Design Firm C = Client

1A D Marlin C Messner Construction 1B D TOKY Branding+Design C Pyramid Companies 1C D Britt Funderburk
2A D MangoGlobal C Metal Innovation Ltd. 2B D dale harris C Bendigo Manufacturing Group 2C D Laura Manthey Design C Monks Project Solutions
3A D Clover Creative Group, LLC C Moorhead Company Inc. 3B D Jane Cameron Design C Mindfield Books 3C D Valhalla | Design & Conquer C Militant Moto
4A D noe design C Metromix 4B D Boston Creative, Inc. C Momentum Strategies 4C D Gardner Design C Mega Metals Group

1

2

3

4

D = Design Firm   C = Client

1A D m-Art C Metro Ferals 1B D Patten ID C Lansing Printing 1C D Sara Delaney Graphic Design C MaestroTec
2A D MondoVox, Inc. C m-systems, inc. 2B D Diagram 2C D Double Brand C www.mlingua.pl
3A D Laura Manthey Design C Monks Project Solutions 3B D VanPaul Design C Visila Design 3C D Element C Midwest Photo Exchange
4A D Iperdesign, Inc. C Mercury 4B D Jelena Drobac C multipano 4C D Gardner Design C Martens Appraisal

A B C

1

2

3

4

D = Design Firm C = Client

1A D Gardner Design C Mitch's 1B D Ray Dugas Design C Charles Muncaster 1C D Advertising Intelligence C Cafe M
2A D Paragon Marketing Communications C Market Maker Fund 2B D Cfx C Momentum Excercise Equipment 2C D Stiles Design C MidFirst Bank/Riester
3A D Remo Strada Design C Maxus Group 3B D Design & Co C Mascoma Corporation 3C D Niedermeier Design C U.S. Dept. of Defense
4A D Lienhart Design C Main America 4B D Lienhart Design C Mutual Bank 4C D Clay McIntosh Creative C Clay McIntosh Creative

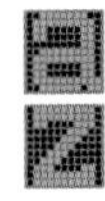

A B C

1

2

3

4

D = Design Firm   C = Client

1A D Demographic Inc. C Camp Manitoqua 1B D Zieldesign C Lillie Ellison 1C D GCG C Mesa View Hospital
2A D Haute Haus Creative C Motorola 2B D Haller Design C Manno's Pro-Fitness 2C D Burocratik–Design C Moonspell
3A D ADC Global Creativity C Corporación Multi Inversiones 3B D Roy Smith Design C Lisa Millett 3C D asmallpercent C Brookwood School
4A D Helius Creative Advertising C Mike Bailey Printing 4B D LogoDesignGuru.com 4C D Mindgruve C Mauzy

A B C

1

2

3

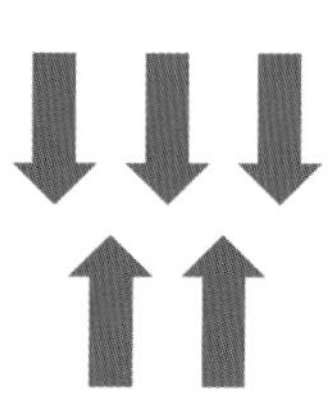

4

D = Design Firm C = Client

1A D KZ creative 1B D R Design LLC C Momentis 1C D grow C Molys
2A D BlueSpark Studios C Moocow Boards 2B D Clutch Design C The Museum of Tolerance 2C D Opolis Design, LLC C The Momentum Group
3A D Pappas Group C M 3B D Menikoff Design C Menikoff Design 3C D gocreativ C Marketing Strategists
4A D Jeffhalmos C Mergency Inc. 4B D Miriello Grafico, Inc. C Qualcomm 4C D Burocratik–Design C Biblioteca EL

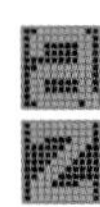

1

2

3

4

D = Design Firm C = Client

1A D 28 LIMITED BRAND C mactastic 1B D 28 LIMITED BRAND C macrebels 1C D Iskender Asanaliev C Bilkay Mobilya
2A D Mindgruve C Dr. Lardon 2B D Spark Studio C MotorOne 2C D Tactix Creative C Quicksilver / Roxy
3A D Tom Law Design C Myrick Real Estate 3B D Beacon Branding LLC C Master Clean 3C D Impressions Design and Print Ltd C Diane Minshull
4A D LogoDesignGuru.com C Mar Media 4B D Ventress Design Group, Inc C Merlin Technologies 4C D Design Fish C Communicaitons and PR consulting group

A B C

1

2

3

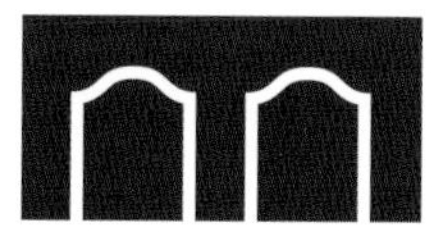

4

D = Design Firm C = Client

1A D Ketch 22 Creative C Wamzle New Media 1B D Sebastiany Branding & Design C M&ASI 1C D Shelley Design+Marketing C Maryland Works
2A D Jelena Drobac C Monus 2B D Pixellente! C Mayte Ramos 2C D Richards Brock Miller Mitchell & Associates C Mitchell Reis Robb
3A D Form G C Mica Craft + Design 3B D Methodologie C WSHM 3C D Marlin C Mediation First
4A D Beveridge Seay, Inc. C MarketResearch.com 4B D Archrival C Federal Apartments 4C D Thomas Cook Designs C Masters Properties

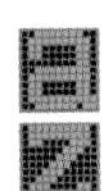

A B C

1

2

3

4

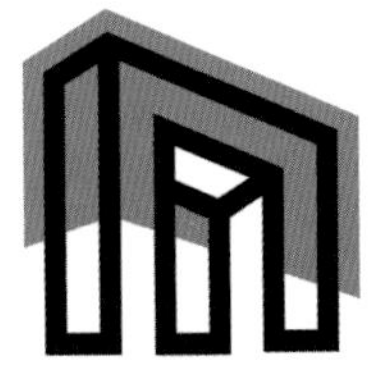

D = Design Firm C = Client

1A D Richards & Swensen C Matthews Enterprises 1B D schaer creative l.l.c. C Richmond American Homes 1C D Creative NRG C McFadden & Co.
2A D Heins Creative, Inc. C McCall Development 2B D Tactical Magic C My Next Phase 2C D Roman Kotikov C Metrinfo.ru
3A D Modern Dog Design Co. C Modern Dog 3B D David Kampa C Studio Maquette 3C D Octavo Design Pty Ltd C i3 Construction
4A D Gardner Design 4B D ADC Global Creativity C Grupo Marhnos 4C D Mindgruve C Dr. Lardon

A B C

1

2

3

4

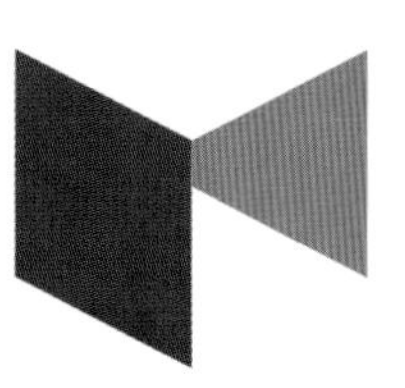

D = Design Firm C = Client

1A D Funnel Design Group C Mehlburger Brawley 1B D MDUK Media 1C D KITA International I Visual Playground C m10 investments
2A D David Kampa C Mann & Mann Custom Homes 2B D Redpoint design C Mid Michigan Masonry 2C D Cocoon C Phil-Mar Trade Bindery
3A D fallindesign studio C NordlWestlMedia 3B D Landkamer Partners, Inc. C Massini 3C D Strategy Studio C Mediling
4A D TOKY Branding+Design C Mackey Mitchell Associates 4B D Steiner&Co. C Millenia, Singapore 4C D D&Dre Creative C MaxInvest Settlements

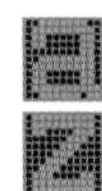

1

2

3

4

D = Design Firm C = Client

1A D Gardner Design C Mega Metals Group 1B D Extraverage Productions C Mayo Chix
1C D Richards Brock Miller Mitchell & Associates C Rails Relationship Marketing
2A D LCD Incorporated C Mavis Media 2B D Taylor Raber C Blue Medora 2C D Dino Design C Magnet Capital
3A D LogoMotto.com C Medicon Marketing 3B D Greteman Group C Messner Architecure 3C D reaves design C McDonald's
4A D Daniel Sim Design C Relationships Matter 4B D Pink Tank Creative C Match.com.au 4C D Juicebox Designs C Manual Therapy of Nashville

A B C

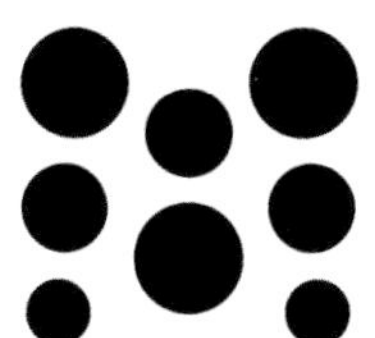

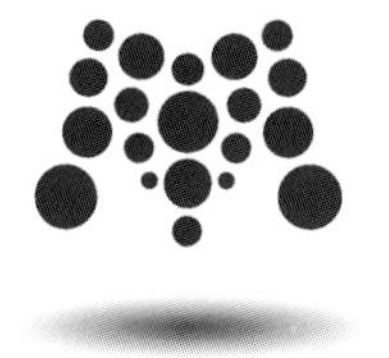

1

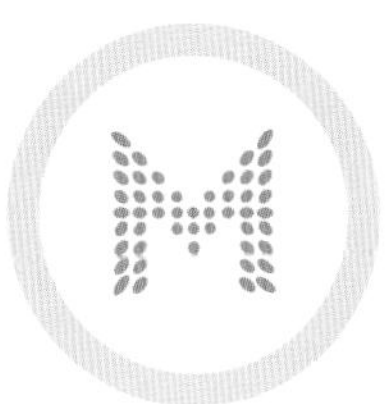

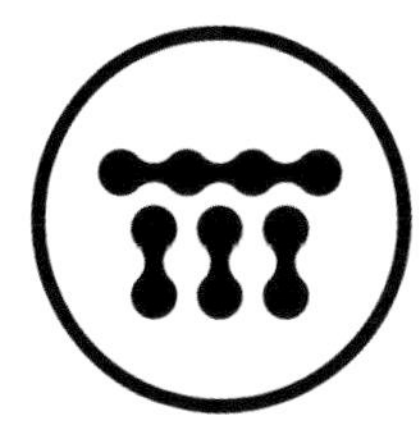

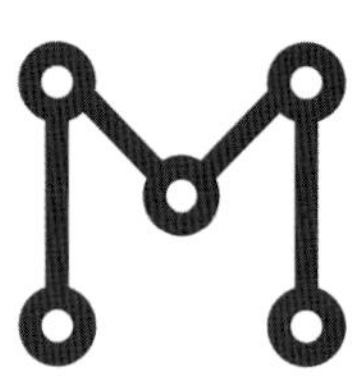

2

3

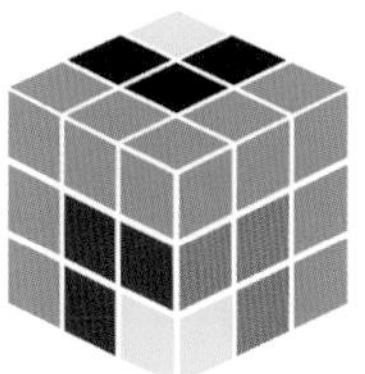

4

D = Design Firm C = Client

1A D Jared Milam Design C Tulsa MetroNet 1B D Gridwerk C Modern Graphics 1C D Prana Design + Art Studios C This is Major Tom
2A D Flywheel Design C M.R.Williams 2B D two tribes gmbh C Mann Blumen & Deco 2C D Tandemodus C The Metro Connection
3A D Dept 3 C Mecury 3B D Design Nut C David L. Marcus 3C D Beacon Branding LLC C Merkury Innovations
4A D LSD C m engineering 4B D Z&G 4C D Offbeat Design C Mosaic Media

A B C

1

D = Design Firm **C = Client**

1A D Lesniewicz Associates C Mohon Realty 1B D Mitchel Design Inc. C Mitchel Design Inc. 1C D Miriello Grafico, Inc. C Qualcomm
2A D schaer creative l.l.c. C Richmond American Homes 2B D moosylvania C City of Maplewood 2C D KTD C Mulberry Publishing
3A D Glitschka Studios C Macore Company 3B D Opolis Design, LLC C The Momentum Group 3C D Sibley Peteet Design—Dallas C Montomery Farm
4A D Karl Design Vienna C Torsten Mueller 4B D Extraverage Productions C Mayo Chix 4C D Tactix Creative C Phillip-Morris

A B C

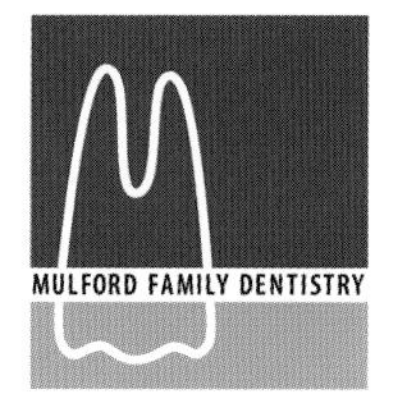

1

2

3

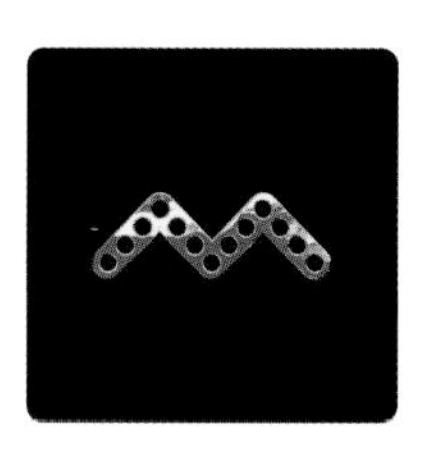

4

D = Design Firm C = Client

1A D Prejean Creative C M Dental Studio / Wright Feigley 1B D ContrerasDesign C Mulford Famiy Dentistry 1C D Jeremy Stott C Arteis
2A D Hayes+Company C Martin Promotional Advertising 2B D monkeygrass C monkeygrass 2C D LSD C gno for women aid
3A D Zapata Design C The Myositis Association 3B D Spangler Design Team C Majesty Companies 3C D Hirshorn Zuckerman Design Group C Ross Development
4A D Gardner Design C Mega Metals Group 4B D Gardner Design C Mega Metals Group 4C D Paradox Box C «Mir» Building company

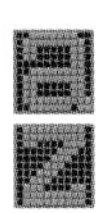

A B C

1

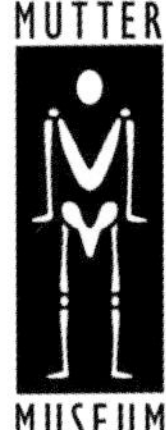

D = Design Firm C = Client

1A D Noble C Noble 1B D Howling Good Designs C Magicris Productions 1C D NOT A CANNED HAM C Matt Stillwell
2A D Schwartzrock Graphic Arts C American Bible Society 2B D Identity33, LLC C Stephen Hernandez 2C D Kradel Design C mutter museum
3A D Studio International C Varteks 3B D Michael Freimuth Creative C Matthieu Chardon and Alexis Garmey 3C D R&R Partners C Meadows Bank
4A D medium control C medium control 4B D Creative NRG C Michael Drescher 4C D lazy snail—art factory C Minoan Lines

A B C

1

2

3

4

D = Design Firm C = Client

1A D Diagram C Media Expert 1B D BrandSavvy, Inc. C Media Furniture 1C D Novasoul
2A D WestmorelandFlint C Liscomb Hood Mason Co. 2B D Rufuturu C Host Max 2C D DBD+A Studio C Michelle, Inc.
3A D Flaherty Robinson Inc. C International Media Service 3B D Courtney & Company C Michael Kleinberg 3C D dache C webmynd
4A D Ulyanov Denis C Minmade 4B D CONCEPTO WORLDWIDE C LMDC 4C D Essex Two C Northwestern Memorial Corporation

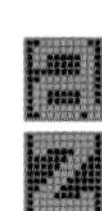

1

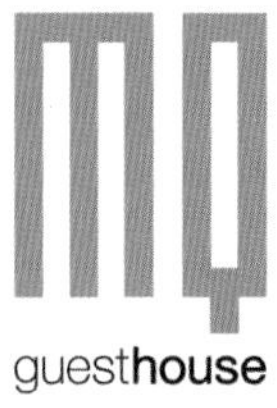

2

3

4

D = Design Firm C = Client

1A D The Office of Art+Logik C Minneapolis Park Lakehawks 1B D VINE360 C Museum Quality, LLC 1C D LeBoYe C MQ Guest House
2A D Phony Lawn C Russell+Mills Studios 2B D rajasandhu.com 2C D Phony Lawn C Russell+Mills Studios
3A D DUEL Purpose C Managed Data Solutions 3B D Offbeat Design C Monsac Handbags 3C D Resin Design C Angela Winter Jewellery
4A D Cisneros Design C Mesilla Valley Mall 4B D Flory Design, Inc. C May-Way Farms 4C D Creative NRG C Miller-Wenzler

A B C

1

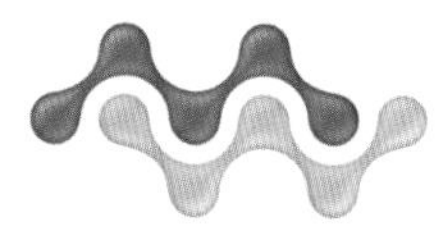

2

3

4

D = Design Firm C = Client

1A D Madomat C Michael Woolley 1B D lunabrand design group C Midwest Chemical 1C D Chris Herron Design C Milky Way Lounge
2A D Gabriel Kalach • V I S U A L communication C Michael Work—Attorney 2B D Hinge Incorporated C Maak1 2C D Kurt for Hire
3A D Anagraphic C Naturhome 3B D Creative NRG C Novotny Landscaping 3C D Richards & Swensen C Dunn Communications
4A D Karl Design Vienna C PfK / Heilmoor Neydharting GmbH Austria 4B D Redbeard Communications Inc. C Nelsons Pool Service 4C D pearpod C Navitas

A B C

1

2

3

4

D = Design Firm C = Client

1A D renaud garnier smart rebranding C Seed Factory 1B D Brandient C Novensys 1C D Bluespace Creative, Inc. C New Way
2A D PETTUS CREATIVE C New Energy Communications 2B D Rhombus, Inc. C NoLimitz Snowboards 2C D Hinge C Nucore Vision
3A D VanPaul Design 3B D CAPSULE C Nortrax 3C D Jerron Ames C Arteis
4A D X RAY C Niks Ltd. 4B D Kevin Creative C Nugen Software 4C D SiglerGroup, Inc. C Neuvie Furniture

A B C

1

2

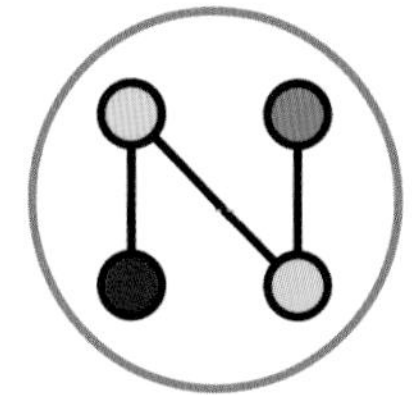

3

4

NationaLease

D = Design Firm **C** = Client

1A **D** Formula Design **C** Nuglu 1B **D** Maycreate **C** Nextlec 1C **D** ANS **C** Advanced Neuromodulation Systems, Inc.
2A **D** LogoDesignGuru.com **C** Netzonehost 2B **D** Peter Gibbons **C** The Social Network Company 2C **D** FigDesign **C** North Texas Tollway Authority
3A **D** CF Napa Brand Design **C** Refreshment Brands 3B **D** CAPSULE **C** North American Banking Company 3C **D** Matthew Wells Design **C** Norwood Resources Ltd.
4A **D** BrandSavvy, Inc. **C** NationaLease 4B **D** Strategy Studio **C** National Transit 4C **D** Ty Wilkins **C** Ty Wilkins

1

2

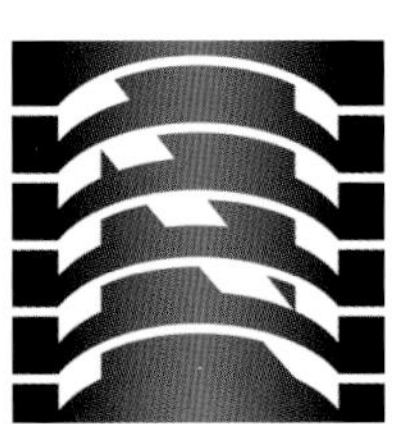

3

4

D = Design Firm C = Client

1A D Rocket Science C Siemens 1B D Rocket Science C Siemens 1C D Funk/Levis & Associates, Inc. C Nielsen Research Labs 2A D Funk/Levis & Associates, Inc. C Payment Insured Plan, Inc. 2B D Essex Two C River North Assn. 2C D Gee + Chung Design C Nanocosm Technologies, Inc. 3A D Beganik Strategy + Design C The Northstar at Siebert Field 3B D AKOFA Creative C University of Delaware/ Self Promotional 3C D Landor Associates C Netscape 4A D Mitre Agency C Peconic Bay Winery 4B D Miles Design C Northwest Advisory Group 4C D Gizwiz Studio C Nivek Services Inc

A B C

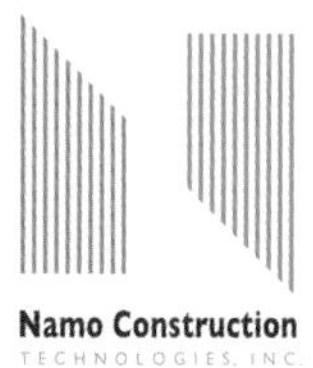

1

2

3

4

D = Design Firm C = Client

1A D Laura Manthey Design C Northern Sky Productions 1B D Living Creative Design C Namo Construction Tech 1C D OzbeyArt C Neo Knit Ltd.
2A D The Office of Art+Logik C Nimble, Inc. 2B D Kate Resnick C Niche 2C D Classic Lines Design C North of England Excellence
3A D GOTCHA DESIGN C NCA, Inc. 3B D Tactical Magic C National Community Services 3C D Mikhail Gubergrits C North Engineering Design
4A D Mad Dog Graphx C Northern Air Cargo 4B D face C Northgate Marketing 4C D Nynas C Nichole Nynas Consulting

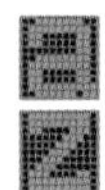

A B C

1

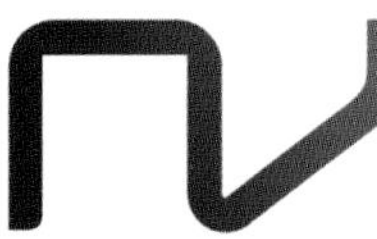

2

3

4

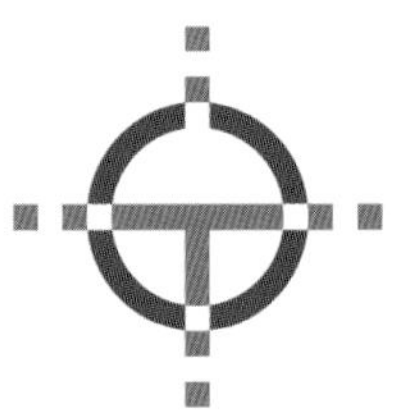

D = Design Firm C = Client

1A D Ulyanov Denis C laboratory information technology 1B D DDB SF C Altavie 1C D Landor Associates C Northwest
2A D Kraftaverk—Design Studio C NÁMSMATSSTOFNUN 2B D Glitschka Studios C One Number 2C D Concussion, llc C N3 Real Estate
3A D B.L.A. Design Company C SC Opera, unused 3B D oneal design C Carrie O'Neal 3C D Diagram
4A D Adept Interactive C Megalan Network 4B D Tomko Design C Orbit 4C D FigDesign C Telematics Research Group

A B C

3

4

D = Design Firm C = Client

1A D DMG Asociados, S.A. C Ocean Realtors 1B D logobyte C Onto Machine 1C D Spoonbend C Olicon
2A D Grey Matters, LLC C Omega Packaging 2B D Sanders Design C Oceania Aviation 2C D Strategy Studio C Offset Online
3A D Paul Black Design C Lehndorff Properties 3B D Sauvage Design C Odyssey House 3C D Gabriel Kalach • V I S U A L communication C Cesar Sotomayor
4A D Funk/Levis & Associates, Inc. C OneLink Corporation 4B D Studio Nine Creative C DesignPoint 4C D Sebastiany Branding & Design C Click Obras

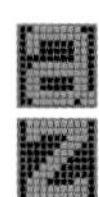

A B C

1

2

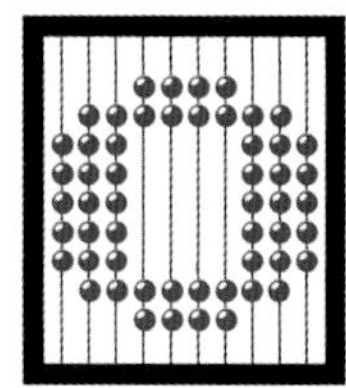

3

4

D = Design Firm C = Client

1A D 3 Advertising LLC C Osuna Nursery 1B D S Design, Inc. C Oklahoma Heritage Association & Museum 1C D Signal Design C Olive Advertising
2A D Studio Simon C Orem Owlz 2B D MetaDesign C The Ocean Conservancy 2C D Hubbell Design Works C David M. Oberheu, CPA
3A D The Martin Group C Odyssey Advisors 3B D Addison Whitney C Wildlife International Network 3C D Stoltze Design C Office Environments of New England
4A D Ventress Design Group, Inc C Oman-Gibson Associates 4B D Essex Two C Corporate Graphic Arts 4C D Steele Design C 0KM Fashion

A B C

1

2

3

4

D = Design Firm C = Client

1A D Fleishman Hillard C Team Phat Girl 1B D br:Verse C Parisi Artisan Coffee 1C D freelancer C Poligraph_Izdat Service
2A D gsFITCH C ATLANTIS DUBAI 2B D Gardner Design C ParkStone 2C D Schwartzrock Graphic Arts C Infinity Direct
3A D Banowetz + Company, Inc. C The Hanover Company 3B D mugur mihai C Pergola 3C D Brian Krezel C Egg Strategy
4A D GingerBee Creative C Placer Club 4B D Liew Design, Inc. C Peakway, Inc. 4C D Tran Creative C Parkside Fitness

1

2

3

4

D = Design Firm C = Client

1A D Purpled : Graphic Design Studio C Professional Reporters, Inc. 1B D Whaley Design, Ltd 1C D Gardner Design C Pivotal Athletic Training
2A D Gardner Design C Pivotal Athletic Training 2B D joe miller's company C Pearson Communications 2C D Minale Tattersfield and Partners Ltd C Principe
3A D Tchopshop Media C Petrotek 3B D LogoDesignGuru.com 3C D Dotzero Design C Pacific Crest Motel
4A D Penhouse Design C Laois Chamber and Laois Tourism 4B D Sire Advertising C Pulse Fitness for Women
4C D Corporate Image Consultants, Inc. C Pallets South, Inc.

A B C

1

2

3

4

D = Design Firm C = Client

1A D Garbow Graphics, Inc. C Farnbacher Loles Motorsports 1B D Double Brand C Biuro Plus 1C D Flow Creative C Physicians Plus
2A D tisha domingo design C Philippine Nursing Institute 2B D Tomko Design C Phatanium 2C D Scott Lewis Design
3A D Koch Creative Group C Koch Industries Inc 3B D Dotzero Design C PayPin 3C D 73ideas C Placebo
4A D LGA / Jon Cain C Park Inc 4B D Hazen Creative, Inc. C The Perfect Petal 4C D Interrobang Design Collaborative, Inc. C IMSA

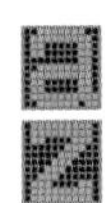

A B C

1

2

3

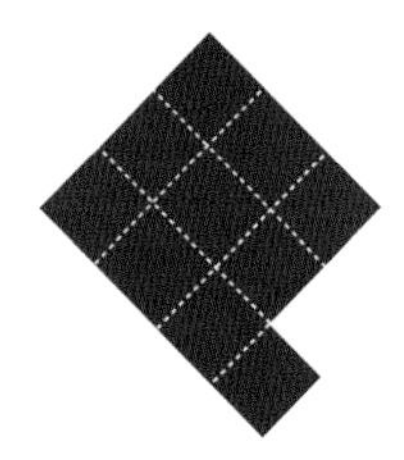

4

D = Design Firm C = Client

1A D Ammunition C Panchang.com 1B D Studio GT&P C Effepi 1C D SoupGraphix Inc. C Parts Direct

2A D Identica Branding and Design C ITA, Industry training Authority 2B D Diagram C Polenergia 2C D Burocratik–Design C Pixel Studio

3A D Laura Manthey Design C Steve Preston 3B D Strange Ideas 3C D FutureBrand BC&H C Politec

4A D Impressions Design and Print Ltd C Premium Watch Financial Services 4B D Chris Yin Design C Pontiac Land 4C D Lienhart Design C The Paradigm Group

A B C

1

2

3

4

D = Design Firm   C = Client

1A D 212-BIG-BOLT C c-base 1B D Lesniewicz Associates C Palmetto Products 1C D Hayes+Company C Paradigm Retail Group
2A D Kevin Creative C Pixellogo Custom 2B D Think Cap Design C Phat Pelican 2C D robert meyers design
3A D Advertising Intelligence C Palazzo Restaurant 3B D Nynas C Public Executions 3C D Schwartzrock Graphic Arts C Pugleasa
4A D Jerron Ames C Arteis 4B D MFDI C Pure Power Products 4C D The Envision Group C Paragon Alliance

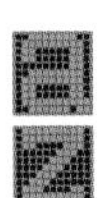

1

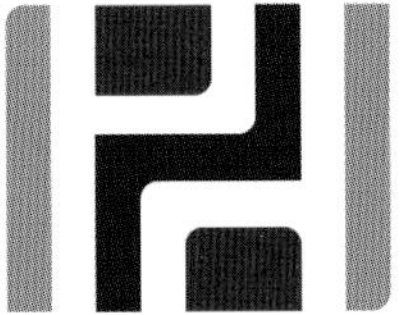

PIAZZA SAN LORENZO

D = Design Firm C = Client

1A D MINE(tm) C Print Alchemy 1B D Q Digital Studio C Project Brillig 1C D Critt Graham
2A D Tran Creative C Parkside Fitness 2B D Doink, Inc. C Pink Gun Brand 2C D Steven O'Connor C Pascal Hong Interiors
3A D Mindgruve C Panish & Hoey 3B D Mindgruve C Panish & Hoey 3C D Giles Design Inc. C Piazza San Lorenzo
4A D TPG Architecture C Picasso Lighting 4B D Tomko Design C Partner Mark 4C D Zapata Design C People & Partners

A | B | C

1

2

3

4

D = Design Firm C = Client

1A D Jeffhalmos C The Providence Corporation 1B D Church Logo Gallery C Petra Christian Fellowship 1C D Ink Graphix C Perola Productions
2A D Janson Straub C Priority Signs 2B D Doink, Inc. C ParkSouth 2C D Sockeye Creative C Portland State University
3A D ARTini BAR C Pitch University (proposed) 3B D Impressions Design and Print Ltd C Premium Watch Financial Services (unused)
3C D Deep Design C Mannington Mills 4A D Pat Taylor Inc. C Queen Ann Press 4B D Phony Lawn C Quintess
4C D Karl Design Vienna C Braue / Q-Bioanalytic

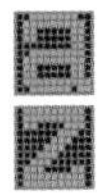

A B C

1

2

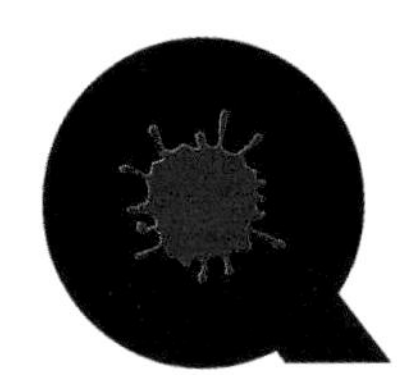

3

4

D = Design Firm C = Client

1A D Truly Design C Personal project 1B D br:Verse C Quixotic 1C D Copperfin C Karin E. Quirk
2A D Mary Hutchison Design LLC C O'Asian Bistro, Inc. 2B D KOESTER design C Q ink 2C D Studio GT&P C Quid
3A D STUBBORN SIDEBURN C Magnet Eyes 3B D Crave, Inc C Questinghound Technologies 3C D Lippincott C Quick Chek
4A D Impressions Design and Print Ltd C Quietly Confident Technology 4B D Nynas C Quady Painting 4C D C.Cady Design C Qingdoa Pavilion

A B C

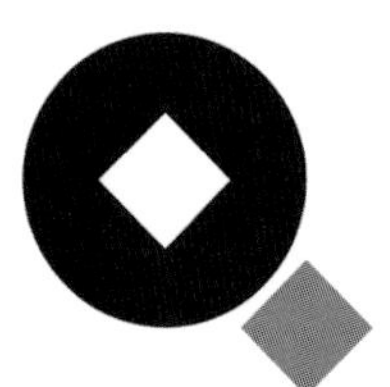

1

2

3

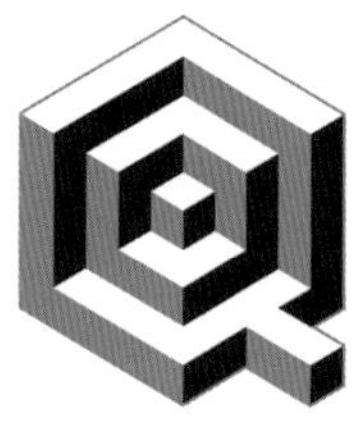

4

D = Design Firm C = Client

1A D Axiom Design Partners C Q Construction 1B D Sauvage Design C Qbik 1C D design:tn C Inquest Media
2A D MDUK Media C Quist Solicitors 2B D Happy Giraffe C Qbeta 2C D Q Design C Q Design
3A D Mattson Creative C Quadra 3B D gsFITCH C ATLANTIS DUBAI 3C D LOCHS
4A D Pherra C Qube9 4B D noe design C Quality Automation Graphics 4C D Karl Design Vienna C Braue / Q-Bioanalytic

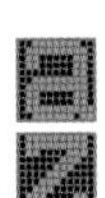

A B C

1

2

3

4

D = Design Firm C = Client

1A D Bruketa & Zinic C Ministry of Sea, Transport and Infrastructure 1B D Daniel Sim Design C Qadrati 1C D demasijones C Q Kitchens
2A D Pat Walsh Design, LLC C Quiet Detective 2B D POLLARDdesign C Quest 2C D Nanantha Shroff C C&D Aerospace
3A D Wox C Maria Antonia 3B D Tesser C Quiznos Sub 3C D Mindgruve C Custom Quilting
4A D Axiom Design Partners C Questus Capital Group 4B D Braue: Brand Design Experts C Q-Bioanalytic 4C D Karl Design Vienna C Braue / Q-Bioanalytic

A B C

1

2

3

4

D = Design Firm C = Client

1A D Vasco Morelli Design C La Honda Winery/Schneider 1B D Double Brand C Letter Shop 1C D Medlahuis C QSN Kwaliteitsmanagement
2A D Sussner Design Company C Reflections 2B D Ulyanov Denis C Radiance 2C D Hubbell Design Works C Rosary Catholic High School
3A D Honey Design C Auburn Developments 3B D Schwartzrock Graphic Arts C Brad Radtke 3C D Tactix Creative C Core Proprties
4A D Francis Hogan C Rancourt 4B D Brains on Fire C South Carolina Department of Health and Environmental Control 4C D Glitschka Studios C Upper Deck Company

1

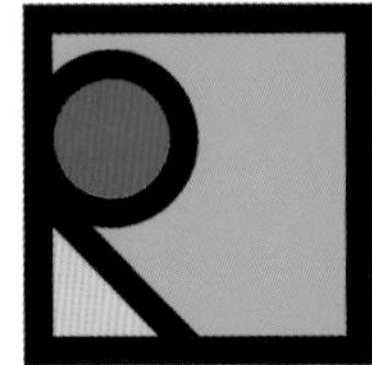

2

3

4

D = Design Firm C = Client

1A D Sussner Design Company C Reflections 1B D R Design LLC C Craig Rouse
1C D Sebastiany Branding & Design C Rede Brasileira de Educação em Direitos Humanos
2A D LSD C Oscar Díez / Microrepublic 2B D Octavo Design Pty Ltd C RedBack Envelopes 2C D Whaley Design, Ltd C Regency Wood Floors
3A D Mojo Solo C Rovrr 3B D Stiles Design C River Rock Construction 3C D DUEL Purpose C Reliable Networks
4A D J6Studios C Ronin Dojo 4B D Paradox Box C Russia 4C D Steve's Portfolio C JEG

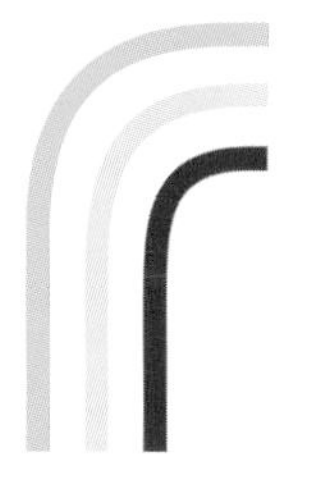

D = Design Firm C = Client

1A **D** Intersection Creative **C** CADRelief 1B **D** Loop Design **C** B3 Productions 1C **D** O!
2A **D** Logan Cantu **C** Rainbow Chemicals 2B **D** Beveridge Seay, Inc. **C** Resource International 2C **D** Scientific Arts **C** The Render Warehouse
3A **D** Prejean Creative **C** Iberia Medical Center 3B **D** Plumbline Studios **C** The Ranch Winery 3C **D** UNIT-Y **C** Army & Air Force Exchange Service
4A **D** Jenny Kolcun Freelance Designer 4B **D** Jan Sabach Design **C** Fresh Research, Jaroslav Cir 4C **D** Twin Engine Creative **C** Real-Lending.com

A B C

1

2

3

4

D = Design Firm C = Client

1A D Richard Rios C Rios Creative 1B D Methodologie C Redley 1C D Carlson Marketing Worldwide C Revolution Health
2A D Gardner Design C Recreational Vehicle Products 2B D Creative Madhouse C Costal Realty 2C D Heisel Design C The Resource Group
3A D UniGraphics C Bowling Green State University 3B D Unibrand Belgrade C ramapo 3C D The Joe Bosack Graphic Design Co. C Keystone Baseball
4A D VanPaul Design C PartsRail.com 4B D Gardner Design C Reno Cooking Conveyors 4C D SPATCHURST C Randwick City Council

A B C

1

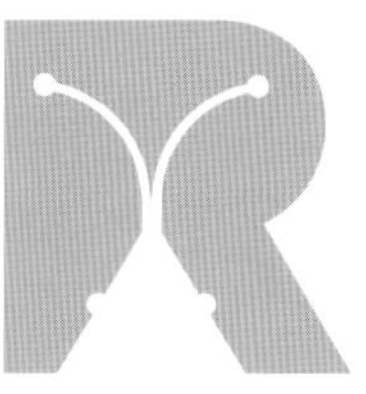

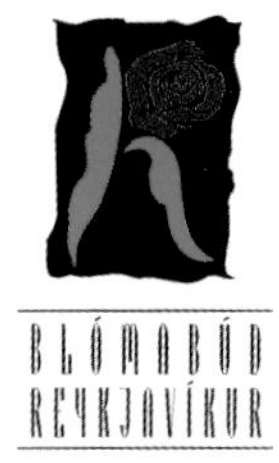

2

3

4

D = Design Firm C = Client

1A D Lesniewicz Associates C Roach Graphics 1B D Tunglið Advertising Agency ehf. C Reykjavik Florist's 1C D Logologik C AIG/Lincoln Poland
2A D Vasco Morelli Design C Rohrer Construction 2B D Jeff Andrews Design C Double R Manufacturing 2C D Richards Brock Miller Mitchell & Associates C Home Depot
3A D Gardner Design C Reno Cooking Conveyors 3B D Whaley Design, Ltd C Regency Wood Floors 3C D ANS C Roger's Hardware
4A D GTA—Gregory Thomas Associates C Remington 4B D Ryan Cooper Design C Archrival 4C D ArtGraphics.ru C Identity magazine

A B C

1

RBt

return design

2

RKI

3

4

D = Design Firm C = Client

1A D Imadesign, Corp. C Russian Business Travel 1B D KTD C Robert Deputy 1C D asmallpercent C Return Design
2A D dmayne design C Risner Group, Inc. 2B D Brian Krezel C the Black Heart Project 2C D fuszion C Robinson Koerner International
3A D Phony Lawn C Russell+Mills Studios 3B D The Laster Group C RMHW 3C D volatile-graphics
4A D Studio Simon C Round Rock Express 4B D Home Grown Logos C RiverRatPokerWear.com 4C D Romulo Moya / Trama C RR Architects

A B C

1

2

3

4

D = Design Firm C = Client

1A D Bertz Design Group C Kostin Ruffkess 1B D DUEL Purpose C Launchpad Creative 1C D Planet Propaganda C Radical Rye
2A D El Paso, Galeria de Comunicacion C Regente Jewellery 2B D Alphabet Arm Design C Jon Letzkus 2C D VanPaul Design C Royal Saxon
3A D MARC USA C Raina Kerman 3B D Corder Philips C Assured Group 3C D R&R Partners C Hampton Roads Transit
4A D Conover C Eldorado Stone 4B D Ad Impact Advertising C Stirling Foods 4C D Tactix Creative C Kyle Scoresby

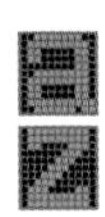

A B C

1

2

3

4

D = Design Firm C = Client

1A D Tactix Creative 1B D Westwerk DSGN C Barger Brewing Co. 1C D Oluzen C Constructora Langa
2A D Studio grafickih ideja C Strugar 2B D Tank Design C tromsø symphony orchestra 2C D McGarrah/Jessee C Hyatt Regency Lost Pines Resort and Spa
3A D Haute Haus Creative C Waterstone Development 3B D Faith C Sacred Lifestyle 3C D Velocity Design Group C Set N' Stone Design
4A D Brian Krezel 4B D Strange Ideas 4C D Chapa Design C Stonecutter Arts

A | B | C

1

2

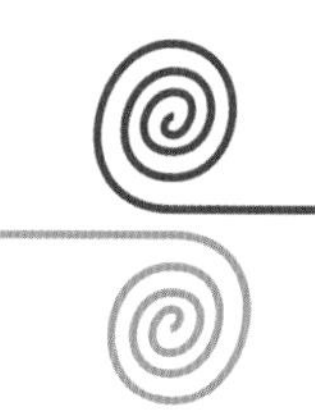

3

4

D = Design Firm C = Client

1A D Giles Design Inc. C Pearl Stable 1B D Power Plus Advertising C Spazio Interno 1C D RICH design studio C Samal Hotel
2A D UlrichPinciotti Design Group C Sunset Retirement Communities 2B D Latinbrand C Savidi 2C D three o'clock I design C Stinson Aerospace
3A D Schwartzrock Graphic Arts C Design Center 3B D For the Love of Creating C Sarah Bussey Photography 3C D squiggle6 C Anthony Spies Landscapes
4A D Fernandez Design C Salcido Photography 4B D ebb+flow design C Suspect Group 4C D Orn Smari I Design C Strikamerki ehf.

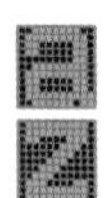

A B C

1

2

3

4

D = Design Firm C = Client

1A D Crave, Inc C Southern Specialties 1B D Glitschka Studios C Mattson Creative 1C D BadGenius C Kahn Development Company
2A D Clockwork Studios C Spectrum Landscaping 2B D David Kampa C Schumann & Company 2C D LogoDesignGuru.com
3A D Ellis Kaiser C Southern Tennessee Medical Center 3B D LGA / Jon Cain C Stedman Realty 3C D The Martin Group C Sonoma
4A D Menikoff Design C UNICEF 4B D Rocket Science C W.Morrison & Co. 4C D Khoa Le C Simple Balance Massage Therapy

A B C

1

2

3

4

Ⓓ = Design Firm Ⓒ = Client

1A Ⓓ stressdesign Ⓒ stressdesign 1B Ⓓ O'Mahony Design LLC Ⓒ Safe Place and Rape Crisis Center 1C Ⓓ Remo Strada Design Ⓒ Synergy Graphix
2A Ⓓ Ulyanov Denis Ⓒ 8800 call centre 2B Ⓓ Spark Studio Ⓒ Sandringham Hospital 2C Ⓓ Gardner Design Ⓒ Signature Bank
3A Ⓓ zakidesign Ⓒ Cash Express Global Money Transfer 3B Ⓓ Gardner Design Ⓒ Signature Bank 3C Ⓓ A. Shtramilo design studio Ⓒ Eka Systems
4A Ⓓ Sparkman + Associates Ⓒ SwissFone 4B Ⓓ Ross Hogin Design Ⓒ The Shepherd Group 4C Ⓓ Phony Lawn Ⓒ SpectraLink

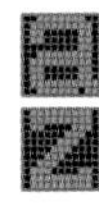

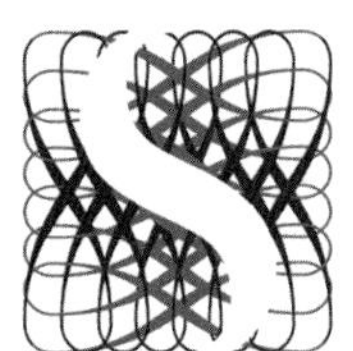

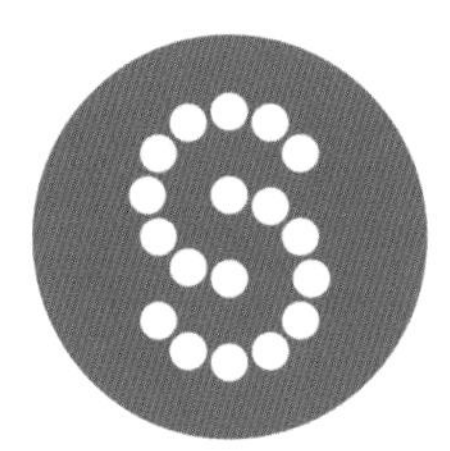

D = Design Firm C = Client

1A D Hubbell Design Works C System Centrix 1B D elf design C Snap Appliance Proposal 1C D imagenation C Synapse
2A D Gardner Design C Signature Bank 2B D Karl Design Vienna C Seydler AG Frankfurt 2C D Opolis Design, LLC C BuySafe
3A D McArtor Design C Softedge 3B D lazy snail—art factory C Gonianakis S.A. 3C D Resin Design C Ninth Floor Project
4A D Maycreate C Smartech 4B D Coolstone Design Works C Seitel Systems, Inc. 4C D Actual Size Creative C SalesGene

A B C

1

2

3

4

D = Design Firm C = Client

1A D Kahn Design C Ultimate Rider 1B D Pear Tree Design C Shine Dance Lounge 1C D The Joe Bosack Graphic Design Co. C SportsTowne
2A D Interbrand São Paulo 2B D KENNETH DISENO C Silueta, Beauty Clinic and Salon 2C D Double Brand C Slodownia
3A D Savacool Secviar Brand Communications C Stingaree 3B D Gabe Re is a designer. 3C D Howling Good Designs C Sprawl Fightwear
4A D SoupGraphix Inc. C Sano Systems 4B D Howling Good Designs C The Boardshop 4C D Gyula Nemeth C Swicon

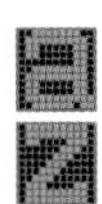

A B C

1

2

3

4

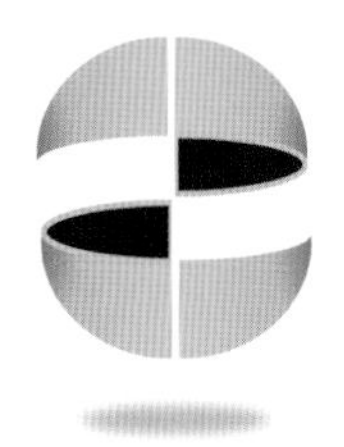

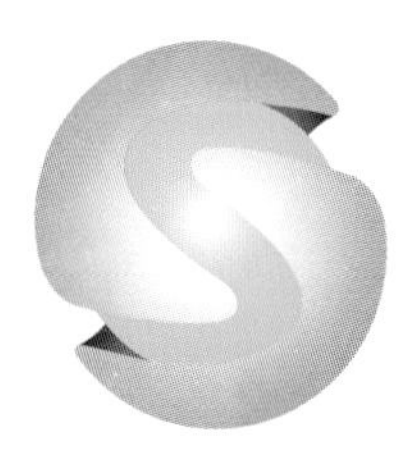

D = Design Firm   C = Client

1A D CAI Communications C Supply Velocity 1B D Gardner Design C shelton collision repair 1C D Letter 7 C SamTec
2A D Blue Clover C Spectrum Capital 2B D noe design C Bill Campie 2C D Sons Of Shin Productions C Samurai Surf Armor
3A D Tilt Design Studio C Stylefetish Design Labs, Hamburg, Germany 3B D Small Dog Design C Soulfree Adventures 3C D gsFITCH C Oman Goverment
4A D Landor Associates C Saba 4B D RedinWyden C Open System Design 4C D helium.design C SinkaCom AG

A B C

1

2

3

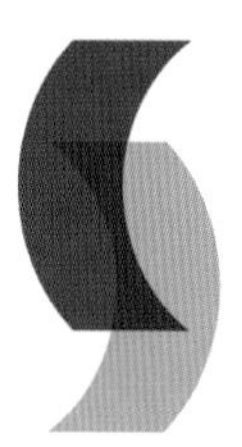

4

D = Design Firm C = Client

1A D AKOFA Creative C Charles Tarver/ Self Promotional 1B D RS Identity Design C RTF Professional Coaching, Inc. 1C D LogoDesignGuru.com C Siraia Networks
2A D Studio GT&P C Sophy Ltd 2B D UNIT-Y C Savus 2C D Tran Creative C Viking Homes
3A D B-Squared Advertising C Naples Bay Resort 3B D Jeffhalmos C Microsoft Canada 3C D Salty Design Foundry C Silverwood Theme Park
4A D Printt Diseñadores, s.c. C Grupo Financiero del Sureste 4B D Gardner Design C Signature Bank 4C D Gary Sample Design C Gary Sample Design

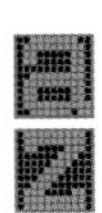

A B C

1

2

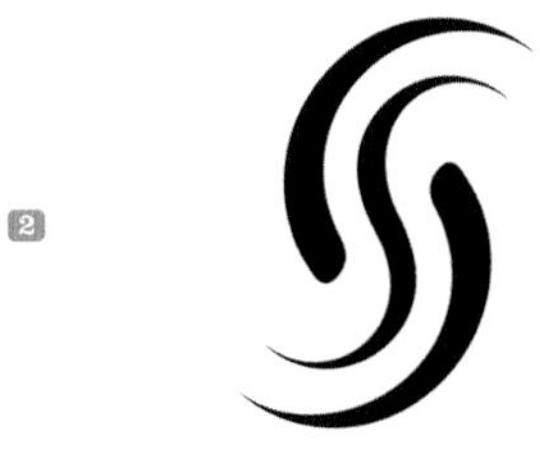

3

4

D = Design Firm C = Client

1A D NeoGrafica C SINAES 1B D Steve Cantrell C Subaqueous Services 1C D Zapata Design C CVX Homes
2A D Subcommunication C François Armanville 2B D Chris Herron Design C Spherics Inc. 2C D RocketDog Communications C Scott Smith DDS
3A D Pagliuco Design Company C Sentinel Technologies 3B D Contenido Neto C Suasor Consultores SC 3C D o graphicstudio C Stimmel Associates
4A D noe design C Concat Systems 4B D SD33/Art Direction & Design C Consumer Directed Services 4C D Sean Daly Design C Personal

A B C

1

2

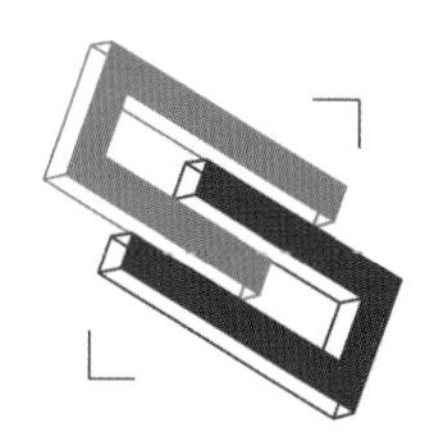

3

4

D = Design Firm C = Client

1A D moko creative C Surface Interiors 1B D A3 Design C DR Horton 1C D Milk Creative Services C Status Insurance Company
2A D Brains on Fire C Schnackel Engineers 2B D Special Modern Design C Sam Saboura 2C D Salty Design Foundry C Don Sutherland Architect
3A D Tower of Babel C Stapleton Planning and Development Services 3B D Creative NRG C SB Framing Gallery 3C D Nynas C Stefano Group
4A D Design Army C VeraSolve 4B D JoshuaCreative C Stanza Systems 4C D Gardner Design C The Standard

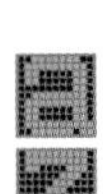

A B C

1

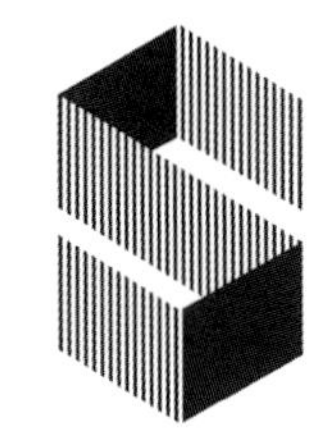

2

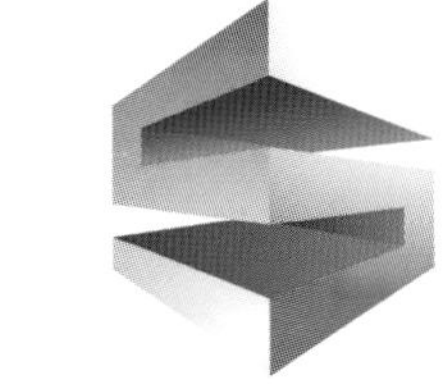

3

4

D = Design Firm C = Client

1A D Dotzero Design C Standard Companies 1B D Strategy Studio C The Shepherd Corporation 1C D Origin C Salhia Real Estate
2A D mugur mihai C Stainless Steel Corp. 2B D Bystrom Design C Systemhause 2C D Roy Smith Design C Somerleyton Hall
3A D Integrated Communications (ICLA) C The Creative Sign Company 3B D Hubbell Design Works C StepPrinting.com 3C D mugur mihai C Stainless Steel Corp.
4A D designfocus C seoul ttc 4B D mugur mihai C Stainless Steel Corp. 4C D Unibrand Belgrade C Idea Plus DDB

A B C

1

2

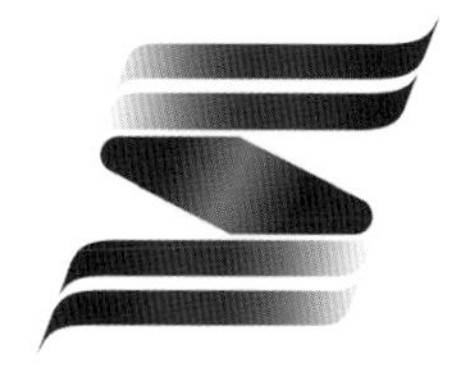

3

4

D = Design Firm C = Client

1A D LEKKERWERKEN C Oliver Foerster 1B D Gardner Design C The Standard 1C D Gardner Design C The Standard
2A D Gardner Design C Signature Bank 2B D Redpoint design C Skinner Law Corporation 2C D Honest Bros. C Struxture
3A D Heins Creative, Inc. C Spanwell 3B D Gardner Design C The Standard 3C D Bridges Design Group C Sydney Harbour
4A D Kevin Creative C Core Associates 4B D A. Shtramilo design studio C Real Steel 4C D Luke Baker C Arteis

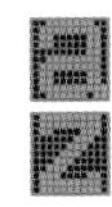

A B C

1

2

3

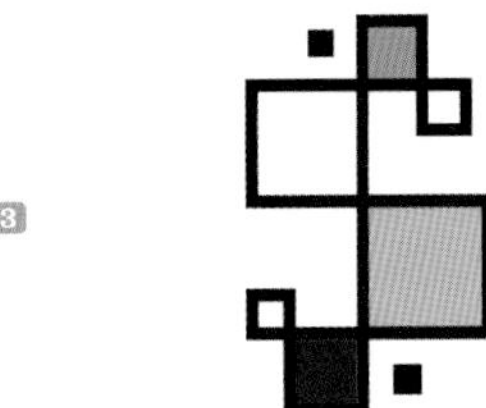

4

D = Design Firm C = Client

1A D St. Dwayne Design C SoftPro Technologies 1B D R&R Partners C Coyote Springs 1C D Curtis Sharp Design C Curtis Sharp Design
2A D Fernandez Design C Spur Interactive 2B D Fusion Advertising C strada 2C D Carmi e Ubertis Milano Srl C Saatco
3A D Karl Design Vienna C Schallehn Financing 3B D KROG, d.o.o. C Government Media Office 3C D Hula+Hula C Cartoon Network Latinamerica
4A D Monster Design Company C Sarai 4B D Union Design & Photo C Saucier Real Estate Analysis 4C D Judson Design

A B C

1

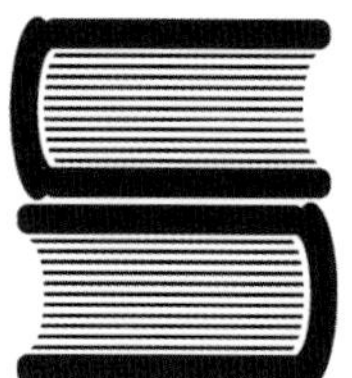

2

3

4

Ⓓ = Design Firm Ⓒ = Client

1A Ⓓ Jeff Fisher LogoMotives Ⓒ Samuels Yoelin Kantor Seymour & Spinrad 1B Ⓓ KROG, d.o.o. Ⓒ Presernova Druzba 1C Ⓓ Jeffhalmos Ⓒ Smart Desktop
2A Ⓓ lunabrand design group Ⓒ Sieb Publishing 2B Ⓓ ArtFly Ⓒ Snyder Advertising 2C Ⓓ Steve's Portfolio Ⓒ Small Planet
3A Ⓓ D&Dre Creative Ⓒ Scott Birds 3B Ⓓ Q Ⓒ Bergal, Nico & Solitaire GmbH 3C Ⓓ wedge.a&d Ⓒ Scachter Asset Management
4A Ⓓ Riccardo Sabioni Ⓒ The Saddlery California 4B Ⓓ STUBBORN SIDEBURN Ⓒ Magnet Eyes 4C Ⓓ Werner Design Werks Ⓒ Style Stretch

1

2

3

4

D = Design Firm   C = Client

1A D Corporate Design Associates 1B D High Tide Creative C Sandler Development Group 1C D Pure Identity Design C Snap-on Incorporated
2A D RIGGS 2B D Studio International C Simecki 2C D Les Kerr Creative C TheSingleScene.com
3A D 3 Advertising LLC C Shelton Jewelers 3B D Strategy Studio C Strategy Studio 3C D Entermotion Design Studio
4A D Glitschka Studios C Shipping Company 4B D Dylan Menges C Surfrider Foundation 4C D Dreamedia Studios C RRY Publications—Spine Technology Summit

A B C

2

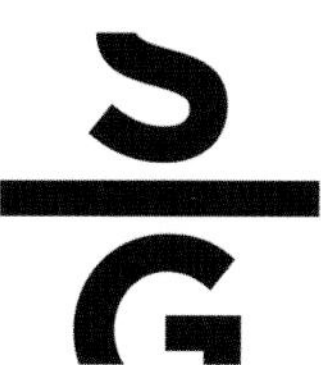

4

D = Design Firm C = Client

1A D o graphicstudio C stimmel & associates 1B D Lucky Dog Graphic Design C Souza & Associates 1C D Stefan Romanu C Saol Serv, Timisoara
2A D baba designs C Rebecca Steele 2B D DotArt Design Solutions C Scanlon Communications 2C D Dessein C sch homes
3A D Gee + Chung Design C Sandra Frank Photography 3B D Integer Group—Midwest C Maytag Commercial 3C D Jan Sabach Design C Shop Gopher, Olivia Song
4A D Zapata Design C Sumpter Gonzalez LLC 4B D Round 2 Integrated C Seva Group 4C D Brainding C Hawkins Saunders

D = Design Firm C = Client

1A D Smyers Design C Sacred Heart School 1B D blueground C InSkin Media Ltd. 1C D The Laster Group C Inn of the Mountain Gods Resort and Casino
2A D 903 Creative, LLC C SlickPixel 2B D DUEL Purpose C Superior Hardwood Floors 2C D cypher13 C Stellar Sounds
3A D Rufuturu C Shock Show 3B D Seagrass Studios C Seagrass Studios 3C D VanPaul Design C Saxon Seats
4A D UNO C Spectrum Sound Studio 4B D David Maloney C Semi Studio Systems 4C D Rufuturu C Shock Show

A B C

1

2

3

4

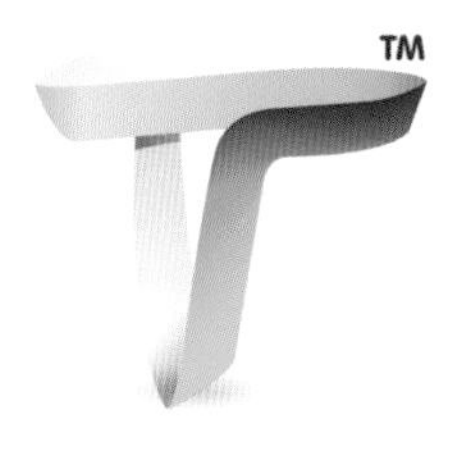

D = Design Firm C = Client

1A D David Kampa C US Creative 1B D 2TREES DESIGN C Springvale Cellars 1C D Salty Design Foundry C Silverwood Theme Park
2A D Niedermeier Design C S.W. Thurston 2B D 01d C True Taste 2C D Taproot Creative C Tallahassee Titans
3A D Glitschka Studios C Talon Boots 3B D Paul Jobson C Tubular Synergy Group 3C D Steven O'Connor C Steven O'Connor
4A D Howerton+White C TriGenex Technologies 4B D Independent C T Communications Community 4C D Gridwerk C Teratron, Inc.

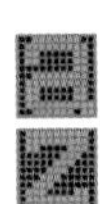

A B C

1

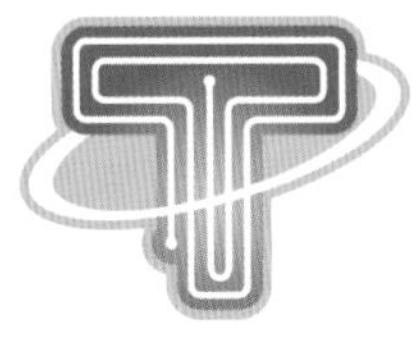

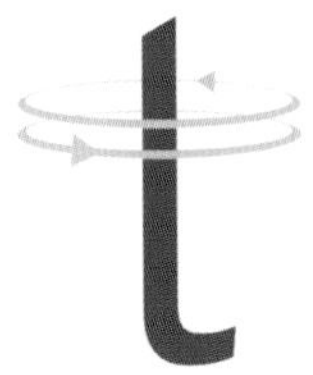

2

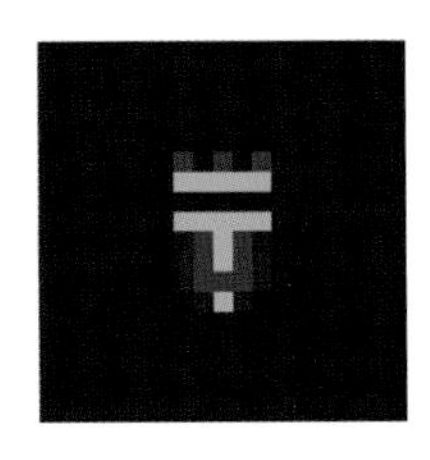

3

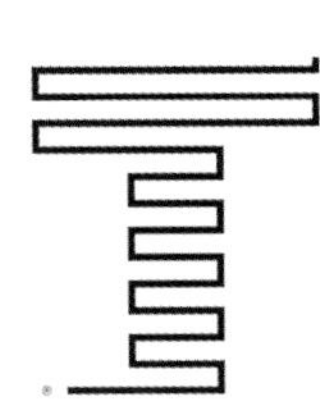

4

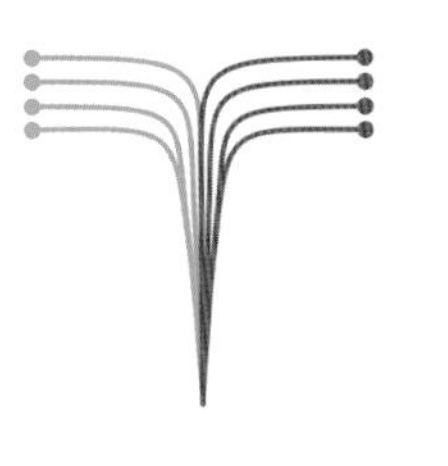

D = Design Firm C = Client

1A D String C Tigar Commerce 1B D monkeygrass C Circle of Trust 1C D McGuire Design C Turnaround
2A D Britt Funderburk 2B D Sanders Design C Tui Consulting 2C D Christopher Labno C T agency
3A D Hoyne Design C Tandou Ltd 3B D Muamer Adilovic DESIGN C TEXTURA fashion 3C D Romulo Moya / Trama C Trama Publishers
4A D AKOFA Creative C AKOFA Creative 4B D Studio International C Radio Trsat 4C D Squires and Company C Tirion Solutions

A B C

1

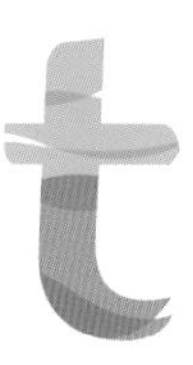

2

3

4

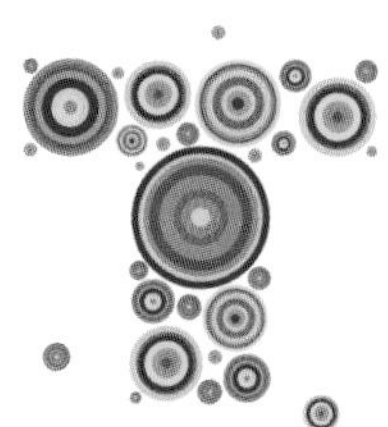

D = Design Firm C = Client

1A D Johnston Duffy C T bar 1B D INDE C Trust Ray 1C D Miller Meiers Design for Communication C Telco Energy
2A D Dickerson C T Bank 2B D Honey Design C Tremware 2C D Lippincott C TransUnion
3A D The Russo Group C Q-Based Healthcare 3B D Carmi e Ubertis Milano Srl 3C D Spohn Design C Technology Group
4A D Johnston Duffy C T bar 4B D MacLaren McCann Calgary C Telphonic 4C D Opolis Design, LLC C Tropolis

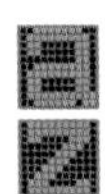

A B C

1

2

3

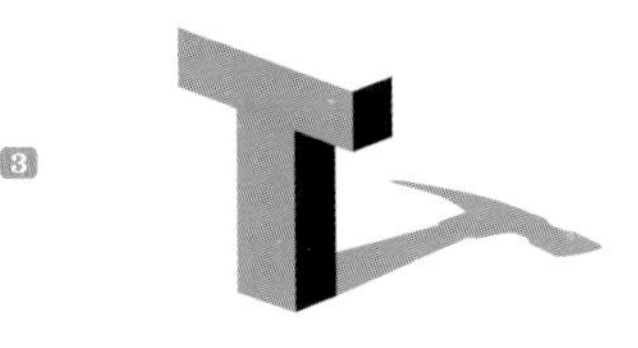

4

Ⓓ = Design Firm Ⓒ = Client

1A Ⓓ Landor Associates Ⓒ Traverse City 1B Ⓓ LGA / Jon Cain Ⓒ Taylor Properties Group 1C Ⓓ KTD Ⓒ Tanknology
2A Ⓓ Braue: Brand Design Experts Ⓒ Thomas Marine Consultants 2B Ⓓ Studio GT&P Ⓒ Tecnokar srl 2C Ⓓ Essex Two Ⓒ Tucker Gallery and Salon
3A Ⓓ Rhombus, Inc. Ⓒ Tremaine Construction 3B Ⓓ Eisenberg And Associates Ⓒ TEXO 3C Ⓓ Infiltrate Media Ⓒ Titus Construction
4A Ⓓ studio-h Ⓒ Towne Tile & Construction 4B Ⓓ Wolken communica Ⓒ Trakleads 4C Ⓓ KROG, d.o.o. Ⓒ Tehcenter, Ptuj

A B C

1

2

3

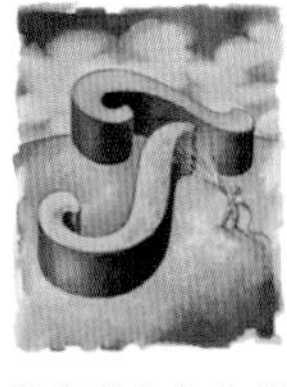

4

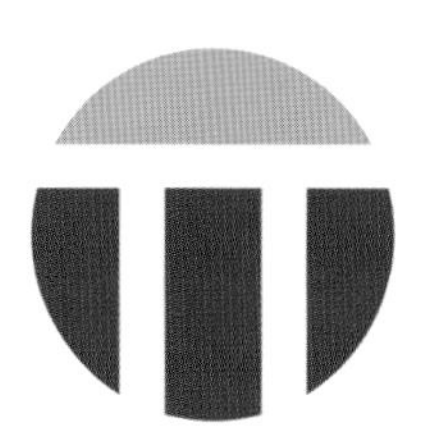

D = Design Firm C = Client

1A D Bunch C Tustica 1B D Dino Design C Steve Welker 1C D Align Design Graphics Studio C Environmental Turf Management
2A D lazy snail—art factory C Tsigenis Carpentry 2B D dandy idea C Tait Moring 2C D Red Clover Studio C pm&j
3A D LeBoYe C Topiary 3B D LeBoYe C Topiary 3C D LeBoYe C Topiary
4A D Davis Design C Thompson Engineering 4B D QUANGO C Thompson Transportation 4C D Liquidgraphic Design Inc. C Trowbridge Consulting

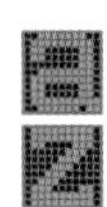

A B C

1

2

3

4

D = Design Firm   C = Client

1A D R&R Partners C Wingfield Group 1B D Tom Law Design C Thornton Metal Works 1C D Bostrom Graphics, LLC C Jonathan Riemer
2A D ohTwentyone C Tidy Tom's Cleaniing Company 2B D Kradel Design C Special Tea 2C D Judson Design
3A D Traction C At The Yard Baseball Training Center 3B D Liska + Associates Communication Design C Tim Bieber 3C D Stiles Design C Team Bonzai
4A D Werner Design Werks C Textbooks.com 4B D David Kampa C Nike 4C D Rhombus, Inc. C Tony DeMarco Homes

A B C

1

2

3

4

D = Design Firm C = Client

1A D Karl Design Vienna C B&K / Nike Deutschland 1B D Kiku Obata & Company C Wolff Properties 1C D Straka-Design
2A D RedSpark Creative C The Hairdresser 2B D Born to Design C tech * knowledge 2C D Go Media C Tony Little
3A D Imulus C Tenge Law Firm 3B D Doink, Inc. C Tania Mastrapa 3C D Boelts Design C Tucson Museum Art
4A D Form C VC Recordings 4B D proteus C Telluride Properties 4C D Crosby Associates C Sachnoff & Weaver, Ltd.

A B C

1

TRA

D = Design Firm C = Client

1A D Effective Media Solutions C Thomson Research 1B D Selikoff+Co C Tipping Sprung 1C D Hornall Anderson C TruckTrax
2A D Rickabaugh Graphics C Tennessee Tech 2B D Ken Shafer Design C Nike 2C D Stefan Romanu C Two
3A D ARTini BAR C charles montoya 3B D fuszion C Hobo International 3C D Olson C Phillips Distilling Company
4A D Daniel Sim Design C Uniadvantage.com 4B D rehab(r) communication graphics C Unionbay Sportswear 4C D Peel C Albuquerque Uptown Progress Team

A B C

1

2

3

4

D = Design Firm C = Client

1A D UTILITY C Utility Design Co. 1B D Bailey Brand Consulting C University of Pennsylvania 1C D Draplin Design Co. C Union Binding Co.
2A D H2 Design of Texas 2B D Mattson Creative 2C D Dotzero Design C Uluru Ascent
3A D Visual Lure, LLC C CR Holland 3B D Ulyanov Denis C Umbra 3C D Pagliuco Design Company C Urban Center
4A D Strategy Studio C City of Utica 4B D Tactix Creative C Unlimited Tech 4C D Lisa Brussell Design C Unique Salon

A B C

1

2

3

4

D = Design Firm C = Client

1A D Jacob Tyler Creative Group C University Thongs 1B D Glitschka Studios C Upper Deck Company 1C D RARE Design C RARE Design
2A D Effective Media Solutions C Vivid Air Inc. 2B D Dotzero Design C Uluru Ascent 2C D A3 Design C urban architectural group
3A D Moscato Design C Union Bank 3B D Glitschka Studios C Union Bay Sportswear 3C D Hubbell Design Works C UC Construction
4A D Designer Case C URBAN DESIGN 4B D Sebastiany Branding & Design C UFS (design Contest) 4C D Creative NRG C Health & Happiness

A B C

1

2

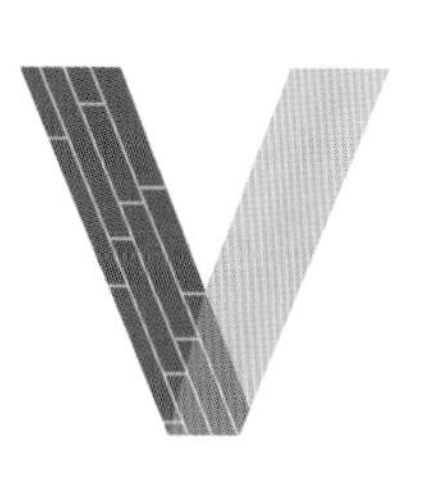

3

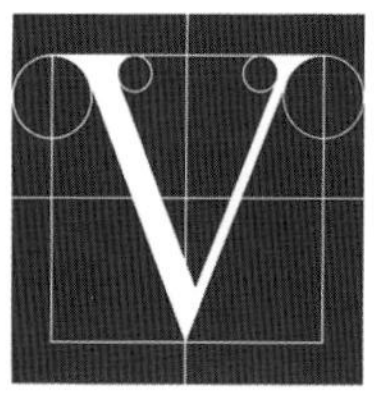

4

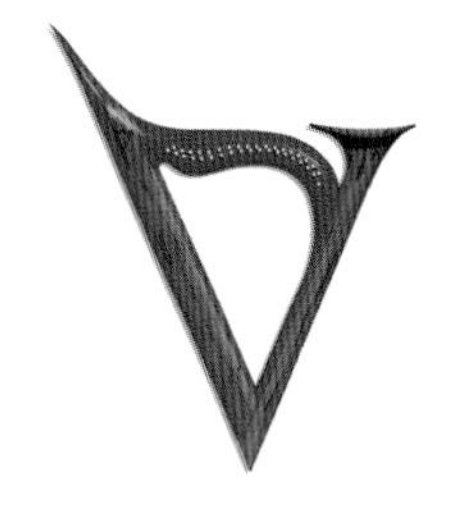

D = Design Firm C = Client

1A D Steven O'Connor C Cruz/Kravetz:Ideas 1B D Matt Johnson C United Petroleum 1C D WhatWorks
2A D Tactical Magic C Union University 2B D BrandExtract C Vision Products 2C D The Adsmith C Venable Flooring
3A D Ditto! C Architectural Woodworking 3B D McMillian Design C Virtual Net Europe 3C D Marc Posch Design, Inc C Vernare, Inc
4A D Fox Fire Creative C Valor Christian High School 4B D Effective Media Solutions C Vivid Design Inc. 4C D Studio Simon C Great Falls Voyagers

A B C

1

2

3

4

D = Design Firm C = Client

1A D Zed+Zed+Eye Creative Communications C Vancouver 2010 Olympic Commitee 1B D Murillo Design, Inc. C Vertical Racing Technologies 1C D MINE™ C San Francisco Vegetarian Society 2A D The Adsmith C Venable Flooring 2B D CF Napa Brand Design C Tuck Beckstoffer Wines 2C D Whole Wheat Creative C Sid Weiss Properties 3A D Hep C Kutahya Vitrifiye 3B D The Logo Factory Inc. 3C D MiresBall C Vulcan Motor Club 4A D Altagraf C DuPont Pharmaceuticals 4B D 1310 Studios C Voltivity 4C D Lapada Solutions C Valerent

B C

Votorantim

1

2

3

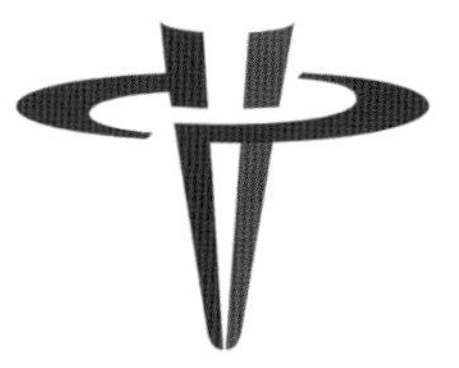

4

D = Design Firm C = Client

1A D FutureBrand BC&H C Votorantim 1B D mugur mihai C Gideon Cardozo Communications 1C D Design One C Vista Systems
2A D Sol Consultores C Vento 2B D Zapata Design 2C D UlrichPinciotti Design Group C Vector Pathology
3A D Logostogo C Troon Golf 3B D markatos I moore 3C D Kurt for Hire C GoIP Global
4A D Gardner Design C Virtual Focus Internet 4B D Intrinsic Design C Verridia 4C D Paradigm New Media Group C ArcVision, Inc.

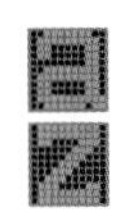

A B C

1

2

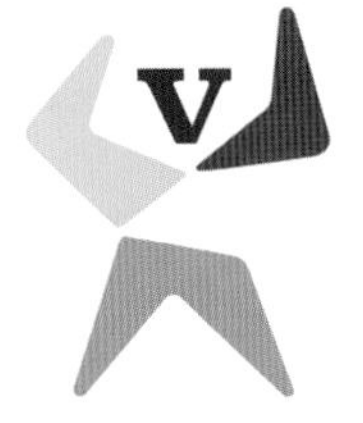

3

4

D = Design Firm C = Client

1A D Gardner Design C versacourt 1B D LogoDesignGuru.com C Viaone 1C D Gardner Design C VizWorz Photo Lab
2A D tomvasquez.com C Thomas Vasquez 2B D Sanders Design C vision schools 2C D Perdue Creative C Verso Paper
3A D Stiles+co C Vertical Networks / Storyhat 3B D Dennard, Lacey & Associates C Vista Ridge Mall 3C D David Kampa C V Tel
4A D ZEBRA design branding C Versus 4B D Eben Design C Versatile Home Improvement 4C D Design Nut C Vivid Edge

A B C

1

2

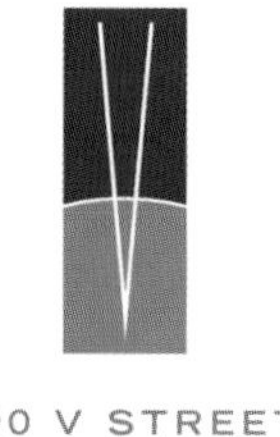

3

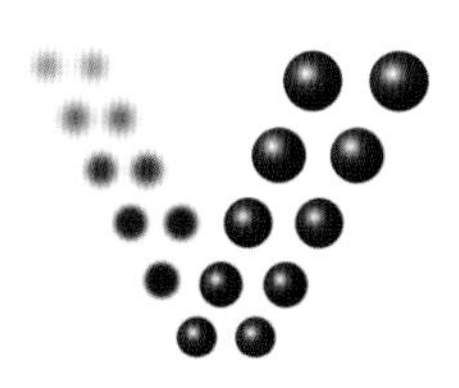

4

D = Design Firm C = Client

1A D Woodward Design C Van Horn Welding Ltd. 1B D Culture Pilot C Vector Financial 1C D Kastelov C Vyron steel
2A D monkeebox inc. C Akeridge 2B D Eisenberg And Associates C Vollmer Public Relations 2C D Brian Blankenship C Verso
3A D Kinesis, Inc. C Vista Pathology 3B D Gardner Design C Virtual Focus Internet 3C D Dotzero Design C Vergence
4A D Vision 3 C Vision 3 4B D Kahn Design C Vital Therapies 4C D James Clark Design C Venture Lab

D = Design Firm C = Client

1A D Whaley Design, Ltd C Visions Web Solutions 1B D O! C Vördur 1C D Bailey Brand Consulting C Vectrix Corporation
2A D Graham Hanson Design C Vanguard Construction 2B D 5 Fifteen Design Group, Inc. 2C D Funk/Levis & Associates, Inc. C Versalogic
3A D Gizwiz Studio C Bob 3B D Porkka & Kuutsa Oy C Valopaino Oy 3C D Glitschka Studios C Cyphon Design
4A D Envizion Dezigns C Vertical Sports Group 4B D LogoDesignGuru.com C Vanguard Solutions 4C D Leah Hartley C SASI Marketing/Valentines Furniture

A B C

1

2

3

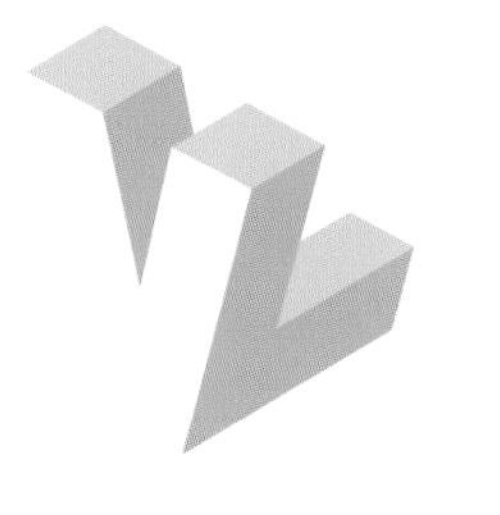

4

D = Design Firm C = Client

1A D R&R Partners C Valley Metro 1B D Driven Communications C Vattikuti Cancer Center 1C D Chris Oth Creative C Valiant Securities
2A D Essex Two C Verakis Associates 2B D Graphic-FX C Van Elkins & Associates 2C D Gee + Chung Design C Vitria Technology, Inc.
3A D Landkamer Partners, Inc. C Vista Financial, Inc. 3B D innfusion studios C Ave 3C D Murillo Design, Inc. C KGB Texas
4A D CONCEPTO WORLDWIDE C Vinicola del Norte 4B D PMKFA C VUJJ™ 4C D DUEL Purpose C Lauchpad Creative

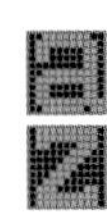

A B C

1

2

3

4

D = Design Firm C = Client

1A D Tactix Creative 1B D David Gramblin C Watermark Construction 1C D Buchanan Design C Waters Edge
2A D David Clark Design C Four Winds Casino/Eslick Design 2B D pat sinclair design C Penn Wynne Civic Assn.
2C D Shelley Design+Marketing C Woodmore Country Club 3A D Creative NRG C The Wicked Garden 3B D Judson Design C Detering Co.
3C D Dotzero Design C WalkerMay Landscape Architects 4A D The Micro Agency C Toronto Waldorf School 4B D Steven O'Connor C Wealth Care Inc.
4C D Josh Higgins Design C Walter Andersons Nusery

A B C

1

2

3

4

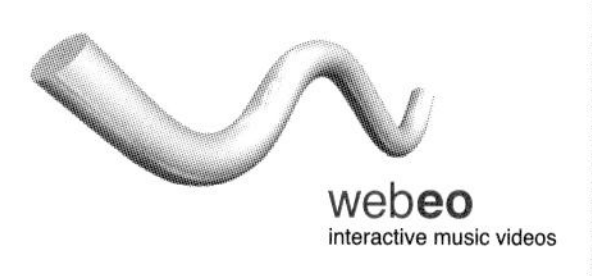

D = Design Firm C = Client

1A D KROG, d.o.o. C Vinovin, Ljubljana 1B D Jan Sabach Design C Unilever 1C D Southside Creative Group C Waterhouse Public Relations
2A D Westwerk DSGN C Fauxkoi Design 2B D Steven O'Connor C Kerry Wallingford 2C D ANS C Waterford Exclusive Residential Community
3A D POLLARDdesign C Wildhaber 3B D ID.Brand C WMP 3C D WestmorelandFlint C University of Minnesota Duluth
4A D Bernhardt Fudyma Design Group C Hudson Williams 4B D RedSpark Creative C Wiggle Wireless 4C D asmallpercent C MTV

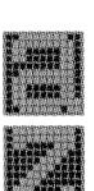

A B C

1

D = Design Firm C = Client

1A D Creative NRG C Wasco Windows 1B D Creative NRG C Wasco Windows 1C D Creative NRG C Waukesha Fence & Deck
2A D Garfinkel Design C Athens Area Chamber of Commerce 2B D Haller Design C West Block Development
2C D Jon Flaming Design C Watermark Community Church 3A D Nynas C Warren Accountants 3B D Ad Impact Advertising C The Wilner Group
3C D Combustion C Wurzburg 4A D Angie Dudley C Primerica 4B D Carlos Bela C Wishlist.nu 4C D Tielemans Design C Wentworth County Libraries

A B C

1

2

3

4

D = Design Firm C = Client

1A D Bluespace Creative, Inc. C Wilsons Bookkeeping & Tax Service 1B D oneal design C Valarie Willis 1C D Funk/Levis & Associates, Inc. C Willamette Valley Company
2A D Shelley Design + Marketing C Codeangel.com 2B D Denis Olenik Design Studio C Warranty.ru 2C D Porkka & Kuutsa Oy C WSOY
3A D maynard kay C Asset International Inc. 3B D Mauck Groves Branding & Design C Wells + Associates 3C D Mindgruve C Waveland
4A D Clutch Design C Weber Printing 4B D maynard kay C Wurld Media Inc. 4C D jeda creative C Westco

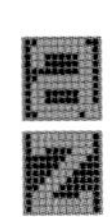

A B C

1

2

3

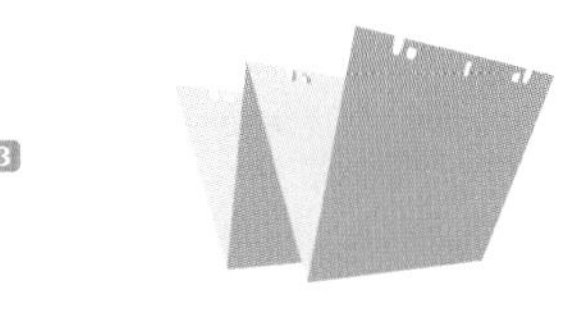

4

D = Design Firm C = Client

1A D Futrell Design Company C University of Washington 1B D Dragulescu Studio C Nevada Cancer Institute, MGM/Mirage 1C D Combustion C Wurzburg
2A D Cristina Lagorio C Whet Design, Inc 2B D Jon Flaming Design C Watermark Community Church 2C D robert meyers design
3A D Braue: Brand Design Experts C Druckhaus Wuest 3B D p11Creative C Westamerica Graphics 3C D brossman design C Wyeth
4A D Jennifer McAlister Graphic Design C Wraith Systems, LLC 4B D twentystar C Colorado Ridge Church 4C D Carousel30 C Whidden's Royal Jelly

A B C

1

2

3

4

D = Design Firm C = Client

1A D Juicebox Designs C WAY FM MEDIA GROUP 1B D Parallele gestion de marques C Watco Web Waves 1C D LaMonica Design C The Wailea Group
2A D Design Army C World Security Institute 2B D Idealogy Design + Advertising C Woman Care 2C D Ulyanov Denis C Wintervoice
3A D Lesniewicz Associates C Wilcox 3B D Whaley Design, Ltd D Whaley Excavating, Inc. 3C D Ulyanov Denis C Winfort
4A D bryon hutchens | graphic design C America West Airlines 4B D Gardner Design C Wichita State University Crew Team
4C D Diana Graham C Kaynee Shirt Company

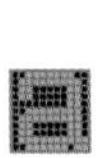

A B C

1

2

3

4

D = Design Firm C = Client

1A D Tower of Babel C Wyatt Fire Protection 1B D Timber Design Company C Walker Racing, Inc 1C D Blue Bee Design C University of Montana Western
2A D elf design C Law Offices of Darcey L. Wong 2B D Fixation Marketing C Webism 2C D Classic Lines Design C Waldrons
3A D Blake BW C Wokabout Travel 3B D R Design LLC C White Lighting Design 3C D Steven O'Connor
4A D Sputnik Design Partners Inc C The Wynford Group 4B D Mitre Agency C WeaverCooke Construction 4C D Tandemodus C Waterford Banquets

A B C

1

2

3

4

D = Design Firm C = Client

1A D Paul Black Design C YWCA of Dallas 1B D switchfoot creative C winspire 1C D UNI-Y C Webster Design
2A D Schwartzrock Graphic Arts C Riverbrand Design 2B D RARE Design C World Events Group 2C D Richards & Swensen C Public Employees Health Program
3A D Denis Olenik Design Studio C Warranty.ru 3B D Delikatessen C Paul Körner Gruppe 3C D Judson Design C The Williams Group
4A D Level B Design C Wells Fargo Financial 4B D Warren Diggles Photography and Design C Western Management
4C D Crosby Associates C Mutual of Omaha's Wild Kingdom

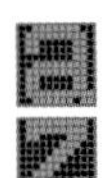

A B C

1

2

3

4

D = Design Firm C = Client

1A D Kevin France Design, Inc. C VF corp 1B D O'Hare Design C Gary L. White Construction 1C D joe miller's company C Works/San José
2A D On Design, Inc. C Wang Associates 2B D Anagraphic C Walz Foundation 2C D 360ideas C Weber & Associates
3A D Gardner Design C Bredar Waggoner Architects 3B D Kendall Creative Shop, Inc. C Woody Candy Company 3C D Nectar Graphics C Oregon Wine Cottage
4A D Evenson Design Group C Waldorf Crawford 4B D David Kampa C Carrington Weems III 4C D Crave, Inc C Widedata

A B C

1

2

3

4

D = Design Firm C = Client

1A D S Design, Inc. C Women's Foundation Of Oklahoma 1B D Perdue Creative C Hope Works Wonders 1C D tub C W Lounge
2A D substance151 C Washington Jewish Women 2B D Tactix Creative 2C D RARE Design C Wealth Management Consultants
3A D Diana Graham C Works New York 3B D rylander design C Wyoming Outfitters 3C D Hyperakt C West Orange, NJ
4A D Sibley Peteet C Sanders\Wingo 4B D Matt Shepherd C Townsend Inc 4C D Bertz Design Group C Pratt & Whitney

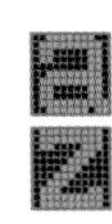

A B C

1

D = Design Firm C = Client

1A D Sheehan Design C Co-Opportunities 1B D THE GENERAL DESIGN CO. C Wilson Woodworks 1C D Hirschmann Design C Wewatta Transfer
2A D rylander design C Without Walls Museum Multimedia 2B D Thomas design C Workingwomen.com Concept 2C D Rocketman Creative C WBW
3A D Judson Design C Robert Wagnon 3B D KTD C American Assurance 3C D Sebastiany Branding & Design C Export Manager
4A D Elevation Creative Studios C XCEED Personal Fitness Solutions 4B D Lichtsignale C Lichtsignale 4C D Infiltrate Media C Tarsus Technologies (Proposed)

A B C

1

2

3

4

D = Design Firm C = Client

1A D Q C XPOLIT! 1B D BBMG C Center on Nonprofit Effectiveness 1C D jing C Cleveland State University
2A D Kendall Creative Shop, Inc. C Drive 2B D Axiom Design Collaborative C Xtreme Gym 2C D The Martin Group C Victory Christian Center
3A D Sebastiany Branding & Design C Export Manager 3B D face C Komori 3C D switchfoot creative C Infommersion, Inc.
4A D Ross Hogin Design C CXO Golf 4B D Kurt for Hire C Glowlab / Conflux 4C D Organic Grid C xhilarate.com

A B C

1

2

3

4

D = Design Firm C = Client

1A D Octavo Design Pty Ltd C Pier 10 Vineyard 1B D A3 Design C Extreme Water Sports 1C D Brainding
2A D CS Design C xTech 2B D Plumbline Studios C XeroCoat 2C D Xfacta C Xfacta
3A D Spire C ConXgen 3B D Diagram C Polpharma 3C D McElveney & Palozzi Design Group, Inc. C Xelus
4A D Rhombus, Inc. C Interactive Exchange 4B D Insight Design C CenterWorks Gym 4C D Mojo Solo C Proxama

A B C

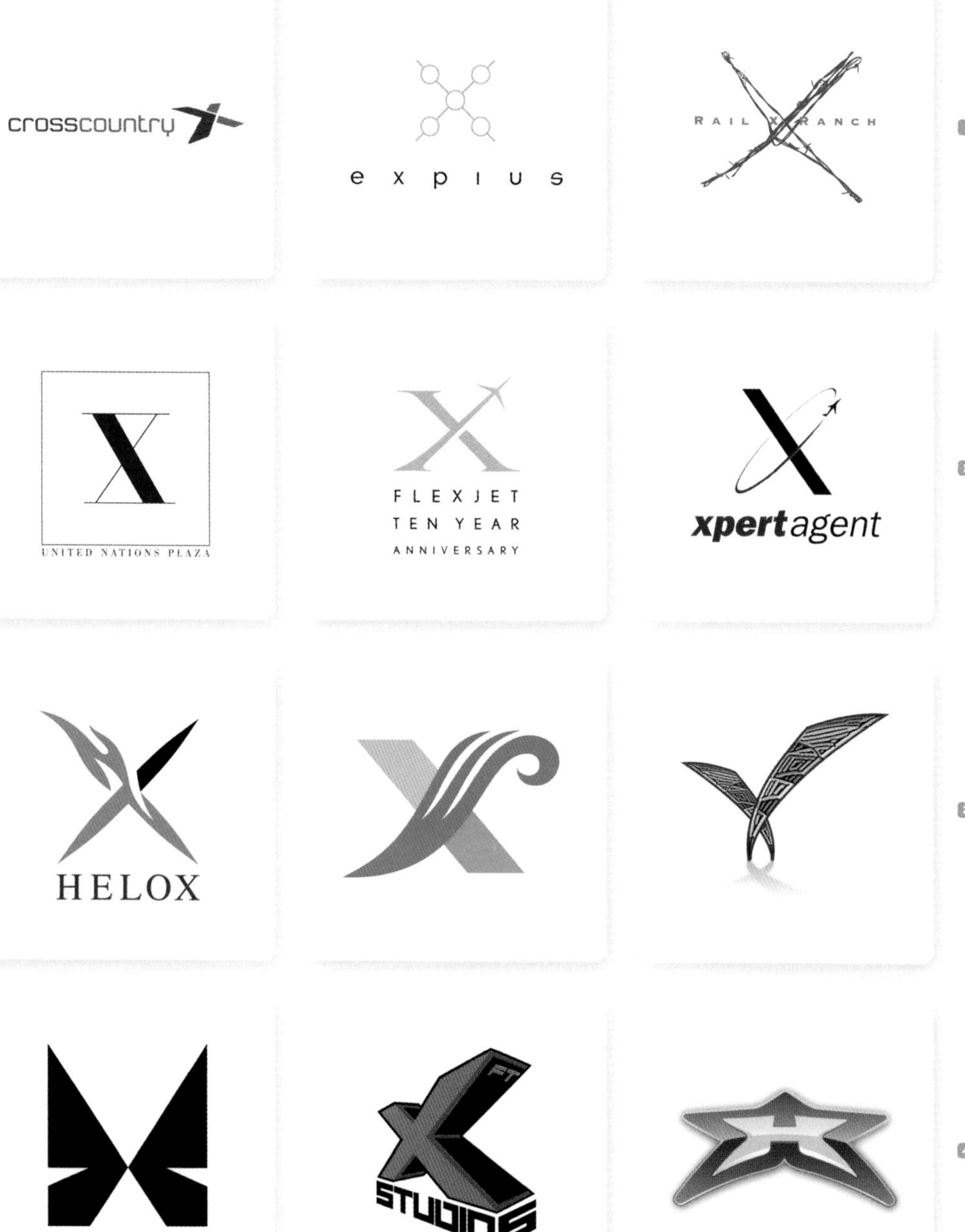

D = Design Firm C = Client

1A D Brand Environment (Be) C CrossCountry trains 1B D Headwerk C Expius 1C D True Perception C Rail X Ranch
2A D Graham Hanson Design C Macklowe Properties 2B D Greteman Group C 2C D Natoli Design Group C Outtask Inc.
3A D Strange Ideas 3B D Greteman Group 3C D Gabriel Kalach • V I S U A L communication C Arrso Restaurants CO.
4A D Pictogram Studio C Mariposa Art Gallery 4B D DUEL Purpose C Tenfoot Studios 4C D VanPaul Design C Hollywood.com

1

2

3

4

D = Design Firm C = Client

1A D Hubbell Design Works C Window Rock Enterprises 1B D Burocratik—Design C CH Business Consulting 1C D Strategy Studio C Xiolink
2A D Ground Zero Communications C Youth Skin Products 2B D Pink Tank Creative C Y Net 2C D Rule29 C Yeti
3A D Tom Law Design C YSA Sport 3B D kickit communications 3C D Effusion Creative Solutions
4A D The Bradford Lawton Design Group C San Antonio Youth Literacy 4B D Adams Design Group C Yoga Unlimited Ltd 4C D wedge.a&d C Chance Saint-Marche

A B C

1

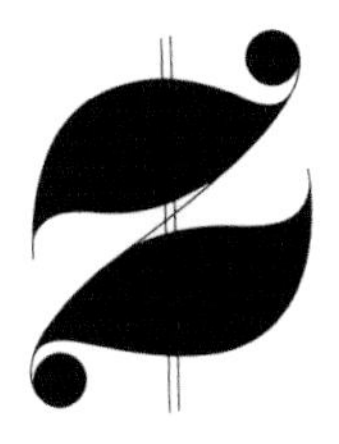

2

3

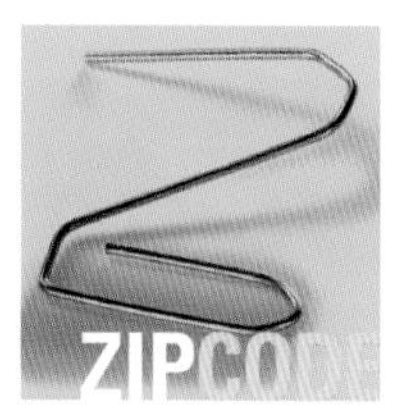

4

D = Design Firm C = Client

1A D Banowetz + Company, Inc. C Hotel ZaZa 1B D KROG, d.o.o. C The Faculty of Law, Ljubljana 1C D Lienhart Design C Zeisler and Associates, Inc.
2A D Richards Brock Miller Mitchell & Associates C Zenta 2B D Diagram C Zeneris Energy Sources 2C D Jennifer Panepinto, LLC C Z Media, LLC
3A D Carmi e Ubertis Milano Srl C Coin 3B D dache C Zipliner 3C D Clusta Ltd C Clusta
4A D 212-BIG-BOLT C Z100 4B D LSD C ctrl Z music band 4C D Jerron Ames C Arteis

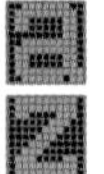

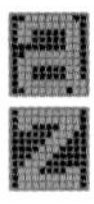

A B C

1

2

3

4

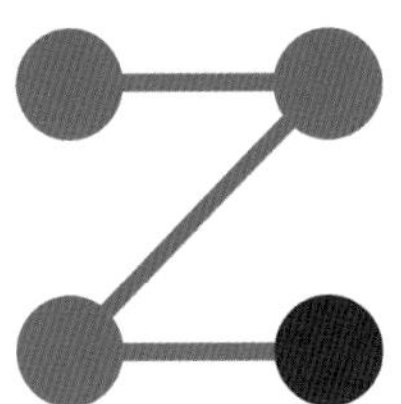

D = Design Firm C = Client

1A D Mitre Agency C ZUM Contract 1B D Range C TuZoom 1C D Snap Creative C Zupon Construction
2A D mIQelangelo C Zmex 2B D Tower of Babel C Zenses 2C D Canvas Astronauts & Agriculture C Zefor Energy
3A D Gardner Design C Zenith Drilling 3B D SUPERRED C Remiks Real Estate 3C D Jenny Kolcun Freelance Designer C Zero Degrees
4A D PosterV.Design Studio C Zalai Printinghouse Ltd. 4B D Pikant Marketing C Regional economy organisation 4C D Jerron Ames C Arteis

A B C

3

4

D = Design Firm C = Client

1A D Z Factory C Z Factory 1B D ContrerasDesign C Zdot Technology 1C D Landor Associates C Zurich
2A D Yantra Design Group Inc C zenotica inc 2B D MangoGlobal C Zeus 2C D Pikant Marketing C Regional economy organisation
3A D Murillo Design, Inc. C HEB Grocery 3B D The Joe Bosack Graphic Design Co. C Whitehall-Coplay School District 3C D VanPaul Design C Zeus MMA
4A D Mindgruve C Zocalo 4B D Tactical Magic C Zambezi Studios 4C D Onoma, LLC C ZWN Mass Transit

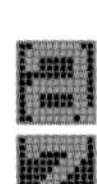

A B C

1

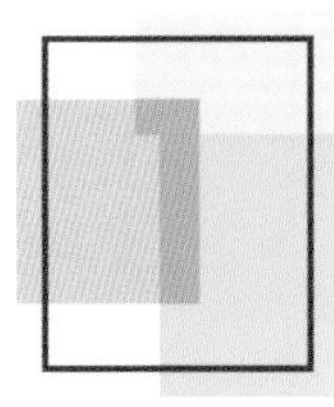

2

3

4

D = Design Firm C = Client

1A D Dotzero Design C Your Half Pictures 1B D Luke Baker C Arteis 1C D Ellen Bruss Design C Perry&Co
2A D Via Grafik C Kanister Records 2B D RICH design studio C In2it 2C D United States of the Art C United States of the Art
3A D Felixsockwell.com C merck 3B D TNOP & bePOSI+IVE C Futatsu Industries, Norway 3C D Alterpop C plus 3
4A D S4LE.com C www.monstercan.com 4B D CAI Communications C 3TEX 4C D Gary Sample Design C Asterix 3 Design

A B C

1

2

3

4

D = Design Firm C = Client

1A D Shawn Huff C Dustin Huff 1B D Shawn Huff 1C D Squarelogo C Third Coast Composites
2A D Bmu Creative Design Agency C 2B D Jerron Ames C Artcis 2C D Ziga Aljaz C exhibition 4
3A D Jesse Kaczmarek 3B D Richards Brock Miller Mitchell & Associates C Channel 5 3C D Jessica Peltz Design
4A D reaves design C the home depot 4B D MSI C 5After5 4C D Sibley Peteet C Austin Hilton

1

2

3

4

D = Design Firm C = Client

1A D MEGA C Kathy Patterson CFP 1B D R&R Partners C Zappos 1C D R&R Partners C Zappos
2A D R&R Partners C Zappos 2B D R&R Partners C Zappos 2C D The Key C Leo Burnett
3A D Peter Gibbons C 7 Ltd 3B D Image Communications, Inc. C Seventh Row 3C D id29 C Scholastic Inc.
4A D BFive C 7I 4B D Fashion Graphics C Alpha 7 Security Astana 4C D 01d C Seven Gnomes

A B C

1

2

3

4

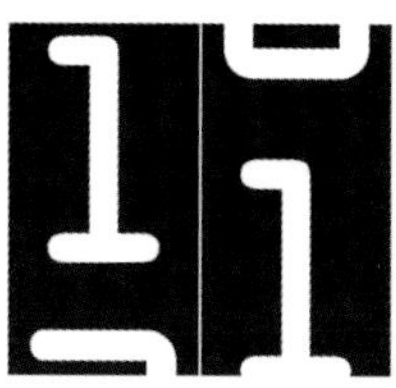

D = Design Firm C = Client

1A D jeda creative C Seven Wire 1B D bartodell.com C Layer8 Consultants 1C D Black Osprey Dead Arts C BURLESQUE OF NORTH AMERICA
2A D Marina Rose C Eight Pounds 2B D Thinking*Room Inc. C SkyEight 2C D UpShift Creative Group C Provence Development Group
3A D Studio Nine Creative C Studio Nine Creative 3B D 7th Street Design C Dragon City Shopping Mall 3C D TOKY Branding+Design C Ninth Street Noodles
4A D The Joe Bosack Graphic Design Co. C The Joe Bosack Graphic Design Co. 4B D 9 Surf Studios C CMP Media 4C D Sanders Design C ASB Properties

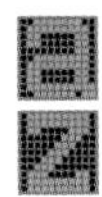

A B C

1

2

3

4

D = Design Firm C = Client

1A D West Reed C Eleven Audio 1B D ZupiDesign C Cooperplus 1C D 9 Surf Studios C Network World
2A D Gardner Design C Cox News 22 2B D Gardner Design C Cox News 22 2C D TracyLocke Dallas C 24/7 Class, Lovers Lane United Methodist Church, Dallas
3A D 9 Surf Studios C Industry Week 3B D BBDO NY C New Jersey Devils 3C D The Brand Union C Emaar
4A D Karl Design Vienna C Charta 77 4B D Lesniewicz Associates C Owens Corning 4C D Eric Baker Design Assoc. Inc C MGM Grand

A B C

1

2

3

4

D = Design Firm C = Client

1A D Tanoshism C Valentin Triponez 1B D The Bradford Lawton Design Group C Kennedy Space Center 1C D joe miller's company C Space 47
2A D Bronson Ma Creative C Highland Baptist Church 2B D Tomko Design C SIX 2C D Essex Two C Printing World Wide
3A D Ikola designs... C Minnesota Orchestra 3B D Pat Taylor Inc. C American Enterprise Institute 3C D Hvita husid C Samtokin 78
4A D Lucero Design C Project 240 Apparel 4B D DAVID BARATH DESIGN C 321 Art of the Sign 4C D Schwartzrock Graphic Arts C 3.2.1, Inc.

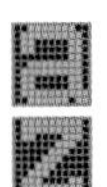

A B C

1

2

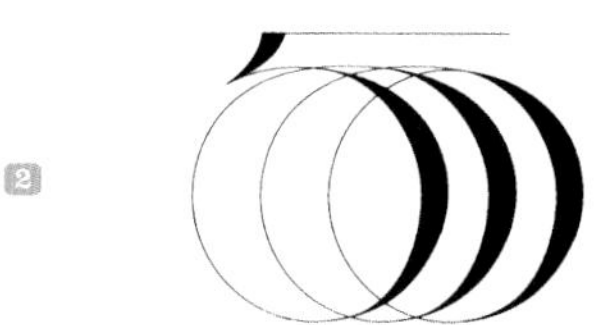

3

4

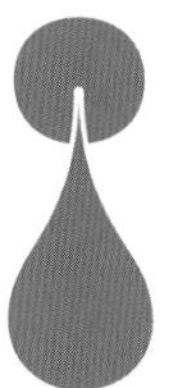

D = Design Firm C = Client

1A D DUEL Purpose C CRBC 1B D 343 Creative C 343 Creative 1C D kaimere C 365 Marketing 2A D Richards Brock Miller Mitchell & Associates C 500 Inc. 2B D 9 Surf Studios C Industry Week 2C D FiveNineteen: a print + motion + interactive design boutique. C Fivenineteen Visual Communication 3A D Kendall Creative Shop, Inc. C Knights of Columbus—799 3B D Karl Design Vienna C Land Niederoesterreich 3C D Hirshorn Zuckerman Design Group C Sidney Fetner Associates, Inc. 4A D Q C Gloria Alvaro 4B D Brian Collins Design C Nathan Olds—Innate Technologies 4C D Bystrom Design C Neos Consulting

crests

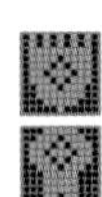

D = Design Firm C = Client

1A D Randy Mosher Design C August Schell Brewing Co. 1B D Eyespike Design C Genuine Old School
1C D Michael Doret Graphic Design C Margarethe Hubauer GmbH
2A D Parachute Design C Lusso Exclusive Residence Collection 2B D MiresBall C Boyds Coffee 2C D UNO C Schreiber Foods
3A D Judson Design 3B D M. Brady Clark Design C The Lab 3C D Steven O'Connor C 11:24 Design / Spike Lee
4A D Squires and Company C Texas Olive Ranch 4B D SoupGraphix Inc. C Cross Domain Solutions 4C D McQuillen Creative Group C Preserve South Dakota

A B C

1

2

3

4

D = Design Firm C = Client

1A D Chip Sheean C Nine North Wines 1B D Guernsey Graphics C Bowdoin College 1C D Karl Design Vienna C Waldorfschule Frankfurt
2A D Sullivan Higdon & Sink C Cargill Meat Solutions 2B D Bobby Magallanes C Stellar Properties 2C D reaves design C IVS
3A D Greg Walters Design C Taphandles 3B D Headwerk C APS—Arizona Public Service 3C D Sanders Design C Wither Hills
4A D Sayles Graphic Design, Inc. C Girl Scouts of Chicago 4B D Extrabrand C Ambartsumyan Family 4C D Howling Good Designs C Long Island Puppet Theatre

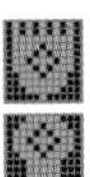

A B C

1

2

3

4

D = Design Firm C = Client

1A D Deep Design C UPS 1B D Mattson Creative C Orange County Water District 1C D SoupGraphix Inc. C Cross Domain Solutions
2A D Dotzero Design C Gresham Station Townhomes 2B D mod&co C mod&co 2C D Colle + McVoy C Colle + McVoy
3A D Gee Creative C Creative Ventures 3B D Gardner Design C Lavish Boutique 3C D Sayles Graphic Design, Inc. C Jimmy's American Cafe
4A D Olson C Premium Beer 4B D McElveney & Palozzi Design Group, Inc. C Wagner Valley Brewing Co. 4C D Storm Design Inc. C The Lakeside Hammers

A B C

1

2

3

4

Ⓓ = Design Firm Ⓒ = Client

1A Ⓓ Haller Design Ⓒ Sportiqe Apparel 1B Ⓓ Red Clover Studio Ⓒ Airtex Design Group 1C Ⓓ Caliber Creative, LLC Ⓒ Austin Dog Walker
2A Ⓓ Erich Brechbuhl [Mixer] Ⓒ Restaurant to the Battle 2B Ⓓ Little Jacket Ⓒ The Jacket 2C Ⓓ Miller Creative LLC Ⓒ Brown Cow Pantry
3A Ⓓ Hausch Design Agency LLC Ⓒ Brew City Bar-B-Q 3B Ⓓ Colle + McVoy Ⓒ Ciatti's Chianti Grill 3C Ⓓ Judson Design Ⓒ Continental Airlines
4A Ⓓ Judson Design Ⓒ Continental Airlines 4B Ⓓ Digital Flannel Ⓒ Okemo Mountain Resort 4C Ⓓ HMK Archive Ⓒ KSYM 90.1 FM

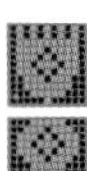

A B C

1

2

3

4

D = Design Firm C = Client

1A D Sayles Graphic Design, Inc. C Iowa Chapter of American Marketing Association 1B D Brand Navigation C Chef Juri Sbandati 1C D Doink, Inc. C Tovar Music Group
2A D Alphabet Arm Design C Georganne Calyanis 2B D Hove Design Works C Sanus 2C D Sayles Graphic Design, Inc. C Zooks Harley Davidson
3A D Extra Point Creative C Mark Cooley 3B D Foundry C ClearChannel 3C D Velocity Design Group C Natural Bread Co.
4A D Jean Peterson Design C Voluntary Protection Programs Participants' Association 4B D Lynch Design C Sherwood Services Club Inc.
4C D Art Chantry C Union Bay

A | B | C

CHARLES LUCK

1

2

3

4

D = Design Firm   C = Client

1A D Tactix Creative C LuckStone 1B D Roskelly Inc. C Preservation Society on Newport 1C D Gardner Design C Scone On the Range
2A D Richards & Swensen C River Wood Boat Company 2B D Paul Black Design C TLP, 7 Eleven 2C D Buffalo Design Group Inc. C Hamburg Oktoberfest
3A D Mark Oliver, Inc. C Ocean Beauty Seafoods 3B D Mez Design C Heckler Brewing Company 3C D Hill Design Studios C Top Dog Sports Bar
4A D Home Grown Logos C Azz & Bzz Apparel 4B D Dennard, Lacey & Associates C Steak & Ale Tavern 4C D Entermotion Design Studio C Scooper Joe's

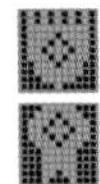

A B C

1

2

3

4

D = Design Firm C = Client

1A D Sheehan Design C The Sea Lodge 1B D Squires and Company C Papou's 1C D Sayles Graphic Design, Inc. C 801 Steak and Chop House
2A D Gardner Design C Excel Corporation 2B D Jean Peterson Design C Voluntary Protection Programs Participants' Association
2C D Sayles Graphic Design, Inc. C Mezzodis Restaurant 3A D Sayles Graphic Design, Inc. C Proctor Mechanical 3B D HOOK C Cigar Factory Charleston
3C D Dustin Commer C Commercial Picture Framing 4A D Brian Collins Design C Pacific Printing Company 4B D Dotzero Design C Boise Paper
4C D Helius Creative Advertising C Big O Tires

A B C

1

2

3

4

D = Design Firm C = Client

1A D Tim Frame Design C Brentwood Builders 1B D Gardner Design C Roosevelts Restaurant 1C D Enforme Interactive C National Association of School Psychologists
2A D Jerron Ames C Arteis 2B D VMA C Brixx an American Grill 2C D CF Napa Brand Design C Judy's Candies
3A D Anabliss Graphic Design C Patriot and Loyalist 3B D 13thirtyone Design C A Delightful Day Weddings And Events
3C D Sayles Graphic Design, Inc. C Modern Age Gallery 4A D David Beck Design C Phil Romano 4B D Gary Sample Design C Gary Sample Design
4C D Max Kelly Design C Jack Russell's Steak House

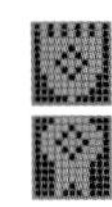

1

2

3

4

D = Design Firm C = Client

1A D Esse Design C Russell Solutions 1B D Archrival C Kopsa Otte 1C D Henjum Creative C Inner Harbor Marina
2A D Visual Lure, LLC C Hong Brothers Martial Arts 2B D Fernandez Design C One Global City 2C D Gary Sample Design C 3rd Rail Design
3A D Tim Frame Design C Lyon's Den 3B D MiresBall C Early V8 Ford Car Club 3C D Clockwork Studios C TXAFL
4A D Matt Whitley C Indy Motor Speedway 4B D Mez Design C Big Island Organics 4C D Sayles Graphic Design, Inc. C Nelson Company

1

2

3

4

D = Design Firm   C = Client

1A D Colle + McVoy C CHS 1B D Scott Oeschger Design C M&M 1C D Jerron Ames C Arteis

2A D co:lab C International paper / with Williams & House 2B D Bryan Cooper Design C Bella Dolce 2C D Design Hub C Hirsh Family

3A D Flaherty Robinson Inc. C Muscular Dystrophy Association 3B D Lisa Wood Design C Roseville, CA

3C D McElveney & Palozzi Design Group, Inc. C HighFalls Brewing Co.

4A D Absolute Design C Sunnyside Hotel 4B D Kiku Obata & Company C Southeast Missourian 4C D Traction C At The Yard Baseball Training Center

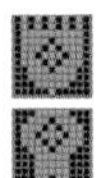

A B C

1

2

3

4

D = Design Firm C = Client

1A D TMCA, Inc. C S.C. Chamber of Commerce 1B D Kendall Creative Shop, Inc. C Walter Exploration 1C D Glitschka Studios C Upper Deck Company
2A D Gary Sample Design C G8S Design Alliance 2B D Canyon Creative C The Parker Companies 2C D Glitschka Studios C Brown and Associates
3A D Parachute Design C Crepuscular Society Show of Comedy 3B D Noble C Tyson Foods Inc. 3C D RAZAUNO C Ecko Unlimited
4A D tomvasquez.com C Miller Lite 4B D Alphabet Arm Design C Tim McCoy 4C D Gary Sample Design C Gary Sample Design

A B C

1

2

3

4

D = Design Firm C = Client

1A D Sayles Graphic Design, Inc. C Iowa State Fair 1B D M3 Advertising Design C Desert Aces Flying School 1C D Michael Doret Graphic Design C General Amusements
2A D Barnstorm Creative Group Inc C Image Engine 2B D Carol Gravelle Graphic Design C Giant Bicycles 2C D Jon Kay Design C Starmen.Net
3A D Brian Collins Design C Dewar's Ice Cream & Candy Shop 3B D Studio Simon C Idaho Falls Chukars 3C D Charles Design C Bandung Restaurant
4A D ANDLAB C Maison Riz 4B D Fleishman Hillard C St. Louis Cardinals 4C D Hinge C Corinthian Realty Partners

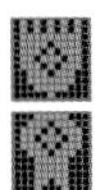

A | B | C

1

2

3

4

D = Design Firm C = Client

1A D Hornall Anderson C Rainier Bank 1B D SoupGraphix Inc. C Broad Display 1C D Sibley Peteet Design—Dallas C Zaragoza Vineyards
2A D Sabingrafik, Inc. C Buck Knives 2B D Sabingrafik, Inc. C San Pacifico 2C D Deep Design C Dr. Smiths Veterinary Collectibles
3A D Paradox Box C 3B D Airtype Studio C JR Motorsports 3C D McQuillen Creative Group C Side Pocket Billiards Club
4A D Threds C SOUTHERN PLAINS OIL 4B D Michael Doret Graphic Design 4C D M3 Advertising Design C Block16

A B C

INTERNATIONAL
GREG ★ DAVIS
PHOTOGRAPHER

1

2

3

4

D = Design Firm C = Client

1A D Spoonbend C Greg Davis 1B D Rhombus, Inc. C Fryer8or 1C D ivan2design
2A D moosylvania C Johnny's Lunch 2B D Sayles Graphic Design, Inc. C Specialty Enterprises 2C D octane inc. C Al Platt Architect
3A D Hornall Anderson C Thomas Maxwell 3B D Alphabet Arm Design C Charlie McEnerney 3C D DUEL Purpose C Roosevelt Elementary
4A D Arena Design C The Body Shop Gym 4B D Brainding 4C D Zync Communications Inc. C Weston Forest Group

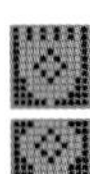

A B C

Ⓓ = Design Firm Ⓒ = Client

1A Ⓓ Tom Law Design Ⓒ Southland Graphics 1B Ⓓ Gardner Design Ⓒ Backroads Traveler 1C Ⓓ Gardner Design Ⓒ Backroads Traveler 2A Ⓓ Gardner Design Ⓒ Emily Bergquist Photography 2B Ⓓ The Office of Art+Logik Ⓒ Williamson Bicycle Works 2C Ⓓ Suburban Utopia Ⓒ Downtown Athens Recording Company 3A Ⓓ josh higgins design Ⓒ whistle Stop Bar 3B Ⓓ Curtis Sharp Design Ⓒ 206HandyMan 3C Ⓓ D&i (Design and Image) Ⓒ Deborah Williams 4A Ⓓ Qualitá Design Ⓒ Fabricio de Macedo 4B Ⓓ Associated Advertising Agency, Inc. Ⓒ KCF Consulting 4C Ⓓ Archrival Ⓒ Kopsa Otte

A B C

1

2

3

4

D = Design Firm C = Client

1A D Logoidentity.com C Luigi's Kitchen & Wine Bar 1B D Green Olive Media C Green Olive Media 1C D Nectar Graphics C Cowgirl Mercantile
2A D NOT A CANNED HAM C Vanessa Montgomery 2B D Red Clover Studio C Liberty Design House 2C D Gardner Design C Piccadilly
3A D Miles Design C Brand Photodesign 3B D Jason Kochis C Gagwear/TCM 3C D Sayles Graphic Design, Inc. C Beaver Avenue Cleaners
4A D Hanna & Associates C North Country Trading Co. 4B D Burd & Patterson C Valley Junction Historical District 4C D Kendall Creative Shop, Inc. C Cowgirl Justice

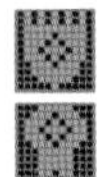

A B C

1

2

3

4

D = Design Firm C = Client

1A D Red Headed Frog Design C Concept Design for Salon and Spa 1B D JM Design Co. C Casa Sorrento Pizzeria 1C D 3 Advertising LLC C Chez Nous
2A D Timber Design Company C IUPUI 2B D Michael Doret Graphic Design C Duty Free Shops 2C D High Fiber Design C Tropiscapes
3A D Sandstrom Partners C Full Sail 3B D Level B Design C Wells Fargo Financial 3C D The Joe Bosack Graphic Design Co. C Arena Football League
4A D Dotzero Design C Bridgetown 4B D RARE Design C Minnesota Wild 4C D Mauck Groves Branding & Design C Iowa's Race 2 Recovery

A B C

1

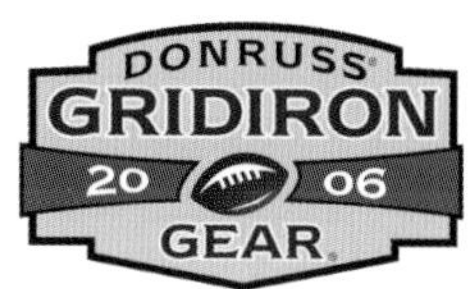

2

3

4

Ⓓ = Design Firm Ⓒ = Client

1A Ⓓ Tactix Creative Ⓒ Tactix Creative 1B Ⓓ Sayles Graphic Design, Inc. Ⓒ Des Moines Park and Recreation 1C Ⓓ Gardner Design Ⓒ Epic
2A Ⓓ Steve's Portfolio Ⓒ JEG 2B Ⓓ Oomingmak Design Company Ⓒ Donruss Trading Card Company 2C Ⓓ Niedermeier Design Ⓒ Red Rocket
3A Ⓓ Level B Design Ⓒ Downtown Community Alliance 3B Ⓓ Mez Design Ⓒ Mountain Village 3C Ⓓ BrainBox Studio Ⓒ Mylifeoftravel.com
4A Ⓓ McGarrah/Jessee Ⓒ Hyatt Regency Lost Pines Resort and Spa 4B Ⓓ schaer creative l.l.c. Ⓒ Chili Davis Premier Baseball 4C Ⓓ Iratxe Mumford

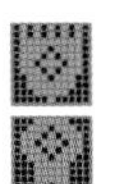

1

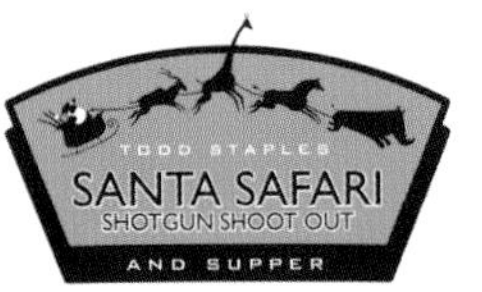

D = Design Firm   C = Client

1A D Spoonbend C Pattern Productions 1B D Sol Consultores C CTPN 1C D 9MYLES, Inc. C WUSA
2A D RADAR Agency C Ag Commissioner Todd Staples 2B D William Fox Munroe Inc C Kunzler & Company, Inc. 2C D 3 Deuces Design, Inc. C Greg Howard
3A D Werner Design Werks C Cliff Rakerd 3B D Ross Creative + Strategy C Ross Creative + Strategy 3C D Triple Frog LLC C Triple Frog
4A D Fresh Oil C Whelihan's Pub 4B D Retro DC C K&K Amusement 4C D 7th Street Design C ShangHai Restaurant

A B C

1

2

3

4

D = Design Firm C = Client

1A D Sabingrafik, Inc. C Helen Woodward Animal Center 1B D Hausch Design Agency LLC C Brew City Bar-B-Q, Milwaukee, Wisconsin 1C D RARE Design C Leatha's
2A D Jonathan Rice & Company C Joshua Experience 2B D Burd & Patterson C Principal Residential Mortgage 2C D Gridwerk C Cross Keys Diner
3A D Mez Design C Mountain Village 3B D Atha Design C Ankeny Class of '82 Reunion Committee 3C D Tim Frame Design C Charley's Steakery
4A D Kendall Creative Shop, Inc. C Woody Candy Company 4B D Storm Design Inc. C Precise Engine 4C D Monster Design Company C Don's Tire Service

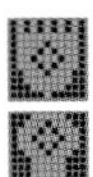

A B C

1

2

3

4

D = Design Firm C = Client

1A D Sayles Graphic Design, Inc. C Principal Bank 1B D Timber Design Company C Fusek's Hardware 1C D McQuillen Creative Group C Northern Route to the Black Hills 2A D Cass Design Co. C The Gideons International 2B D pearpod C association of gospel rescue missions 2C D McGarrah/Jessee C McGarrah/Jessee 3A D Giles Design Inc. C Pearl Brewery 3B D Fleishman Hillard C St. Louis Cardinals 3C D Chameleon Design Group, LLC C Activate Sports & Entertainment for Delaware North Companies 4A D Kiku Obata & Company C St. Louis Zoo 4B D Ad Impact Advertising C Silver Sponge Hand Car Wash 4C D Hotiron Creative, LLC C Lauer-Krauts

A B C

1

2

3

4

D = Design Firm C = Client

1A D SoupGraphix Inc. C Broad Display 1B D LogoDesignGuru.com C Dawson King International 1C D Sayles Graphic Design, Inc. C Dave Carlson
2A D Alphabet Arm Design C Sue Christian / Donna Benson 2B D Tactix Creative C A T Meridian 2C D Gardner Design C BG Bolton's Bar Grille and Tavern
3A D Sayles Graphic Design, Inc. C Phil Goode 3B D Brady Design Ltd C The Chicago Fury 3C D Dr. Alderete C FMI—Bunbury
4A D Compass Design C Jacks Toolbox 4B D Element C Finish Line Custom Building 4C D Sayles Graphic Design, Inc. C The Adventure Institute

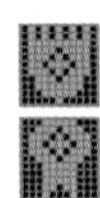

A B C

1

2

3

4

D = Design Firm C = Client

1A D Tim Frame Design C OnMessage 1B D Chip Sheean C CF Napa 1C D Alphabet Arm Design C Mr. Lif
2A D Insight Design C Lofts at Old Town Square 2B D Sayles Graphic Design, Inc. C Blue Ribbon Steak House 2C D MFDI C Luxor Cab Company
3A D Gardner Design C Cargill 3B D Rickabaugh Graphics C Big East Conference 3C D Tim Frame Design
4A D Level B Design C Riverside Casino Resort 4B D Koch Creative Group C Koch Industries Inc. 4C D Pale Horse Design C Blackout Creations

A B C

1

2

3

4

D = Design Firm C = Client

1A D Mark Oliver, Inc. C Ocean Beauty Seafood 1B D 9 Surf Studios C Source Media 1C D Richards Brock Miller Mitchell & Associates C Vinny Testa's
2A D Sabingrafik, Inc. C CountryCritter.com 2B D HOOK C Sucker Jeans 2C D Sharisse Steber Design C Jake Leg Stompers
3A D Periscope C Speedco 3B D 9 Surf Studios C NFL 3C D 9 Surf Studios C Air Age Media
4A D Kevin Creative C Tsunami Marketing 4B D Mystic Design, Inc. C Beermann's 4C D wray ward C WIX

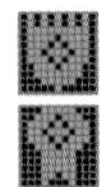

A B C

1

2

3

4

D = Design Firm C = Client

1A D DesignPoint, Inc. C Gateway Communications 1B D Sharisse Steber Design C Bella Luna 1C D R&R Partners C Vegas Rock Dog
2A D Insight Design C The Hayes Company, Inc. 2B D Insight Design C The Hayes Company, Inc 2C D GTC Media
3A D Timber Design Company C Walker Racing, Inc 3B D Moss Creative C Foutz Stone 3C D Vivitiv C Signatures/BDA
4A D Pale Horse Design C Mercitron Design 4B D Ulyanov Denis C Bankhouse Erbe 4C D Gardner Design C City of Newton, KS

A B C

1

2

3

4

D = Design Firm C = Client

1A D HMS Design C LabattUSA 1B D Blacktop Creative C Kansas City City Market 1C D Cashmere Creative C Erick LeFevre Masonry
2A D Gardner Design C City of Newton, KS 2B D Juancazu C asados eco 2C D noe design C Screenscape Studios
3A D Goldforest C The Four Twenty Co. 3B D Mez Design C Deloitte 3C D Gardner Design C Avalanche Popcorn
4A D Actual Size Creative C AIGA Pittsburgh 4B D Gardner Design C BG Bolton's Bar and Grill 4C D LGA / Jon Cain C Amras Inc

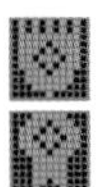

A B C

1

2

3

4

D = Design Firm C = Client

1A D Judson Design C Unused 1B D Design Hub C Lb. Brewing Co. 1C D Jon Kay Design C Starmen.Net
2A D reaves design C jcpenny 2B D RARE Design C University of Southern Mississippi 2C D James Olson Design C Creative Labs
3A D SoupGraphix Inc. C Adio Footwear 3B D Valhalla I Design & Conquer C the Shadow Conspiracy 3C D Opolis Design, LLC C ESPN
4A D Patten ID C Cadillac Club 4B D KBO PROTOTYPES C Hacendadas Mazatepec 4C D JP Global Marketing, Inc. C Ingram Ranch

A B C

1

2

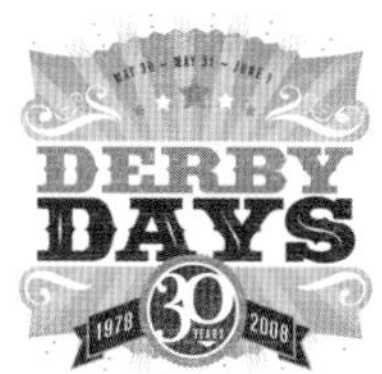

3

4

Ⓓ = Design Firm Ⓒ = Client

1A Ⓓ Muku Studios Ⓒ Quarter Lives 1B Ⓓ Mystic Design, Inc. Ⓒ American Cancer Society 1C Ⓓ SoupGraphix Inc. Ⓒ Adio Footwear
2A Ⓓ Jon Kay Design Ⓒ Starmen.Net 2B Ⓓ Tim Frame Design Ⓒ OnMessage 2C Ⓓ Jajo, Inc. Ⓒ City of Derby
3A Ⓓ DUSTIN PARKER ARTS Ⓒ Paul D. McKee 3B Ⓓ Church Logo Gallery Ⓒ Solana Beach Presbyterian Church 3C Ⓓ Sayles Graphic Design, Inc. Ⓒ East Village
4A Ⓓ Bureau Blank Ⓒ Evil Empire 4B Ⓓ Black Osprey Dead Arts Ⓒ ISIS 4C Ⓓ Hybrid Design Ⓒ Super 7

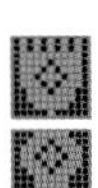

A B C

1

2

3

4

D = Design Firm C = Client

1A **D** Black Osprey Dead Arts **C** FLIP SKATEBOARDS 1B **D** Airtype Studio **C** Pinedale Student Ministries 1C **D** SoupGraphix Inc. **C** Fly Racing
2A **D** Fons Schiedon **C** Museum Princessehof 2B **D** 9 Surf Studios **C** Big Brothers Big Sisters of the Greater Seacoast 2C **D** Delikatessen **C** City of Hamburg, Germany
3A **D** CDI Studios **C** 3B **D** Michael Doret Graphic Design **C** The Hershey Co. 3C **D** 9 Surf Studios **C** Stuff
4A **D** Scott Carroll Designs, Inc. **C** The National WWII Museum 4B **D** 9 Surf Studios **C** Source Media 4C **D** Mitre Agency **C** Hog's Head Beer Cellars

A B C

1

2

3

4

D = Design Firm C = Client

1A D Rickabaugh Graphics C Delaware 4-H 1B D Barnstorm Creative Group Inc C Image Engine 1C D Matt Whitley C Wal-Mart
2A D Swingtop C Ohio High School Athletic Association 2B D BlueSpark Studios C Coca-Cola, Albertsons 2C D Alphabet Arm Design C Big Honcho Media
3A D Jon Kay Design C Starmen.Net 3B D Burton (Snowboards) Corp. C Burton Snowboards 3C D HOOK C Fez
4A D Brian Collins Design C Kern Co. Youth Mariachi Foundation 4B D DTM_INC C HomeBrew Records 4C D Daggerfin C AlixPartners

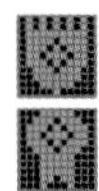

A B C

1

2

3

4

D = Design Firm C = Client

1A D Michael Doret Graphic Design C Fuddruckers 1B D 9 Surf Studios C Popular Photography 1C D Rickabaugh Graphics C ICLA
2A D 2TREES DESIGN C 2TREES DESIGN 2B D SoupGraphix Inc. C Adio Footwear 2C D Pelco C Pelco
3A D 9 Surf Studios C Source Media 3B D 9 Surf Studios C CMP Media 3C D 9 Surf Studios C Design News Magazine
4A D 9 Surf Studios C McGraw-Hill 4B D TMCA, Inc. C S.C. Chamber of Commerce 4C D 9 Surf Studios C Small Business Opportunity

A  C

1

2

3

4

D = Design Firm **C** = Client

1A **D** 9 Surf Studios **C** Small Business Opportunity 1B **D** 9 Surf Studios **C** Small Business Opportunity 1C **D** 9 Surf Studios **C** Gray / Hasbro
2A **D** 9 Surf Studios **C** Cavalcade of Sports 2B **D** 9 Surf Studios **C** 9 Surf Studios 2C **D** 9 Surf Studios **C** HSR / Hobart
3A **D** Pagliuco Design Company **C** Van Gorp International, Inc. 3B **D** Endura **C** FamilyLife 3C **D** Fargo Design Co., Inc **C** PA Council Against the Drink Tax
4A **D** Purpled : Graphic Design Studio **C** Stuph Clothing 4B **D** DUEL Purpose **C** Bricktown Association 4C **D** Rickabaugh Graphics **C** Phil Hellmuth Poker Challenge

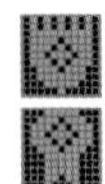

A B C

1

2

3

4

D = Design Firm C = Client

1A D J6Studios C Houston Area Knife Stickers 1B D TBF Creative C 1C D Visual Inventor Ltd. Co. C Union Mutual insurance Company
2A D Michael Doret Graphic Design C Ricardo Rousselot 2B D Michael Doret Graphic Design C Bloomingdale's 2C D Urban Influence C Urban Industries
3A D Schwartzrock Graphic Arts C Blackwood Management Group 3B D Jon Flaming Design C The Covenant School
3C D Sayles Graphic Design, Inc. C Lloyd's of Des Moines 4A D Insight Design C The Hayes Company, Inc. 4B D joni dunbar design C Sidelines Sports Cafe
4C D Brown Ink Design C Eureka Tiles

A B C

1

2

3

4

D = Design Firm C = Client

1A **D** Delikatessen **C** fashion label 1B **D** Stiles Design **C** Texas Department of Transportation/Sherry Matthews
1C **D** McQuillen Creative Group **C** NX 10-31 Entertainment 2A **D** Sussner Design Company **C** AIGA MN 2B **D** Digital Flannel **C** KAF
2C **D** Gizwiz Studio **C** Bob 3A **D** Fresh Oil **C** Mass. General Hospital Cancer Center 3B **D** Shift **C** Dutch Communications 3C **D** POLLARDdesign **C** NBC
4A **D** Double Brand **C** Foudation 4B **D** Doink, Inc. **C** Belen Jesuit Preparatory School 4C **D** JG Creative

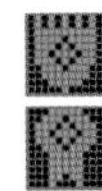

1

2

3

4

D = Design Firm C = Client

1A D VanPaul Design C Streetside 1B D Sayles Graphic Design, Inc. C Eagle Investment Resources 1C D The Greater Good Design C Big City Barbers
2A D Miles Design C Wheel Tags 2B D Paragon Marketing Communications C Zodiac Saloon 2C D Urban Influence C 59 Limousine
3A D Clockwork Studios C Youth Basketball League of Salt Lake City 3B D Gardner Design C T B Guide Company
3C D Tandem Design Agency C Gaylord Country Club 4A D Westwerk DSGN C Blueye 4B D Bukka Design C Bukka Design
4C D Sarah grimaldi C Bambistar Clothing

A | B | C

1

2

3

4

D = Design Firm C = Client

1A **D** The Laster Group **C** Inn of the Mountain Gods Resort and Casino 1B **D** Synthetic Infatuation **C** Kelly Sperl Associates 1C **D** JG Creative
2A **D** Schwartzrock Graphic Arts **C** Freshwater Community Church 2B **D** Studio Simon **C** Dayton Dragons 2C **D** Sayles Graphic Design, Inc. **C** Zook's Harley Davidson
3A **D** POLLARDdesign **C** Hot Rods USA 3B **D** GCG **C** American Advertising Federation 3C **D** Fresh Oil **C** Tender by Choice
4A **D** McQuillen Creative Group **C** City of Aberdeen 4B **D** seesponge **C** DaimlerChrysler 4C **D** Jennifer Braham Design **C** AA Lotus

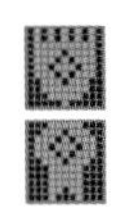

A B C

1

2

3

4

D = Design Firm C = Client

1A **D** Mazemedia 1B **D** Design Partners Inc. **C** Tenneco Automotive 1C **D** Cacao Design **C** Eulda Books
2A **D** Delikatessen **C** HTS GmBH 2B **D** Sabingrafik, Inc. **C** The Peterson Family 2C **D** Capisce Design Inc. **C** Coco Johnsen
3A **D** Oxide Design Co. **C** Polyfro Event Management 3B **D** Extraverage Productions **C** Personal 3C **D** Hove Design Works **C** Absolute inc
4A **D** Topo **C** Dolls 4B **D** Ross Creative + Strategy **C** Caterpillar 4C **D** Brand Anarchy Group **C** Bond By Oath

A B C

1

2

3

4

D = Design Firm C = Client

1A D BrandSavvy, Inc. C Floyd Medical Center 1B D SoupGraphix Inc. C Fly Racing 1C D Design Hub C Lb. Brewing Co.
2A D LogoDesignGuru.com 2B D Fossil C Fossil 2C D RedBrand C PLSE
3A D Karl Design Vienna C Pig Bike GmbH 3B D Kendall Creative Shop, Inc. C Saint Thomas Aquinas School 3C D Gardner Design C Epic
4A D DUEL Purpose C Brian's Automotive 4B D Reactive Mediums C Auto Credit Express, Inc. 4C D Sabingrafik, Inc. C Gordon Screen Printing

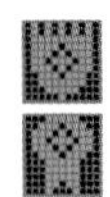

A B C

1

2

3

4

D = Design Firm C = Client

1A D Gabriel Kalach • V I S U A L communication 1B D LGA / Jon Cain C Eddie Littlefield 1C D Fossil C Fossil
2A D SCORR Marketing C Budke's Power Sports 2B D Bluespace Creative, Inc. C Chrome Coalition 2C D Buffalo Design Group Inc. C Bikes Around the Burg Logo
3A D Extraverage Productions C RideHouse, Austria 3B D henriquez lara C Vico Equense 3C D RDQLUS Creative C VNDK8 Freestyle Equipment Co.
4A D MSI C Tractor Supply 4B D Kuznets C Phillip Morris 4C D Monster Design Company C McCallum Cabinets

B C

1

2

3

4

D = Design Firm   C = Client

1A D MLS Creative Services C Rich Levy Productions 1B D Caotica C Pequenas Raposas 1C D United States of the Art
2A D Brian Collins Design C The Bakersfield Californian 2B D Kiku Obata & Company C St. Louis Zoo 2C D R&R Partners C Patty Zimmer
3A D Tran Creative C Viking Homes 3B D Oakley Design Studios C Delrosa International 3C D delphine C Here Comes The Bride
4A D Tran Creative C Viking Homes 4B D Advent Creative C Sonora Grill 4C D Hinge C Hinge

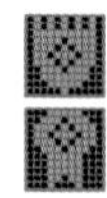

A B C

1

2

3

4

D = Design Firm C = Client

1A D HKLM C InterContinental 1B D 7th Street Design C Courtney Reed 1C D For the Love of Creating C David Schwartz Photography
2A D Freshwater Design C Emile DeFelice 2B D Extraverage Productions C Mayo Chix 2C D Diagram C Gruszecki
3A D Shoofly C Soul Gardener 3B D Essex Two C HearthStone Development, Inc. 3C D Timber Design Company C PolicyFind, Inc
4A D Mingovits Design C Thirsty Girl Productions 4B D TOKY Branding+Design 4C D Murillo Design, Inc. C Misi Woolard

A B C

1

2

3

4

D = Design Firm C = Client

1A D Konstellation C Riva Riva 1B D jing C jing inc. 1C D Howerton+White C Dress For Success
2A D Hornall Anderson C Cold Standard 2B D Corporate Image Consultants, Inc. C Treasure Island Beach Resort 2C D Studio No. 6 C THOMPSON HOUSE INN
3A D Hornall Anderson C Holland America Line 3B D Rusty George Creative C The Roberson 3C D lunabrand design group C Fain Signature Group
4A D Mitre Agency C Opie's Southbound Grille 4B D Airtype Studio C Pinedale Church 4C D Hubbell Design Works C BBB Entertainment

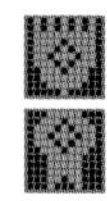

A B C

1

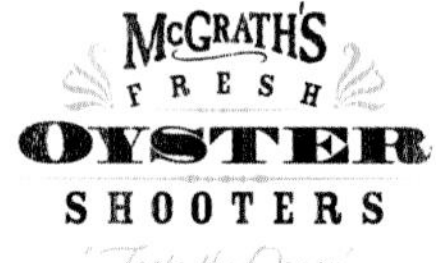

2

3

4

D = Design Firm C = Client

1A D Mauck Groves Branding & Design C Adara Estates 1B D DesignPoint, Inc. C McGrath's Fish House 1C D Schwartzrock Graphic Arts C Windworks
2A D Nectar Graphics C Ghost Hills Cellars 2B D Illustra Graphics C Mansion Farm 2C D LogoDesignGuru.com C Amish Avenue
3A D iDgital Design Studio, Inc. C Cohen & Co. Creative 3B D TOKY Branding+Design C Pappy's Barbeque 3C D Urban Influence C Arctic Club Hotel
4A D Fernandez Design C Steer Branding 4B D MUELLER design C Losson Ranch and Vineyard 4C D lunabrand design group C Harry's

A B C

1

2

3

4

D = Design Firm C = Client

1A D Burd & Patterson C Field Paper Company 1B D Gardner Design C Allied Crane 1C D Kiku Obata & Company C St. Louis Zoo
2A D Corder Philips C Crecent Communities 2B D Gardner Design 2C D Gardner Design
3A D Pale Horse Design C Blackout Creations 3B D Kristian Andersen + Associates C Lights Out Marketing 3C D MiresBall C YMCA
4A D WORK Labs C Steve Berg 4B D Draward 4C D Jackrabbit Design C Boston Yacht Haven

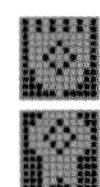

A B C

1

2

3

4

D = Design Firm   C = Client

1A D Banowetz + Company, Inc. C Hotel ZaZa 1B D Miles Design C 12 Gauge Wakeskates 1C D Deep Design C Surface, Inc.
2A D Capisce Design Inc. C Emmylou Harris 2B D Holmberg Design, LLC C Hewitt Studios 2C D Looney Ricks Kiss Architects, Inc. C Gagne Development
3A D Randy Mosher Design C North Shore Brew Dreamers 3B D Entropy Brands C Warehouse Bistro 3C D Velocity Design Group C Southwest Masonry
4A D Passing Notes, Inc. C Jamie Zollars 4B D Moonlit Creative Group C Modern Tribe 4C D Hornall Anderson C Holland America Line

A B C

1

2

3

4

D = Design Firm   C = Client

1A D Gardner Design C The Lone Ranger 1B D Archrival C Kopsa Otte 1C D morrow mckenzie design C Rogue Creamery
2A D Duffy & Partners C Dickson's 2B D Trapdoor Studio C Ride Me 2C D Glitschka Studios C Sequoia Financial Group
3A D lunabrand design group C Augie's Restaurant 3B D Scott Oeschger Design C M&M 3C D Dotzero Design C West Oaks Mall
4A D Simon & Goetz Design C frank kuhlmann 4B D Banowetz + Company, Inc. C Jack Hollingsworth 4C D HMK Archive C The Dorado Partners

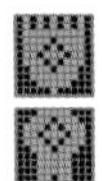

A B C

1

2

3

4

D = Design Firm C = Client

1A D Gardner Design C Gavin Peters 1B D Steve's Portfolio C JEG 1C D Flaxenfield, Inc. C Flaxenfield, Inc.
2A D LGA / Jon Cain C Amras Inc 2B D Louise Fili C Sfoglia 2C D Colle + McVoy C Greater Minneapolis Crisis Nursery
3A D Goodform Design C Only the Blog Knows Brooklyn 3B D Indigo Creative C Casa Brioche 3C D Entermotion Design Studio C Booties
4A D Home Grown Logos C St. Francis School, Sonoma 4B D Sibley Peteet C Rochiolis 4C D Tribe Design Houston C AIGA

A B C

1

2

3

4

D = Design Firm C = Client

1A D Timber Design Company C AMACO, Inc 1B D hnd C Visionary subText 1C D Michael Doret Graphic Design C ViaWest
2A D Randy Mosher Design C Lincoln Station 2B D Tip Top Creative C Boulangerie Nantaise, Biofournil 2C D R Design LLC C Design Council of the Denver Art Museum
3A D moosylvania C Johnny's Lunch 3B D Hove Design Works C Sanus 3C D Fargo Design Co., Inc. C PA Council Against the Drink Tax
4A D Idea Bank Marketing C Equitable Federal Savings Bank 4B D Ambassadors C Isuzu 4C D Jon Flaming Design C Watermark Community Church ministry program

A B C

1

D = Design Firm C = Client

1A D Sabingrafik, Inc. C Morrow Development 1B D Judson Design 1C D Judson Design C Uncle Billy's Brew and Que
2A D Judson Design 2B D Marc Posch Design, Inc C Ebell Club/Jon Nickson 2C D Designbolaget C Granola
3A D Olson C Phillips Distilling 3B D Level B Design C Jasper Winery 3C D Sockeye Creative C MacTarnahan's Brewing Company
4A D JASON GRUBE DESIGN C Keller Williams Realty 4B D The Robin Shepherd Group C Jacksonville Historical Society 4C D Smith Design C Arla

A | B | C

1

2

3

4

D = Design Firm C = Client

1A D Fitting Group C PUMP (Pittsburgh Urban Magnet Project) 1B D TOKY Branding+Design C Contemporary Art Muesum St. Louis 1C D björn soneson C varieties
2A D Chameleon Design Group, LLC C NZP Naturals 2B D MSI C Tractor Supply 2C D mugur mihai
3A D Extra Point Creative C University of Central Florida 3B D Hickabaugh Graphics C Opera Columbus
3C D McQuillen Creative Group C Red Nation Gaming 4A D Jean Peterson Design C Voluntary Protection Programs Participants' Association
4B D Jean Peterson Design C Voluntary Protection Programs Participants' Association 4C D Kendall Creative Shop, Inc. C St. Thomas Aquinas

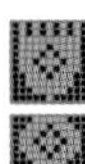

A B C

1

2

3

4

D = Design Firm C = Client

1A D R&R Partners C R&R Partners 1B D seesponge C Mick's Custom Bars and Barstools 1C D R&R Partners C Las Vegas Convention & Visitors Authority
2A D Blik C San Diego College Area Business District 2B D Blacktop Creative C American Jazz Museum 2C D Gardner Design C Printmaster
3A D Tower of Babel C Portland International Raceway 3B D Gesture Studio C Dirty's Maid Service, Inc. 3C D Novasoul C Autumn Leaves
4A D Segura Inc. C MCA 4B D TOKY Branding+Design C Food Outreach of St. Louis 4C D Threds C Capone's Windy City Eatery

index

directory of contributors

01d
Belarus
www.01d.ru
1310 Studios
USA
www.1310studios.com
13thirtyone Design
USA
www.13thirtyone.com
20FIRST
Germany
www.20first.de
212-BIG-BOLT
USA
www.bigbolt.com
28 LIMITED BRAND
Germany
www.twenty-eight.de
2TREES DESIGN
USA
www.2treesdesignco.com
3 Advertising LLC
USA
www.whois3.com
3 Deuces Design, Inc.
USA
719-232-5411
343 Creative
USA
www.343creative.com
360ideas
USA
www.360ideas.com
38one
USA
38one.com
5 Fifteen Design Group, Inc.
USA
www.5-fifteen.com
5Seven
USA
www.fivesevendesign.com
73ideas
USA
480-993-1473
7th Street Design
USA
626-202-4528
9 Surf Studios
USA
www.9surf.com
903 Creative, LLC
USA
www.903creative.com
9MYLES, Inc.
USA
9myles.com
A. Shtramilo design studio
Ukraine
www.shtramilodesign.com
A3 Design
USA
www.athreedesign.com
Abiah
USA
www.abiah.com
Absolute Design
UK
www.absolutedesign.co.uk
Acme Graphic Design
USA
503-872-8940
Actual Size Creative
USA
www.thisisactualsize.com
Acute Cluster
Thailand
www.acutecluster.com
Ad Impact Advertising
Australia
www.adimpact.com.au
Adams Design Group
New Zealand
6449710182
ADC Global Creativity
USA
www.adc-inc.com
Addison Whitney
USA
www.addisonwhitney.com

ADDWATER2
USA
www.addwater2.com
Adept Interactive
Bulgaria
www.adeptplayground.com
The Adsmith
USA
www.theadsmith.com
Adstract Art
Australia
www.adstract.com.au
Advent Creative
USA
www.adventcreative.com
Advertising Intelligence
Kazakhstan
www.artrafael.narod.ru
Ahab Nimry
USA
www.ahabnimry.com
Airtype Studio
USA
www.airtypestudio.com
AKOFA Creative
USA
www.akofa.com
Alambre Estudio
Spain
www.alambre.net
Alan Barnett, Inc.
USA
www.alanbarnett.com
Alice Chae
USA
847-942-7906
Align Design Graphics Studio
USA
678-904-2807
Alin Golfitescu
Romania
40729937251
Allen Creative
USA
www.allencreative.com
Alphabet Arm Design
USA
www.alphabetarm.com
Altagraf
USA
267-342-3815
Alterpop
USA
415-558-1515 ext. 201
Ambassadors
USA
949-219-8663
America Online
USA
614-262-1476
Ammunition
UK
www.ammunition.tv
Anabliss Graphic Design
USA
303-825-4441
Anagraphic
Hungary
www.anagraphic.hu
ANDLAB
USA
323-222-2225
Angie Dudley
USA
www.angiedudley.com
Anoroc
USA
anorocagency.com
ANS
USA
972-526-9642
Archrival
USA
www.archrival.com
Ardoise Design
Canada
ardoise.com
Arena Design
USA
www.arenadesign.com

ars graphica
USA
arsgraphica.net
Art Chantry
USA
253-310-3993
ArtFly
USA
www.artfly.com
ArtGraphics.ru
Russia
www.artgraphics.ru
ARTini BAR
USA
www.artinibar.com
Artrinsic Design
USA
www.artrinsic.com
asmallpercent
USA
www.asmallpercent.com
Associated Advertising Agency, Inc.
USA
www.associatedadv.com
Atha Design
USA
641-673-2820
Atomic Wash Design Studio
USA
www.atomicwash.com
August Design Studio
USA
augustds.com
avenue:b
USA
415-457-0275
Axiom Design Collaborative
USA
801-532-2442
Axiom Design Partners
Australia
www.axiomdp.com.au
B.L.A. Design Company
USA
803 518-4130
b5 Marketing & Kommunikation GmbH
Germany
www.b5-media.de
baba designs
USA
248-514-9427
Back2Front
Australia
395840692
baCreative
USA
www.aitchisonlee.com
BadGenius
USA
www.badgenius.com
Bailey Brand Consulting
USA
610-940-9030
ballard::creative
USA
www.ballardcreative.com
Banowetz + Company, Inc.
USA
www.banowetz.com
Barnstorm Creative Group Inc
Canada
www.barnstormcreative.com
bartodell.com
USA
www.bartodell.com
BBDO NY
USA
212-459-5000
BBMG
USA
www.bbmg.com
Beacon Branding LLC
USA
www.beaconbranding.com
Bean Graphics
USA
www.beangraphics.com
Beganik Strategy + Design
USA
www.beganik.com

Bernas Design
USA
bernasdesign.com
Bernhardt Fudyma Design Group
USA
www.bfdg.com
Bertz Design Group
USA
www.bertzdesign.com
Beveridge Seay, Inc.
USA
www.bevseay.com
BFive
Russia
www.bfive.ru
Biamerikan Inc.
USA
biamerikan.com
Billingsley Concepts, Inc
USA
828-698-5560
björn soneson
USA
319-404-8495
Black Osprey Dead Arts
USA
Blacktop Creative
USA
www.blacktopcreative.com
Blake BW
Argentina
www.blakebw.com
BLANK, Inc.
USA
www.blankblank.com
Blattner Brunner, Inc.
USA
412-995-9529
Blik
USA
619-234-4434
Blink Media Group
USA
www.blinkmg.com
Blue Bee Design
USA
bluebdesign.com
Blue Beetle Design
Singapore
www.bluebeetledesign.com
Blue Clover
USA
www.blueclover.com
blueground
USA
210-738-8200
Bluespace Creative, Inc.
USA
www.bluespacecreative.com
BlueSpark Studios
USA
310-394-9080
Bmu Creative Design Agency
Turkey
www.bmucreative.com
bob neace graphic design, inc
USA
316-264-4952
Bobby Magallanes
USA
www.bobbymagallanes.com
Boelts Design
USA
www.boeltsdesign.com
Boom Creative
USA
www.boom-creative.com
Born to Design
USA
317-838-9404
Boston Creative, Inc.
USA
314-962-5222
Bostrom Graphics, LLC
USA
www.bostromgraphics.com
br:Verse
USA
www.bernstein-rein.com

Brad Norr Design
USA
612-298-7599
The Bradford Lawton Design Group
USA
www.bradfordlawton.com
Brady Design Ltd
USA
www.bradydesignltd.com
BrainBox Studio
Israel
+972 4 9907 933
Brainding
Argentina
www.brainding.com.ar
Brains on Fire
USA
www.brainsonfire.com
Brand Anarchy Group
USA
www.brandanarchygroup.com
Brand Bird
USA
www.brandbird.com
Brand Environment (Be)
UK
www.be-uk.com
Brand Navigation
USA
www.brandnavigation.com
The Brand Union
United Arab Emirates
97144393744
BrandBerry
Russia
www.brand-berry.ru
BrandEquity
USA
www.brandequity.com
BrandExtract
USA
713-942-7959
Brandient
Romania
www.brandient.com
BrandSavvy, Inc.
USA
www.brandsavvyinc.com
Brandstorm Creative Group
USA
305-960-2038
Braue: Brand Design Experts
Germany
www.braue.info
Brian Blankenship
USA
www.brianblankenship.com
Brian Collins Design
USA
417-459-5346
Brian Krezel
USA
briankrezel.com
Bridge Creative
USA
www.bridgecreative.com
Bridges Design Group
USA
www.bridgesdesigngroup.com
Britt Funderburk
USA
brittfunderburk.com
Bronson Ma Creative
USA
www.bronsonma.com
Brook Group, LTD
USA
www.brookgroup.com/branding
brossman design
USA
www.brossman.com
Brown Ink Design
Australia
www.brownink.com.au
BRUEDESIGN
USA
www.nickbrue.com
Bruketa & Zinic
Croatia
00385 99 2117 507

Bryan Cooper Design
USA
www.cooperillustration.com

bryon hutchens | graphic design
USA
310-621-0677

B-Squared Advertising
USA
www.b2ads.com

Buchanan Design
USA
www.buchanandesign.com

Buffalo Design Group Inc.
USA
www.buffalodesigngroup.com

Bukka Design
USA
www.bukkadesign.com

Bunch
UK
www.bunchdesign.com

Burd & Patterson
USA
www.burdandpatterson.com

Bureau Blank
USA
512-557-6010

Burocratik—Design
Portugal
www.burocratik.com

Burton (Snowboards) Corp.
USA
802-652-3777

Business Identity Design
Australia
02 9555 5232

BXC nicelogo.com
USA
www.nicelogo.com

Bystrom Design
USA
www.bystromdesign.com

C.Cady Design
USA
423-326-7329

Cacao Design
Italy
www.cacaodesign.it

CAI Communications
USA
www.caicommunications.com

Caliber Creative, LLC
USA
214-741-4488

The Caliber Group
USA
calibergroup.com

Campbell Fisher Design
USA
www.thinkcfd.com

Canvas Astronauts & Agriculture
USA
www.bethecanvas.com

Canyon Creative
USA
702-262-9901

Caotica
Brazil
www.caotica.com.br

Capisce Design Inc.
USA
310-216-7042

Cappelli Communication Italy
Italy
www.ccommunication.it

CAPSULE
USA
www.capsule.us

Carlos Bela
Brazil
www.carlosbela.com

Carlson Marketing Worldwide
USA
763-212-8318

Carmi e Ubertis Milano Srl
Italy
www.communicationdesign.it

Carol Gravelle Graphic Design
USA
www.carolgravelledesign.com

Carousel30
USA
www.carousel30.com

Carrie Dennis Design
USA
www.carriedennisdesign.com

Carrihan Creative Group
USA
www.carrihan.com

Cashmere Creative
USA
585-300-7876

Cass Design Co.
USA
www.cassdesignco.com

Cassie Klingler Design
USA
www.cassieklingler.com

Catalyst Logo Design
USA
www.catalystlogos.com

Cause Design Co.
USA
215-886-0697

CDI Studios
USA
www.cdistudios.com

ceb design
Canada
www.cebdesign.com

CF Napa Brand Design
USA
cfnapa.com

Cfx
USA
www.cfx-inc.com

Chameleon Design Group, LLC
USA
www.chameleondg.com

Chapa Design
USA
www.chapadesign.com

Charles Design
USA
www.charlesdesigninc.com

Charles Henry Graphic Arts
USA
www.chgarts.com

Chase Design Group
USA
margochase.com

Chermayeff & Geismar Inc.
USA
www.cgstudionyc.com

Chimera Design
Australia
www.chimera.com.au

Chip Sheean
USA
707-225-4164

chirag ahir design
USA
www.relaxiamhere.com

Chris Herron Design
USA
www.chrisherrondesign.com

Chris Oth Creative
USA
www.chrisothcreative.com

Chris Rooney Illustration/ Design
USA
www.looneyrooney.com

Chris Yin Design
China

Christian Palino Design
USA
www.christianpalino.com

christiansen : creative
USA
715-381-8480

Christopher Labno
Poland
www.crislabno.com

Church Logo Gallery
USA
www.churchlogogallery.com

Cidma Group
Canada
514-524-4149

cincodemayo
Mexico
www.cincodemayo.com.mx

Cinnamon Design
USA
909-621-2975

Cinq Partners
USA
cinqpartners.com

Cisneros Design
USA
505-471-6699

Clarke/Thompson Advertising
USA
clarkethompson.com

Classic Lines Design
UK
www.classiclinesdesign.com

Clay McIntosh Creative
USA
www.claymcintosh.com

Clive Jacobson Design
USA
clivejacobson.com

Clockwork Studios
USA
210-545-3415

Clover Creative Group, LLC
USA
www.clovercreativegroup.com

Clusta Ltd
UK
www.clusta.com

Clutch Design
USA
www.clutchla.com

co:lab
USA
www.colabinc.com

Coastal Communities
USA
910-620-2542

Cocoon
Canada
www.cocoonbranding.com

Collaboration Reverberation
USA
www.thecrstudio.com

Colle + McVoy
USA
www.collemcvoy.com

Combustion
USA
www.thesparkmachine.com

Compass Design
USA
compassdesigninc.com

CONCEPTiCONS
USA
www.concepticons.net

CONCEPTO WORLDWIDE
Dominican Republic
809 965 6592

Concussion, llc
USA
817-336-6824 ext. 207

Conduit Studios
USA
616-454-6121

Conover
USA
www.studioconover.com

Contenido Neto
Mexico
www.contenidoneto.com.mx

ContrerasDesign
USA
www.contrerasdesign.com

Coolstone Design Works
USA
www.coolstone.com

Copia Creative, Inc.
USA
www.copiacreative.com

Copperfin
USA
425-881-3302

Corder Philips
USA
corderphilips.com

Corporate Design Associates
USA
cdaorlando.com

Corporate Image Consultants, Inc.
USA
www.cibydesign.com

Cosmic Egg Studios
USA
781-393-1949

Courtney & Company
USA
www.courtneyco.com

Crackerbox
USA
www.crackerbox.us

Crave, Inc
USA
www.cravebrands.com

Creative House
Canada
www.creativehouse.com

Creative Madhouse
USA
www.creativemadhouse.com

Creative NRG
USA
www.creative-nrg.com

Creative Soapbox
USA
www.creativesoapbox.com

Cristina Lagorio
USA
crislagorio.com

Critt Graham
USA
404-519-2158

Crosby Associates
USA
www.crosbyassociates.com

CrossGrain Creative Studios
USA
crossgrain.com

CS Design
USA
320-420-4392

Culture Pilot
USA
713-868-4100

Curtis Sharp Design
USA
www.curtissharpdesign.com

cypher13
USA
www.cypher13.com

D&Dre Creative
USA
www.deandrecreative.com

D&i (Design and Image)
USA
www.seebrandgo.com

dache
Switzerland
www.dache.ch

Daggerfin
USA
248-659-1010

DAGSVERK—Design and Advertising
Iceland
www.dagsverk.is

dale harris
Australia
www.daleharris.com

dandy idea
USA
www.dandyidea.com

Daniel Matthews
UK
www.danielmatthews.net

Daniel Sim Design
Australia
www.danielsim.com/landing.html

Dara Creative
Ireland
www.daracreative.ie

DAS Creative
Vietnam
www.dascreative.com

David Airey
UK
www.davidairey.com

DAVID BARATH DESIGN
Hungary
www.davidbarath.com

David Beck Design
USA
214-828-9622

David Clark Design
USA
davidclarkdesign.com

David Gramblin
USA
918-261-2042

David Kampa
USA
512-636-3791

David Maloney
USA
www.david-maloney.com

Davina Chatkeon Design
USA
www.davinachatkeon.com

Davis Design
USA
303-399-8111

DBD+A Studio
USA
www.dbdastudio.com

DDB SF
USA
www.ddbsf.com

Deep Design
USA
deepdesign.com

Deere Design Group
USA
410-693-8098

Default
Thailand
www.defaultbkk.org

DeFord Designs
USA
defordesigns.com

Delikatessen
Germany
www.delikatessen-hamburg.com

delphine
USA
858-759-7181

demasijones
Australia
www.demasijones.com

Demographic Inc.
USA
www.demographicinc.com

Denis Olenik Design Studio
Belarus
denisolenik.com

Dennard, Lacey & Associates
USA
www.dennardlacey.com

Dept 3
USA
www.dept3.com

Design & Co
USA
617-524-1856

Design Army
USA
www.designarmy.com

Design Fish
USA
www.designfish.com

Design Hub
USA
www.dessinfournir.com

design june
France
www.designjune.com

Design Matters Inc!
USA
www.designmattersinc.com

Design Nut
USA
www.designnut.com

Design One
USA
www.d1inc.com

Design Partners Inc.
USA
www.design-partners.com

design:tn
USA
www.designtn.com

Designbolaget
Denmark
www.designbolaget.dk

Designer Case
Poland
www.designercase.net

designfocus
Korea
www.designfocus.co.kr

designlab,inc
USA
www.designlabinc.com

DesignPoint, Inc.
USA
www.designpointinc.com

Dessein
Australia
www.dessein.com.au

Diagram
Poland
www.diagram.pl

Diana Graham
Germany

Dickerson
USA
817-207-9009

Did Graphics
Iran
www.didgraphics.com

Digital Flannel
USA
digitalflannel.com
DikranianDesign
USA
203-767-3964
Dill and Company
USA
301-760-7282
Dino Design
USA
www.dinodesign-o.com
Ditto!
USA
www.dittodoesit.com
Diva Design
USA
divadesign.com
dmayne design
USA
www.dmaynedesign.com
DMG Asociados, S.A.
Panama
Doink, Inc.
USA
www.doinkdesign.com
DotArt Design Solutions
USA
www.dotartdesignsolutions.com
Dotzero Design
USA
www.dotzerodesign.com
Double A Creative
USA
www.doubleacreative.com
Double Brand
Poland
www.doublebrand.pl
Douglas Beatty
UK
+44 079 603 007 12
Dr. Alderete
Mexico
www.jorgealderete.com
Dragulescu Studio
USA
www.dragulescu.com
Dragyn Studios
USA
www.dragynstudios.com
Draplin Design Co.
USA
www.draplin.com
Draward
Latvia
www.draward.com
Dreamedia Studios
USA
www.dreamediastudios.com
Driven Communications
USA
248-703-5762
DTM_INC
The Netherlands
075 635 52 46
DUEL Purpose
USA
www.duelpurpose.com
Duffy & Partners
USA
www.duffy.com
Dustin Commer
USA
www.dustincommer.com
DUSTIN PARKER ARTS
USA
www.dustinparkerarts.com
Dylan Menges
USA
www.dylanmenges.com
e-alw.com
Poland
e-alw.com
ebb+flow design
USA
www.eandfdesign.com
Eben Design
USA
www.ebendesign.com
Effective Media Solutions
Canada
www.thinkeffective.com
Effusion Creative Solutions
USA
www.effusiondesign.com
EFL Design, LLC
USA
www.efldesign.com

eggnerd
USA
www.eggnerd.com
Eggra
Macedonia
www.eggra.com
eight a.m. brand design (shanghai) Co., Ltd
China
www.8-a-m.com
Eisenberg And Associates
USA
www.eisenberg-inc.com
El Creative
USA
www.elcreative.com
El Paso, Galeria de Comunicacion
Spain
www.elpasocomunicacion.com
Element
USA
www.elementville.com
Elevation Creative Studios
USA
www.elevationcreative.com
elf design
USA
650-358-9973
Elixir Design
USA
www.elixirdesign.com
ellen bruss design
USA
www.ebd.com
Ellis Kaiser
USA
www.elliskaiser.com
Emu Design Studio
USA
www.emudesign.com
Endura
USA
501-217-9191
Enforme Interactive
USA
www.8vodesigns.com
Enlightened Design
USA
www.enlightened-design.com
ENNEMM Ad Agency
Iceland
3545708700
Entermotion Design Studio
USA
www.entermotion.com
Entropy Brands
USA
www.entropybrands.com
The Envision Group
USA
www.envision-grp.com
Envizion Dezigns
USA
www.enviziondezigns.com
ER Marketing
USA
www.ermarketing.net
Eric Baker Design Assoc. Inc
USA
www.ericbakerdesign.com
Erich Brechbuhl [Mixer]
Switzerland
www.mixer.ch
ErikArt Design
USA
www.erikart.com
Esse Design
USA
970-925-9578
Essex Two
USA
www.sx2.com
EvenDesign
USA
310-379-4000
Evenson Design Group
USA
evensondesign.com
Extra Point Creative
USA
www.extrapointcreative.com
Extrabrand
Russia
www.extrabrand.ru
Extraverage Productions
Hungary
www.extraverage.net

eye4 inc.
USA
www.eye4.com
Eyebeam Creative LLC
USA
www.eyebeamcreative.com
Eyescape
Malaysia
design.eyescape.co.uk
Eyespike Design
USA
www.eyespike.com
Ezzo Design
Portugal
+351 229969263
face
UK
www.face-group.co.uk
Factor Tres
Mexico
www.factortres.com.mx
Factory Creative
USA
972-624-5568
Faith
Canada
www.faith.ca
fallindesign studio
Russia
www.faldin.ru
Fandam Studio
South Africa
+27(0)829017699
Fangman Design
USA
www.fangmandesign.com
Fargo Design Co., Inc.
USA
www.fargodesignco.com
Fashion Graphics
Russia
www.f-gr.com
Fekete + Company
USA
www.feketeco.com
Felixsockwell.com
USA
www.felixsockwell.com
Fernandez Design
USA
www.fernandezdesign.com
FigDesign
USA
www.figdesign.com
Finch Creative
USA
www.finchcreative.com
Fine Dog Creative
USA
www.finedogcreative.com
Fiton
Iceland
fiton.is
Fitting Group
USA
www.fittingroup.com
FiveNineteen: a print + motion + interactive design boutique.
USA
www.fivenineteen.com
Fixation Marketing
USA
www.fixation.com
Flaherty Robinson Inc.
USA
401-245-4236
Flaxenfield, Inc.
USA
www.flaxenfield.com
Fleishman Hillard
USA
314-982-9149
Flipcide
USA
www.flipcide.com
The Flores Shop
USA
www.thefloresshop.com
Flory Design, Inc.
USA
florydesign.com
Flow Creative
USA
www.flowcreative.net
Flying Mouse Studio
USA
269-857-7411

Flywheel Design
USA
919-683-8164
Fons Schiedon
Germany
www.fonztv.nl
For the Love of Creating
USA
www.fortheloveofcreating.com
Form
UK
www.form.uk.com
Form G
USA
www.formgdesign.com
Formula Design
USA
www.formuladesign.com
Fossil
USA
972-699-4923
Foundry
USA
foundryadco.com
Fox Fire Creative
USA
www.foxfirecreative.com
Francis Hogan
Canada
www.francishogan.com
Freakstyle Media Group
USA
www.thefmgroup.net
Fredrik Lewander
Sweden
www.portfolios.com/
fredriklewander
Fresh Oil
USA
www.freshoil.com
Freshwater Design
USA
www.rhondafreshwater.com
Fumiko Noon
USA
619-261-7118
Funk/Levis & Associates, Inc.
USA
www.funklevis.com
Funnel Design Group
USA
www.funneldesigngroup.com
Fusion Advertising
USA
www.fusionista.com
fuszion
USA
fuszion.com
Futrell Design Company
USA
www.tomfutrell.com
FutureBrand BC&H
Brazil
www.futurebrand.com
G&G Advertising
USA
505-843-8113
Gabe Re is a designer.
USA
gabere.com
Gabriel Kalach • V I S U A L communication
USA
786-866-5956
Galperin Design, Inc.
USA
www.galperindesign.com
Garbow Graphics, Inc.
USA
203-733-0673
Gardner Design
USA
316-691-8808
www.gardnerdesign.com
Garfinkel Design
USA
www.garfinkeldesign.com
Gary Sample Design
USA
513-271-7785
Garza-Allen Designs
USA
281-804-9436
GCG
USA
817-332-4600

Gee + Chung Design
USA
www.geechungdesign.com
Gee Creative
USA
843-853-3086
THE GENERAL DESIGN CO.
USA
www.generaldesignco.com
Gesture Studio
USA
www.gesturestudio.com
Giles Design Inc.
USA
210-224-8378
GingerBee Creative
USA
406-443-3032
Gingerbread Lady
UK
www.gingerbread-lady.co.uk
Gizwiz Studio
Malaysia
www.logodesigncreation.com
Glitschka Studios
USA
www.glitschka.com
Go Media
USA
216-939-0000
gocreativ
USA
301-331-3614
Goldforest
USA
www.goldforest.com
Goodform Design
USA
www.goodformdesign.com
GOTCHA DESIGN
USA
www.gotchadesign.com
GrafiQa Creative Services
USA
www.grafiqa.com
Graham Hanson Design
USA
www.grahamhanson.com
Grapefruit
Romania
www.grapefruit.ro
Graphic-FX
USA
865-983-0363
Green Olive Media
USA
www.greenolivemedia.com
Greg Walters Design
USA
206-362-1310
The Greater Good Design
USA
www.greatergooddesign.com
Greteman Group
USA
316-263-1004
Grey Matter Group
USA
www.greymattergroup.com
Grey Matters, LLC
USA
314-772-1331
Gridwerk
USA
www.gridwerk.net
Ground Zero Communications
USA
678-461-5634
grow
Qatar
www.growqatar.com
gsFITCH
United Arab Emirates
www.gsfitch.com
GTA—Gregory Thomas Associates
USA
www.gtabrands.com
GTC Media
USA
305-608-7269
Guernsey Graphics
USA
207-829-4023
Gyula Nemeth
Hungary
seadevilworks.blogspot.com

H2 Design of Texas
USA
www.h2dot.com
Habitat Design
USA
www.designbyhabitat.com
Haller Design
USA
480-390-8722
Hallmark Cards, Inc
USA
www.hallmark.com
Hand dizajn studio
Croatia
www.hand.hr
Hanna & Associates
USA
208-667-2428
Happy Giraffe
UK
happy-giraffe.com
Harkey Design
USA
harkeydesign.com
harlan creative
USA
714-469-0795
Hausch Design Agency LLC
USA
www.hauschdesign.com
Haute Haus Creative
USA
www.hahacreative.com
Haven Productions
USA
www.havenproductions.net
Hayes+Company
Canada
416-536-5438
Hazen Creative, Inc.
USA
www.hazencreative.com
Headwerk
USA
www.headwerk.com
Hecht Design
USA
www.hechtdesign.com
Heck Yeah!
USA
www.heckyeah.com
Heins Creative, Inc.
USA
www.heinscreative.com
Heisel Design
USA
www.heiseldesign.com
helium.design
Germany
www.heliumdesign.de
Helius Creative Advertising
USA
www.freewebs.com/utahrugbyguy/index.htm
Henjum Creative
USA
www.henjumcreative.com
henriquez lara
Mexico
www.henriquezlara.com
Hep
Turkey
www.hep.com.tr
HERMANO S TALASTAS
USA
703-966-3312
Hexanine
USA
www.hexanine.com
Hiebing
USA
hiebing.com
High Fiber Design
Switzerland
www.highfiberdesign.com
High Tide Creative
USA
www.hightidecreative.com
Hill Design Studios
USA
www.hilldesignstudios.com
Hinge
USA
www.pivotalbrands.com
Hinge Incorporated
USA
www.pivotalbrands.com

Hirschmann Design
USA
303-449-7363
Hirshorn Zuckerman Design Group
USA
hzdg.com
HKLM
South Africa
27114616890
HMK Archive
USA
hmktest.blogspot.com
HMS Design
USA
203-831-8600
hnd
USA
562-237-1243
HOLAGRAPHIC
USA
www.hellographic.com
Holmberg Design, LLC
USA
www.holmbergdesign.com
Home Grown Logos
USA
www.homegrownlogos.com
Honest Bros.
USA
303-847-8225
Honey Design
Canada
www.honey.on.ca
HOOK
USA
www.hookusa.com
Hornall Anderson
USA
www.hadw.com
Hotiron Creative, LLC
USA
www.hotironcreative.com
Hove Design Works
USA
www.hovedesignworks.com
Howerton+White
USA
www.howertonwhite.com
Howling Good Designs
USA
howlinggooddesigns.com
Hoyne Design
Australia
www.hoyne.com.au
Hubbell Design Works
USA
www.hubbelldesignworks.com
huber+co.
USA
www.huberandco.com
HuebnerPetersen
USA
970-219-8904
Hula+Hula
Mexico
www.hulahula.com.mx
humanot
USA
www.humanot.com
Hutchinson Associates, Inc.
USA
www.hutchinson.com
Hvita husid
Iceland
+354 562 1177
Hybrid Design
USA
www.hybrid-design.com
Hyperakt
USA
www.hyperakt.com
ID.Brand
Indonesia
www.idbrand.co.id
id29
USA
www.id29.com
Idea Bank Marketing
USA
www.ideabankmarketing.com
Idealogy Design + Advertising
USA
812-981-4675
Identica Branding and Design
Canada
www.identica.com

Identity Kitchen
USA
818-459-3993
Identity33, LLC
USA
www.identity33.com
iDgital Design Studio, Inc.
USA
954-701-8913
IE Design + Communications
USA
310-376-9600
IF marketing & advertising
USA
512-930-5558
IGLOO57 Limited
UK
www.igloo57.com
Ikola Designs
USA
763-533-3440
Illustra Graphics
USA
www.illustra-graphics.com
Imadesign, Corp.
Russia
www.imadesign.ru
Image Communications, Inc.
USA
www.imagecom.net
The Image Group
USA
www.imagegroup.com
IMAGEHAUS
USA
612-377-8700
imagenation
USA
317-681-1710
Imaginaria
USA
www.imaginariacreative.com
I-MANIFEST
USA
www.i-manifeststudio.com
Impressions Design and Print Ltd
UK
www.impressionsdesignandprint.co.uk
Imulus
USA
303-247-0550
Incitrio
USA
858-202-1822
INDE
Greece
www.behance.net/inde_graphics
Independent
Philippines
www.tinged.org
Indicia Design Inc
USA
www.indiciadesign.com
Indigo Creative
USA
indigocreativestudio.com
Infiltrate Media
South Africa
www.infiltratemedia.co.za
Ink Graphix
Sweden
www.inkgraphix.com
innfusion studios
USA
www.innfusionstudios.com
Insight Design
USA
316-262-0085
Integer Group—Midwest
USA
ww.integer.com
Integrated Communications (ICLA)
USA
310-851-8066
icla.com
Integrated Media, Inc.
USA
317-508-5022
Interbrand São Paulo
Brazil
www.interbrand.com

Interrobang Design Collaborative, Inc.
USA
www.interrobangdesign.com
Intersection Creative
USA
www.intersectioncreative.com
Intrinsic Design
USA
www.intrinsic-design.biz
Invisible Associates
USA
www.invisibleassociates.com
Iperdesign, Inc.
USA
www.iperdesign.com
Iratxe Mumford
USA
www.iratxedesigns.com
Iron Creative Communication
USA
www.ironcreative.com
Iskender Asanaliev
Turkey
www.behance.net/iskender
ivan2design
USA
www.ivan2.com
j1s designs
USA
www.tracyjones.org
J6Studios
USA
www.j6studios.com
Jackrabbit Design
USA
www.jumpingjackrabbit.com
Jackson Spalding Creative
USA
www.jacksonspaldingcreative.com
Jacob Tyler Creative Group
USA
619-379-0007
Jajo, Inc.
USA
www.jajo.net
James Clark Design
USA
206-623-0908
James Olson Design
USA
612-618-3159
Jan Sabach Design
Czech Republic
www.sabach.cz
Jan Vranovsky
Czech Republic
ra30412.com
Jane Cameron Design
Australia
61882272078
Janson Straub
USA
920-217-0847
Jared Milam Design
USA
www.jaredmilamdesign.com
Jarek Kowalczyk
Poland
www.jarekkowalczyk.com
Jason Drumheller
USA
www.jasondrumheller.com
JASON GRUBE DESIGN
USA
www.jasongrubedesign.com
Jason Kochis
USA
www.jasonkochis.com
Jason Pillon
USA
925-243-1936
Javen Design
USA
www.javendesign.com
Jawa and Midwich
UK
www.jawa-midwich.com
Jean Peterson Design
USA
301-631-2401
jeda creative
USA
jedacreative.com
Jeff Andrews Design
USA
www.jeffandrewsdesign.com

Jeff Fisher LogoMotives
USA
www.jfisherlogomotives.com
Jeff Kern Design
USA
www.jeffkerndesign.com
Jeffhalmos
Canada
www.jeffhalmos.com
Jelena Drobac
Serbia
www.d-ideashop.com
Jenn David Design
USA
www.jenndavid.com
Jennifer Braham Design
USA
512-707-9023
Jennifer McAlister Graphic Design
USA
817-598-8662
Jennifer Panepinto, LLC
USA
201-321-8994
Jenny Kolcun Freelance Designer
USA
415-331-7202
Jenny Ng
USA
646-283-6878
Jeremy Stott
USA
801-334-5499
Jerron Ames
USA
801-636-7929
Jesse Kaczmarek
USA
917-657-6925
Jessica Peltz Design
USA
310-994-5109
JG Creative
USA
www.jgc.me
jing
USA
216-272-7398
JK Design
USA
www.jkdesign.com
jKaczmarek
USA
www.jkaczmarek.com
JM Design Co.
USA
www.jmdesignco.net
The Joe Bosack Graphic Design Co.
USA
www.joebosack.com
joe miller's company
USA
joemillersco.com
Joel Krieger
USA
www.joelkrieger.com
Johnston Duffy
USA
www.johnstonduffy.com
Jon Flaming Design
USA
jonflaming.com
Jon Kay Design
USA
jonkaydesign.com
Jonathan Rice & Company
USA
www.jriceco.com
joni dunbar design
USA
601-520-3309
Josh Higgins Design
USA
www.joshhiggins.com
JoshuaCreative
USA
559-906-0504
Jovan Rocanov
Serbia
www.rocanov.com
JP Global Marketing, Inc.
USA
jpglobalmarketing.com

Juancazu
Columbia
313 350 40 44
Judson Design
USA
www.judsondesign.com
Juicebox Designs
USA
615-297-1682
juis design inc
USA
www.julsdesign.com
justpixels.com
USA
703-266-8535
Kahn Design
USA
www.kahn-design.com
kaimere
United Arab Emirates
kaimere.com
Karl Design Vienna
Austria
www.karl-design-logos.com
Karmalaundry
USA
www.karmalaundry.com
Kastelov
Bulgaria
www.kastelov.com
Kate Resnick
USA
202-487-1414
KBO PROTOTYPES
Mexico
7711299228
Ken Dyment
Canada
www.kennyd.ca
Ken Shafer Design
USA
www.kenshaferdesign.com
Kendall Creative Shop, Inc.
USA
214-827-6680
KENNETH DISENO
Mexico
www.kengraf.net
Kern Design Group
USA
www.kerndesigngroup.com
Kessler Digital Design
USA
www.kesslerdigital.com
Ketch 22 Creative
USA
917-450-9314
Kevin Creative
Canada
www.kevincreative.com
Kevin France Design, Inc.
USA
336-765-6213
The Key
Australia
www.whproject.com
Keyword Design
USA
www.keyworddesign.com
Khoa Le
USA
512-350-6718
kickit communications
USA
www.kickit.biz
Kiku Obata & Company
USA
www.kikuobata.com
Kinesis, Inc.
USA
www.kinesisinc.com
King Design Office
USA
www.kingdesignoffice.com
KITA International | Visual Playground
Germany
www.kita-berlin.com
Kloom
Brazil
+55 (11) 3884-0549
Koch Creative Group
USA
www.kochcreativegroup.com
KOESTER design
USA
www.koesterdesign.com

Koetter Design
USA
502-515-3092
KONG Design Group
USA
www.kennyong.com
Konstellation
Denmark
www.konstellation.dk
Kradel Design
USA
610-505-0121
Kraftaverk—Design Studio
Iceland
www.kraftaverk.is
Krghettojuice
Italy
www.krghettojuice.com
Kristian Andersen + Associates
USA
www.kristianandersen.com
KROG, d.o.o.
Slovenia
www.krog.si
KTD
USA
www.designluminosity.com
Kurt for Hire
USA
www.kurtforhire.com
Kuznets
Russia
www.kuznets.net
KZ creative
USA
www.kzcreative.com
The Laing Group
USA
717-526-4702
LaMonica Design
USA
lamonicadesign.com
Landkamer Partners, Inc.
USA
landkamerpartners.com
Landor Associates
USA
www.sfo.landor.com
Lapada Solutions
USA
www.lapadasolutions.com
The Laster Group
USA
www.lastergroup.com
Latinbrand
Ecuador
www.latin-brand.com
Laura Coe Design Associates
USA
619-223-0909
Laura Manthey Design
USA
lauramantheydesign.com
lazy snail—art factory
Greece
+30 2810285037
LCD Incorporated
USA
415-902-5642
Leah Hartley
Australia
leahhartley.com
LeBoYe
Indonesia
62 21 7199676
LEKKERWERKEN
Germany
www.lekkerwerken.com
Les Kerr Creative
USA
www.leskerr.net
Lesniewicz Associates
USA
www.designtoinfluence.com
Letter 7
USA
212-595-7445
Letterbox Design
Canada
www.letterboxdesign.com
Level B Design
USA
www.levelbdesign.com
Leytonmedia
Chile
www.leytonmedia.com

LGA / Jon Cain
USA
www.joncain.com
Lichtsignale
Germany
www.lichtsignale.de
Lichtwitz—Buro fur Visual Kommunikation
Austria
www.lichtwitz.com
Lienhart Design
USA
www.lienhartdesign.com
Liew Design, Inc.
USA
www.liewdesign.com
LIFT HERE, Inc.
USA
www.lifthere.com
Lippincott
USA
www.lippincott.com
Liquidgraphic Design Inc.
USA
www.liquidgraphic.com
Lisa Brussell Design
USA
415-454-7519
Lisa Wood Design
USA
916-961-8744
Liska + Associates Communication Design
USA
www.liska.com
Little Jacket
USA
www.little-jacket.com
Living Creative Design
USA
www.livingcreative.com
Living Creative Design
USA
www.livingcreative.com
Lizette Gecel
USA
804-359-1711
LOCHS
The Netherlands
www.lochs.nl
Logan Cantu
USA
210-396-1908
Logoboom
USA
www.logoboom.com
logobyte
Turkey
www.logobyte.com
LogoDesignGuru.com
USA
www.logodesignguru.com
Logoidentity.com
USA
www.logoidentity.com
Logologik
Poland
48602152695
LogoMotto.com
Brunei
www.logomotto.com
Logostogo
Australia
07 38140802
The Logo Factory Inc.
Canada
www.thelogofactory.com
Looney Ricks Kiss Architects, Inc.
USA
303-882-2448
Loop Design
USA
www.loopdesigngroup.com
Louise Fili
USA
www.louisefili.com
LSD
Spain
www.lsdspace.com
Lucero Design
USA
505-459-8112
Lucky Dog Graphic Design
USA
323-882-8241

Lukatarina
Slovenia
www.lukatarina.net
Luke Baker
USA
www.creativehotlist.com/lbaker2
Luke Despatie & The Design Firm
Canada
www.thedesignfirm.ca
lunabrand design group
USA
www.lunabrands.com
Lynch Design
Australia
www.lynchdesign.com.au
Lysergid
France
www.lysergid.com
M. Brady Clark Design
USA
www.mbradyclark.com
M3 Advertising Design
USA
www.m3ad.com/new
MacLaren McCann Calgary
Canada
403-261-7155
Mad Dog Graphx
USA
www.thedogpack.com
Madomat
UK
4.4207229707 ext. 011
Maida Design
USA
203-431-4352
MangoGlobal
Hong Kong
www.mangoglobal.com
MANMADE
USA
www.manmade.com
Marc Posch Design, Inc
USA
www.marcposchdesign.com
MARC USA
USA
412-512-3563
Marina Rose
UK
www.marinarose.co.uk
Mariqua Design
USA
www.mariqua.com
Mark Oliver, Inc.
USA
805-686-5166
markatos | moore
USA
www.mm-sf.com
Marlin
USA
www.marlinco.com
m-Art
USA
www.m-art.org
The Martin Group
USA
www.martingroupmarketing.com
Mary Hutchison Design LLC
USA
www.maryhutchisondesign.com
Matt Johnson
USA
www.ceciliaparkerjohnson.com
Matt Shepherd
USA
www.msadvdesign.com
Matt Whitley
USA
501-542-4073
Matthew Wells Design
Canada
www.matthewwells.ca
mattisimo
USA
www.mattisimo.com
Mattson Creative
USA
www.mattsoncreative.com
Mauck Groves Branding & Design
USA
www.mauckgroves.com
Max Kelly Design
USA
www.maxkelly.com

maximo, inc.
USA
www.maximoinc.com
Maycreate
USA
www.maycreate.com
maynard kay
USA
maynardk.com
Mazemedia
USA
www.mazemedia.com
McArtor Design
USA
www.mcartordesign.com
McConnell Creative
USA
248-420-9148
mccoycreative
USA
www.mccoycreative.com
McElveney & Palozzi Design Group, Inc.
USA
585-473-7630
McGarrah/Jessee
USA
www.mc-j.com
McGuire Design
USA
www.mcguiredesign.com
McMillian Design
USA
www.mcmilliandesign.com
McQuillen Creative Group
USA
www.mcquillencreative.com
McRae Creative Group, Inc.
USA
704-342-2880
MDUK Media
UK
www.mdukmedia.com
Mediahuis
The Netherlands
www.mediahuis.nl
medium control
USA
mediumcontrol.com
MEGA
USA
www.mollyeckler.com
Meir Billet Ltd.
Israel
Menikoff Design
USA
206-383-0380
MetaDesign
USA
www.metadesign.com
Methodologie
USA
www.methodologie.com
Mez Design
USA
www.mezdesign.com
MFDI
USA
570-372-4623
MGPdesign
USA
www.mgpdesign.com
Michael Doret Graphic Design
USA
michaeldoret.com
Michael Freimuth Creative
USA
www.michaelfreimuth.com
Michael O'Connell
USA
904-705-4437
The Micro Agency
Canada
www.themicroagency.com
Mikhail Gubergrits
Russia
www.linii.ru
Miles Design
USA
www.milesdesign.com
Milk Creative Services
Ukraine
www.milk.ua
Miller Creative LLC
USA
www.yaelmiller.com

Miller Meiers Design for Communication
USA
www.millermeiers.com
Minale Tattersfield and Partners Ltd
UK
www.mintat.co.uk
Mindgruve
USA
www.mindgruve.com
MINE™
USA
www.minesf.com
Mingovits Design
USA
www.mingovits.com
mIQelangelo
Serbia
www.miqelangelo.com
MiresBall
USA
www.miresball.com
Miriello Grafico, Inc.
USA
www.miriellografico.com
Mirko Ilić Corp
USA
www.mirkoilic.com
Mitchel Design Inc.
USA
www.mitcheldesign.com
Mitre Agency
USA
www.mitreagency.com
The Mixx
USA
212-695-6663
MLS Creative Services
USA
www.mlsnet.com
mod&co
USA
www.modandco.com
Modern Dog Design Co.
USA
www.moderndog.com
Mojo Solo
USA
651-789-6656
Moker Ontwerp
The Netherlands
www.mokerontwerp.nl
moko creative
Australia
www.moko.com.au
MondoVox, Inc.
USA
312-224-8869
Monigle Associates Inc.
USA
www.monigle.com
monkeebox inc.
USA
703-606-9044
monkeygrass
USA
www.monkeygrass.us
Monster Design Company
USA
www.monsterdesignco.com
Moonlit Creative Group
USA
770-978-0116
moosylvania
USA
moosylvania.com
More Branding+Communication
USA
918-519-1605
morrow mckenzie design
USA
www.morrowmckenzie.com
Mortensen Design
USA
650-988-0946
Moscato Design
USA
moscatodesign.blogspot.com
Mosmondesign
Australia
www.home.netspeed.com.au/mosmondesign
Moss Creative
USA
www.mosscreative.com

MSI
USA
312-946-6146
Muamer Adilovic DESIGN
Bosnia & Herzegovina
logotip.ba
MUELLER design
USA
www.muellerdesign.com
mugur mihai
ROMANIA
www.mugurmihai.com
Muku Studios
USA
www.mukustudios.com
MultiAdaptor
UK
www.multiadaptor.com
Mungioli Design
USA
609-680-6960
Murillo Design, Inc.
USA
www.murillodesign.com
Mystic Design, Inc.
USA
www.mysticdesign.net
Nanantha Shroff
USA
562-858-4858
Nastasha Beatty Designs
USA
201-234-7560
Natasha Mileshina
USA
www.flickr.com/photos/bubbo-tubbo
Natoli Design Group
USA
www.natolidesign.com
Nectar Graphics
USA
www.nectargraphics.com
neodesign
Taiwan
+886.7.554.8657
NeoGine Communication Design Ltd
New Zealand
www.neogine.co.nz
NeoGrafica
Costa Rica
506-24400061
Newhouse Design
USA
406-600-6532
Nicole Romer
Australia
www.nicoleromer.com.au
Niedermeier Design
USA
206-351-3927
Noble
USA
417-875-5353
noe design
USA
www.noedesign.com
Nordyke Design
USA
860-233-8874
NOT A CANNED HAM
USA
404-316-2132
Novasoul
USA
818-753-4175
Nynas
USA
214-566-5166
o graphicstudio
USA
www.ographicstudio.com
O!
Iceland
www.oid.is
Oakley Design Studios
USA
oakleydesign.com
Octane
USA
www.octanestudios.com
octane inc.
USA
hi toctdocign.com
Octavo Design Pty Ltd
Australia
www.octavodesign.com.au

Offbeat Design
USA
734-214-1996
The Office of Art+Logik
USA
612-599-0286
O'Hare Design
USA
oharedesign.com
ohTwentyone
USA
www.ohtwentyone.com
Olson
USA
www.oco.com
Oluzen
Dominican Republic
www.oluzen.com
O'Mahony Design LLC
USA
www.omahonydesign.com
On Design, Inc.
USA
www.ond.com
oneal design
USA
www.onealdesigns.com
Onoma, LLC
USA
onomadesign.com
Oomingmak Design Company
USA
817-983-0142
Opolis Design, LLC
USA
www.opolisdesign.com
Organic Grid
USA
www.organicgrid.com
Origin
United Arab Emirates
9716248499
Orn Smari I Design
Iceland
www.ornsmari.net
Oscar Morris
USA
512-293-5954
Oxide Design Co.
USA
www.oxidedesign.com
OzbeyArt
USA
703-973-1551
p11creative
USA
714-641-2090
Pagliuco Design Company
USA
www.pagliuco.com
Pale Horse Design
USA
www.palehorsedesign.com
Pappas Group
USA
703-349-7227
Parachute Design
USA
612-359-4387
Paradigm New Media Group
USA
www.pnmg.com
Paradox Box
Russia
www.paradoxbox.ru
Paragon Marketing Communications
Kuwait
www.paragonmc.com
paralleldesigned
USA
www.paralleldesigned.com
Parallele gestion de marques
Canada
www.parallele.ca
ParkerWhite
USA
www.parkerwhite.com
Passing Notes, Inc.
USA
www.passing-notes.com
pat sinclair design
USA
610-896-8618
Pat Taylor Inc.
202-338-0962

Pat Walsh Design, LLC
USA
440-995-5118
Patten ID
USA
pattenid.com
Patterson Visual
USA
www.pattersonvisual.com
Paul Black Design
USA
www.paulblackdesign.com
Paul Jobson
USA
www.pauljobson.com
pb&j creative
USA
302-836-5838
Pear Tree Design
USA
www.triciahamon.com
pearpod
USA
949-212-7681
Peel
USA
505-400-6426
Pelco
USA
www.pelco.com
Penhouse Design
Ireland
www.penhouse.ie
Pennebaker
USA
www.pennebaker.com
People Design
USA
www.peopledesign.com
Pepe Menendez
Cuba
537 831 1759
Perdue Creative
USA
www.perduecreative.com
Periscope
USA
612-399-0461
Peritus Public Relations
USA
502-618-5886
Peter Gibbons
UK
www.petergibbons.net
PETTUS CREATIVE
USA
860-778-5112
Pherra
Romania
www.pherra.com
Philip J Smith
Australia
61415897004
Phony Lawn
USA
www.phonylawn.com
Pictogram Studio
USA
301-962-9630
Pikant marketing
Croatia
38548222127
Pink Tank Creative
Australia
www.pinktank.com.au
Pinnacle Design Center
USA
www.pinnacledesigncenter.com
Pivot Lab
USA
www.pivotlab.com
PixelGood.
USA
www.pixelgood.com
Pixellente!
USA
www.pixellente.com
Pixelube
USA
www.pixelube.com
Planet Propaganda
USA
www.planetpropaganda.com
Plumbline Studios
USA
www.plumbline.com

PMKFA
Japan
www.pmkfa.com
POLLARDdesign
USA
www.pollarddesign.com
Porkka & Kuutsa Oy
Finland
www.porkka-kuutsa.fi
PositiveZero Ltd.
Czech Republic
www.positivezero.co.uk
PosterV.Design Studio
Hungary
www.pocsposters.hu
Power Plus Advertising
Kuwait
00965 7231371
Prana Design + Art Studios
Australia
www.pranastudios.com.au
Prejean Creative
USA
www.prejeancreative.com
Primarily Rye LLC
USA
primarilyrye.com
Printt Diseñadores, s.c.
Mexico
(525) 55 5520 6001
proteus
USA
www.proteusdesign.com
Pure Fusion Media
USA
www.purefusionmedia.com
Pure Identity Design
USA
www.pureidentitydesign.com
Purpled : Graphic Design Studio
USA
www.purpledcreative.com
Q
Germany
www.q-home.de
Q Design
USA
773-383-5601
Q Digital Studio
USA
www.qdigitalstudio.com
Qualitá Design
Brazil
www.qualitadesign.com.br
QUANGO
USA
www.quangoinc.com
R Design LLC
USA
720-933-3816
R&R Partners
USA
702-228-0222
RADAR Agency
USA
www.radaragency.com
Rainy Day Designs
USA
rainydaydesigns.org
rajasandhu.com
Canada
www.rajasandhu.com
Ramp
USA
www.rampcreative.com
Randy Mosher Design
USA
randymosherdesign.com
Range
USA
www.rangeus.com
RARE Design
USA
www.raredesign.com
Ray Dugas Design
USA
cadc.auburn.edu/graphicdesign/ray.html
RAZAUNO
USA
www.razauno.com
RDQLUS Creative
USA
www.rdqlus.com
RDY
Macedonia
www.myspace.com/rushers dieyoung

Reactive Mediums
USA
517-290-6156

reaves design
USA
www.wbreaves.com

Red Clover Studio
USA
206-683-2314

Red Headed Frog Design
UK
07838 45 52 15

Red Studio Inc
USA
503-228-9493

Redbeard Communications Inc.
USA
www.redbeard.com

RedBrand
Russia
www.golovach.ru/works/

RedinWyden
USA
www.redinwyden.com

Redpoint design
USA
989-837-5999

RedSpark Creative
New Zealand
www.redspark.co.nz

rehab(r) communication graphics
USA
rehabgraphics.com

Remo Strada Design
USA
www.remostrada.com

renaud garnier smart rebranding
USA
510-653-8809

Resin Design
Australia
www.resindesign.com.au

Retro DC
USA
www.retrodc.com

Rhombus, Inc.
USA
www.rhombusdesign.net

Rhumb Designs, Inc.
USA
www.rhumbdesigns.com

Riccardo Sabioni
USA
www.yeslulu.com

RICH design studio
Kazakhstan
www.richdesign.kz

Richard Rios
USA

richard zeid design
USA
www.rzdesign.com

Richards & Swensen
USA
801-930-9862

Richards Brock Miller Mitchell & Associates
USA
www.rbmm.com

Rick Carlson Design & Illustration
USA
rcarlsondesign.com

Rickabaugh Graphics
USA
rickabaughgraphics.com

RIGGS
USA
www.riggspeak.com

robert meyers design
USA
412-288-9933

The Robin Shepherd Group
USA
904-359-0981

Robot Creative
USA
www.robotcreative.com

Rocket Science
USA
www.rocketsciencedesign.net

RocketDog Communications
USA
www.rocketdog.org

Rocketman Creative
USA
www.rocketmancreative.com

Roman Design
USA
303-526-5740

Roman Kotikov
Russia
www.kotikov.ru

Romulo Moya / Trama
Ecuador
www.trama.ec

Roskelly Inc.
USA
www.roskelly.com

Ross Creative + Strategy
USA
309-680-4143

Ross Hogin Design
USA
206-605-1420

Ross Levine Design
USA
www.rosslevinedesign.com

Rotor Design
USA
www.rotordesign.net

Round 2 Integrated
USA
410-327-0007 ext. 1246

Roy Smith Design
UK
www.roysmithdesign.com

RS Identity Design
USA
www.rsiddesign.com

Rufuturu
Russia
www.rufutu.ru; www.zambezy.ru

Rule29
USA
www.rule29.com

The Russo Group
USA
www.therussogroup.com

Rusty George Creative
USA
www.rustygeorge.com

Ryan Cooper Design
USA
www.visualchili.com

rylander design
USA
www.rylanderdesign.com

S Design, Inc.
USA
www.sdesigninc.com

S4LE.com
Canada
s4le.com

Sabet Branding
USA
www.sabet.com

Sabin Design
USA
www.sabindesign.com

Sabingrafik, Inc.
USA
tracy.sabin.com

Sage Corporation
USA
www.sageisland.com

Saltree Pty Ltd
Australia
saltreecreative.com

Salty Design Foundry
USA
www.saltydf.com

Sanders Design
New Zealand
www.sandersdesign.co.nz

Sandpaper Studio
USA
www.sandpaperstudio.com

Sandstorm Design
USA
773-348-4200

Sandstrom Partners
USA
www.sandstrompartners.com

Sara Delaney Graphic Design
USA
www.delaneygroup.com

Sarah grimaldi
Italy
www.xister.com

Sauvage Design
New Zealand
www.sauvage.co.nz

Savacool Secviar Brand Communications
USA
www.savacoolsecviar.com

Savage-Olsen Design Engineering Inc.
USA
251-344-4001

Sayles Graphic Design, Inc.
USA
www.saylesdesign.com

schaer creative l.l.c.
USA
480-766-6034

Schwartzrock Graphic Arts
USA
www.schwartzrock.com

Scientific Arts
Australia
www.xyarts.com.au

SCORR Marketing
USA
www.scorrmarketing.com

Scott Carroll Designs, Inc.
USA
www.scottcarrolldesigns.com

Scott Lewis Design
USA
www.lewisdesign.net

Scott Oeschger Design
USA
www.scottoeschger.com

SD33/Art Direction & Design
USA
www.sd33.com

Seagrass Studios
USA
www.seagrasstudios.com

Sean Daly Design
USA
716-479-5945

Sebastiany Branding & Design
Brazil
www.sebastiany.com.br

Second Shift Design
USA
www.secondshiftdesign.com

seesponge
USA
586-255-6514

Segura Inc.
USA
www.segura-inc.com

Selikoff+Co
USA
www.selikoffco.com

Sellier Design, Inc.
USA
770-428-8668

Sharisse Steber Design
USA
615-945-1099

Shawn Huff
USA
www.shawnhuff.info

Sheehan Design
USA
619-328-6990

Shelley Design+Marketing
USA
shelleyllc.com

ShenZhen Tusk Advertising &Brand design Co.,Ltd
China
www.sztusk.com

Shift
USA
303-440-2901

Shoofly
USA
541-482-6675

Sibley Peteet
USA
www.spdaustin.com

Sibley Peteet Design—Dallas
USA
214-969-1050

SiglerGroup, Inc.
USA
805-647-8383

Signal Design
Canada
www.signaldesignworks.com

Simon & Goetz Design
Germany
www.simongoetz.de

Sire Advertising
USA
www.sireadvertising.com

Skybend
USA
801-983-6760

skyymedia
USA
www.skyymedia.com

Small Dog Design
Australia
www.smalldog.com.au

SmartArt Design Inc.
USA
www.nancyrockwood.com

Smith Design
USA
www.smithdesign.com

Smyers Design
USA
202-329-7038

Snap Creative
USA
314-482-6438

Sockeye Creative
USA
sockeyecreative.com

Sol Consultores
Mexico
www.solconsultores.com.mx

Sonia Jones Design
USA
www.soniajonesdesign.com

Sons Of Shin Productions
USA
www.sonsofshin.com

SoupGraphix Inc.
USA
www.soupgraphix.com

Southside Creative Group
USA
www.southsidecreative.com

Spangler Design Team
USA
www.spanglerdesign.com

Spark Studio
Australia
+6139686 4703

Sparkman + Associates
USA
www.sparkmandesign.com

SPATCHURST
Australia
www.spatchurst.com.au

Spec Creative
USA
405-206-1088

Special Modern Design
USA
specialmoderndesign.com

Spectrum Brands / Schultz Creative
USA
brianschultzdesign.com

Spin Design
USA
314-922-6819

Spinutech, Inc.
USA
www.spinutech.com

Spire
USA
214-393-5222

Splash:Design
Canada
splashdesign.biz

Splinter Group
USA
www.splintergrp.com

Spohn Design
USA
www.spohndesign.com

Spoonbend
USA
www.spoonbend.com

Spork Design, Inc.
USA
www.sporkdesign.com

Sputnik Design Partners Inc
Canada
www.sputnikart.com

Squarelogo
USA
www.squarelogo.com

squiggle6
Australia
www.squiggle6.com

Squires and Company
USA
www.squirescompany.com

St. Dwayne Design
USA
www.stdwayne.com

Steele Design
USA
www.briansteeledesign.com

Stefan Romanu
Romania
www.stefanromanu.com

Steiner&Co.
Hong Kong
www.steiner.hk

Stellar Debris, Inc.
Japan
www.stellardebris.com

Stephen Averitt
USA
702-452-2951

Steve Cantrell
USA
954-574-0601

Steve Smith
Australia
412022914

Steven O'Connor
USA
323-779-5600

Steve's Portfolio
USA
www.stevesportfolio.net

Stiles Design
USA
brettstilesdesign.com

Stiles+co
USA
www.danstiles.com

Stoltze Design
USA
www.stoltze.com

Storm Design Inc.
Canada
www.stormdesigninc.com

Straka-Design
Germany
www.straka-design.net

Strange Ideas
USA
baileylauerman.com

Strategy Studio
USA
strategy-studio.com

stressdesign
USA
www.stressdesign.com

String
Serbia
38110322370

Struck
USA
801-531-0122

STUBBORN SIDEBURN
USA
www.stubbornsideburn.com

Studio G
USA
970-393-2012

Studio grafickih ideja
Croatia
www.sgi.hr

Studio GT&P
Italy
www.tobanelli.it

Studio International
Croatia
www.studio-internaional.com

Studio Limbus
Croatia
www.studiolimbus.com

Studio Nine Creative
USA
www.studioninecreative.com

Studio No. 6
USA
www.studiono6.com

Studio Simon
USA
www.studiosimon.com

studio sudar d.o.o.
Croatia
www.iknowsudar.com

Studio Tandem
USA
404-819-4117

Studio18Group
USA
studio18group.com

studio-h
USA
856-686-1185

StudioNorth
USA
www.studionorth.com

Stygar Group, Inc.
USA
804-288-4688

Subcommunication
Canada
www.subcommunication.com

substance151
USA
www.substance151.com

Suburban Utopia
USA
www.suburbanutopia.com

Sudduth Design Co.
USA
sudduthdesign.com

Sullivan Higdon & Sink
USA
www.wehatesheep.com

SUPERRED
Russia
www.superred.ru

Sussner Design Company
USA
612-339-2886

Swanson Russell
USA
www.swansonrussell.com

Swingtop
USA
www.swing-top.com

switchfoot creative
USA
www.switchfootcreative.com

Synthetic Infatuation
USA
synth.tc

T H Gilmore
USA
513-240-5111

Tactical Magic
USA
www.tacticalmagic.com

Tactix Creative
USA
www.tactixcreative.com

Tandem Design Agency
USA
www.tandemthinking.com

Tandemodus
USA
www.tandemodus.com

Tank Design
Norway
www.tank.no

Tanoshism
Japan
www.tanoshism.com

Taproot Creative
USA
www.taprootcreative.com

Taylor Martin Design
USA
www.taylormartindesign.com

Taylor Raber
USA
616-745-1650

TBF Creative
USA
www.tbfcreative.com

Tchopshop Media
USA
504-891-0940

Tesser
USA
415-541-9999

Theory Associates
USA
www.theoryassociates.com

Think Cap Design
USA
713-854-8873

Think Tank Creative
USA
www.think-tank-creative.com

Thinking Caps
USA
www.thinkingcaps.net

Thinking*Room Inc.
Indonesia
www.thinkingroominc.com

THINQ
USA
www.thinqdifferent.com

this is nido
UK
www.thisisnido.com

Thomas Cook Designs
USA
www.thomascookdesigns.com

Thomas design
USA
www.thomasdesign.me

Thread Design
China
www.threaddesign.com.cn

Threds
USA
865-525-2830

three o'clock I design
Mexico
www.3oclockdesign.com

Tielemans Design
USA
www.tielemansdesign.com

Tilt Design Studio
Germany
www.tiltdesignstudio.com

Tim Frame Design
USA
www.timframe.com

Timber Design Company
USA
www.timberdesignco.com

Tip Top Creative
USA
www.tiptopcreative.com

tisha domingo design
USA
214-502-2863

TMCA, Inc.
USA
www.tmcadesign.com

TNOP & bePOSI+IVE
USA
www.tnop.com

Todd M. LeMieux Design
USA
www.toddlemieux.com

TOKY Branding+Design
USA
www.toky.com

Tom Law Design
USA
tomlawdesign.com

Tom Welch
USA
310-854-2441

Tomko Design
USA
www.tomkodesign.com

tomvasquez.com
USA
tomvasquez.com

Tony Fletcher Design, LLC
USA
tonyfletcher.com

Topo
Spain
www.topo.bz

Totem
Ireland
www.totem.ie

Tower of Babel
USA
www.babeldesign.com

TPG Architecture
USA
www.tpgarchitecture.com

Traction
USA
www.teamtraction.com

TracyLocke Dallas
USA
www.tracylocke.com

Tran Creative
USA
www.tran-creative.com

Trapdoor Studio
USA
www.trapdoorstudio.com

Travers Collins & Company
USA
716-842-2222

Tribe Design Houston
USA
www.tribedesign.com/branding/logos/home.htm

Trilix Marketing Group
USA
515-974-4705

Triple Frog LLC
USA
triplefrog.com

True Perception
USA
480-236-6479

Truly Design
Italy
www.truly-design.com

tub
USA
804-306-5630

Tunglid Advertising Agency ehf.
Iceland
www.tungl.is

Turnstyle
USA
www.turnstylestudio.com

twentystar
USA
www.twentystar.com

Twin Engine Creative
USA
626-852-7922

two tribes gmbh
Germany
www.twotribes.de

Ty Wilkins
USA
tywilkins.com

UlrichPinciotti Design Group
USA
www.updesigngroup.com

Ulyanov Denis
Russia
www.caspa.ru

Unibrand Belgrade
Serbia
www.unibrand360.com

UniGraphics
USA
419-372-7418

Union Design & Photo
USA
www.uniondesignphoto.com

United States of the Art
Germany
www.unitedstatesoftheart.com

United States of the Art
Germany
www.unitedstatesoftheart.com

UNIT-Y
USA
www.unit-y.com

UNO
USA
unoonline.com

UpShift Creative Group
USA
www.upshiftcreative.com

Urban Influence
USA
www.urbaninfluence.com

UTILITY
USA
www.utilitydesignco.com

Valhalla I Design & Conquer
USA
www.valhallaconquers.com

Valladares, diseño y comunicacion
Spain
www.valladaresdc.net

Valmont Comunicación
Spain
www.valmontcomunicacion.com

VanPaul Design
USA
www.vanpaul.com

Vasco Morelli Design
USA
vascomorelli.com

Velocity Design Group
USA
www.velocitybrand.com

Ventress Design Group, Inc
USA
www.ventress.com

Vestigio—Consultores de Design, Lda.
Portugal
www.emanuelbarbosa.com

Via Grafik
Germany
www.vgrfk.com

Victor Goloubinov
Russia
www.revision.ru/authors/3187/

VINE360
USA
www.vine360.com

Vision 3
USA
317-269-0556

Visual Inventor Ltd. Co.
USA
www.visualinventor.com

Visual Lure, LLC
USA
www.visuallure.com

Visualliance
USA
415-218-1335

Vivid Envisions
USA
608-346-8804

Vivitiv
USA
www.artomatdesign.com

Viziom
USA
www.viziom.com

VMA
USA
vmai.com

volatile-graphics
UK
www.volatile-graphics.co.uk

Walsh Branding
USA
www.walshbranding.com

Warren Diggles Photography and Design
USA
www.warrendiggles.com

wedge.a&d
Canada
403-215-4030

Welcome Moxie
USA
917-385-2314

Werner Design Werks
USA
www.wdw.com

West Reed
USA
www.westreed.com

WestmorelandFlint
USA
www.westmorelandflint.com

Westwerk DSGN
USA
www.westwerkdesign.com

Whaley Design, Ltd
USA
651-645-3463

WhatWorks
USA
718-310-3000

Whole Wheat Creative
USA
www.wholewheatcreative.com

William Fox Munroe Inc
USA
www.wfoxm.com

Wolken communica
USA
www.wolkencommunica.com

Woodward Design
Canada
www.woodwarddesign.ca

WORK Labs
USA
804-385-9372

Wox
Brazil
wox.com.br

wray ward
USA
wrayward.com

Wrijfhout
The Netherlands
www.wrijfhout.nl

X RAY
Latvia
www.xray.lv

Xfacta
South Africa
+27 82 8814621

Y&R Dubai
United Arab Emirates
www.yr.com

Yantra Design Group Inc
USA
www.yantradg.com

yarimizoshintaro
Japan
www.yarimizo.com

Yoshi Tajima
Japan
www.radiographics.jp

Z Factory
USA
773-975-4280

Z&G
Russia
www.zg-company.ru

zakidesign
USA
www.zakidesign.com

Zaman
United Arab Emirates
97142824333

Zapata Design
USA
www.zapatadesign.com

ZEBRA design branding
Russia
+7 8482 538000

Zed+Zed+Eye Creative Communications
USA
www.zedzedeye.com

Zieldesign
USA
www.zieldesign.net

Ziga Aljaz
Slovenia
www.aljaz.org

ZONA Design, Inc
USA
212-244-2900

ZORRAQUINO
Spain
www.zorraquino.com

ZupiDesign
Brazil
www.zupidesign.com

Zync Communications Inc.
Canada
www.zync.ca

about the authors

Bill Gardner is president of Gardner Design and has produced work for Cessna, Learjet, Thermos, Pepsi, Pizza Hut, Kroger, Hallmark, Cargill Corporation, and the 2004 Athens Olympics. His work has been featured in *Communication Arts*, *Print*, *Graphis*, the Museum of Modern Art, and New York Art Director publications, as well as many other national and international design exhibitions. He is the founder of LogoLounge.com and the author of *LogoLounge 1, 2, 3, 4,* and *5*, as well as the Master Library Series. He lives in Wichita, Kansas.

Catharine Fishel specializes in working with and writing about designers and their work. A contributing editor to *Print* magazine, she has written for many leading design publications. She is the editor of LogoLounge.com and is author of many books about design, including *LogoLounge 1, 2, 3, 4,* and *5*; *Inside the Business of Graphic Design*; *How to Grow as a Graphic Designer*; *The In-House Design Handbook*; *The Freelance Design Handbook*; and the Master Library Series.